REEL V. REAL

Books by Frank Sanello

The Opium Wars: The Addiction of One Empire and the Corruption of Another
The Knights Templar: God's Warriors, the Devil's Banker
Reel v. Real: How Hollywood Turns Fact into Fiction
Spielberg: The Man, the Movies, the Mythology
Jimmy Stewart: A Wonderful Life
Eddie Murphy: The Life and Times of a Comic on the Edge
Stallone: A Rocky Life

Upcoming Books

Faith and Finance in the Renaissance: The Rise and Ruin of the Fugger Empire
To Kill a King: The Murder of God's Anointed

REEL V. REAL

How Hollywood Turns Fact into Fiction

Frank Sanello

TAYLOR TRADE PUBLISHING

Lanham • New York • Oxford

First Taylor Trade Publishing edition 2003

This Taylor Trade Publishing softcover edition of *Reel v. Real* is an original publication. It is published by arrangement with the author.

Photos on pages 4, 8, 18, 29, 35, 37, 40, 41, 44, 46, 59, 76, 90, 91, 94, 95, 98, 102, 108, 113, 122, 136, 140, 163, 169, 173, 177, 183, 188, 192, 234, 238, 239, and 246 appear courtesy of J. C. Archives

Photos on pages 116, 132, 198, 218, and 228 appear courtesy of Larry Edmonds

Published by Taylor Trade Publishing
A Member of the Rowman & Littlefield Publishing Group
4720 Boston Way
Lanham, Maryland 20706

Distributed by National Book Network

Library of Congress Cataloging-in-Publication Data
Sanello, Frank.
    Reel v. real : how hollywood turns fact into fiction / Frank Sanello
      p. cm.
    Includes bibliographical references and index.
    ISBN 0-87833-268-5 (pbk : alk.paper)
      1. Historical films—History and criticism.   2. Motion pictures and history.   I. Title: Reel
versus real.   II. Title.

PN41995.9.H5 S26 2001
791.43'658—dc21   2001027525

For Christina Madej

"Those who do not learn the mistakes of the past
are condemned to repeat them on film."

—Santayana & Ebert at the Movies

CONTENTS

III. AMERICAN HISTORY

INTRODUCTION

Gibbon said that history is little more than the register of the crimes, follies, and misfortunes of mankind, but when fictionalizing history, writers often feel such dramatic fare needs a tweaking for maximum theatricality. The real events, however stormy, seem to require more *stürm und drang*.

The great German playwright Friedrich von Schiller once wrote that "in order to tell the truth sometimes you have to lie." He amply demonstrated this in his 1803 play *The Maid of Orleans*, at the end of which Joan of Arc escapes imminent immolation and gains her freedom! Schiller was attempting to get at some deeper philosophical truth rather than the well-known facts of Joan's life, including her iconic death. But more often and with less noble goals, history for centuries has been twisted and distorted beyond recognition for a much simpler reason. As the old newspaper hack once urged, "Never let the facts get in the way of a good story."

Ever since Homer used rhyme to jog his memory and Suetonius put stylus to parchment in his gossipy, ahistorical *Lives of the Caesars*, writers have been using history for purposes other than the obvious—accurate re-creations of the past. But the greatest gap between the actual past and fictionalized accounts of it may lie in Hollywood's marzipan-and-truffles treatment of history. Never, indeed, let historical truth get in the way of a good, two-hour blockbuster that earns $200 million domestic.

I hope this work serves as more than a "gotcha!" catalogue of movie missteps proving the already proven: that Hollywood treats history like an ugly stepchild that needs to be tarted up with fictional additions. Or, as *The Times* (London) said,

"No historical drama can be said to have done its job unless it causes at least half a dozen historians to tear their hair out." There's also an old saying that when one walks through history, one should be careful not to trip. Critics would say that Hollywood has been stumbling over its feet since the day it began making period films.

The stakes are higher than the frivolous nature of popular entertainment makes them seem at first glance. As John Harlow and Nicholas Hellen wrote in *The Times* (London), movies are often the only way kids learn history:

> Dramatists have long sacrificed fact in pursuit of art, and much of the time it can be shrugged off . . . but there is a growing concern that in a "post-literate" society, where children get more information from films and television than books, the routine distortion of history in Hollywood films is becoming pernicious. Films are no longer mere entertainments: they are a prime and often sole source of information for many young minds.

Consider these sad surveys of the state of young American minds: Shortly before the release of *Schindler's List* in 1993, a Gallup poll revealed that eighty percent of children had never heard of Auschwitz. Other polls show that youngsters think Lenin, not Stalin, led the Soviet Union during World War II, and that some think the first name of the leader of the Russian Revolution was John. And, no doubt, that Groucho wrote *Das Kapital*.

"Highly fictionalized treatments of the past are being accepted as historical truth by students," reports history professor Judith MacKinlay, who recalls that one of her college students "reproduced whole chunks of dialogue almost verbatim from the film *Michael Collins*," the 1996 epic about the birth of the Irish Republic, which was widely criticized for its pro-IRA, anti-British slant. "Students would rather watch movies than wade through a textbook, without realizing that directors are twisting the facts. Hollywood leaves behind powerful images," MacKinlay says.

The New York Times agrees. "More people are getting their history, or what they think is history, from the movies these days than from the standard history books," Richard Bernstein wrote in 1990. Things have improved a bit since then, as people now learn about the past from sound bytes on the History Channel.

But it's not just our youth who swell the ranks of the historically confused. Here's another bit of embarrassing trivia: The American distributor of the British-made *The Madness of King George III* demanded that the Roman numeral be removed from the title so frustrated audiences wouldn't think they were watching a sequel whose first two installments they had missed.

If Santayana was correct that those who do not learn the mistakes of the past are condemned to repeat them, we're in big trouble.

Commercial imperatives most often fuel cinematic rewrites of history. Complex economic and social issues are puréed into easily digestible bits of information intended for consumption by Hollywood's most sought-after demographic: the lowest common denominator.

The entertainment industry's traditional liberalism also nurtures historical solipsism. American historian James Bowman says:

> The deeper sin is to make every historical character, from Merchant/Ivory's *Jefferson in Paris* to *Elizabeth I*, sound like a modern liberal. They distort in subtle as well as obvious ways, such as making us feel superior to Nazis and slave-traders rather than questioning if, in another life, we might have been Nazis and slavers. It gets in the way of understanding the foreign country that is the past.

This historical solipsism goes beyond politics. Writing in *The Los Angeles Times*, film critic Jack Matthews said, "Period movies inevitably reflect more the period in which they're made than the period of their subject."

In his *Poetics*, Aristotle said that art is more real than life. If the fourth century B.C. philosopher had lived in our times, he might have been even more convinced of the truth of his words when "real" figures appear on movie screens two stories high, making them more real and literally bigger than life. Hollywood's iconization of historical figures has validated Aristotle's claim in spades.

Rather than point out historical inaccuracies in films and turn this work into a pseudo-scholarly, high-brow variation of Trivial Pursuit, I have tried to reveal why filmmakers have played fast and loose with the facts, that is, what greater truth or dramatic benefit was achieved by distorting the past.

"The past is a foreign country. They do things differently there." So goes the opening line of L. P. Hartley's 1953 cult novel, *The Go-Between*. In the case of Hollywood's re-creation of historical events, sometimes it seems that the past took place on another planet. Planet Hollywood? But don't take my word for it. Check out the following other worldly visions of the past recorded on film.

FRANK SANELLO
Los Angeles, California
September 2002

PREHISTORY, ANCIENT TIMES, AND THE BIBLE

Quest for Fire
(1981)

Directed by Jean-Jacques Annaud
Written by J. H. Rosny, Sr., Gerard Brach

CAST

Everett McGill (Naoh)
Ron Perlman (Amoukar)
Rae Dawn Chong (Ika)
Gary Schwartz (Rouka)
Franck-Olivier Bonnet (Aghoo)
Jean-Michel Kindt (Lakar)

Critics couldn't agree if *Quest for Fire* was a laudable attempt to popularize the arcane subject of paleoanthropology or an example of disposable flick-your-Bic filmmaking.

In 80,000 B.C., the world was a very cold place. It wasn't called the Ice Age for nothing. In that frigid time and climes, fire was as essential to life as food and water. If you had it, you could cook meat, repel beasts and unfriendly neighbors, and make an inhabitable cave a home. The Cro-Magnon Ulam tribe in *Quest for Fire* has fire, provided by trees ignited by lightning, but doesn't know how to create it. When their only torch goes out during a fight with a tribe of Neanderthals, the Ulam seem doomed. So they send three of their clan across the permafrost of what would one day be called Western Europe to find fire—and better yet, learn how to make it. During this primeval quest for a burning grail, they battle saber-toothed tigers, woolly mammoths, a tribe of really scary cannibals called the Kzamm and rescue a captive girl the flesheaters are about to dish up as an entrée. Along the way, centuries

Rae Dawn Chong and Everett McGill play a cave couple seeking a reliable source of light and central heating in *Quest for Fire*.

if not millennia of human discoveries occur during their three-month journey, including the birth of slapstick (a food fight and a rock falling on a caveman's head), the convenience of footwear and female orgasms (introducing the missionary position). Oh, and they learn how to rub two sticks together to make fire.

Academics came out of the woodwork en masse to slam *Quest for Fire*'s factual flaws, but their arguments didn't seem to prove anything more than the quip attributed to Dwight Eisenhower, "All generalizations are inaccurate, including this one."

The biggest complaints revolved around so many epoch-making discoveries occurring over such a short time span. Director Jean-Jacques Annaud countered that his timetable was symbolic, not historical. "*Quest for Fire* doesn't try to be *true*, only plausible. It is a symbolic approach to man's development. In a few days, these people make progress that might really have taken several generations," Annaud said.

Paleoanthropologists also had trouble with the approximate date, 80,000 B.C., of the primary event in *Quest for Fire*, i.e., how to make it. Excavations in China in the early part of the 20th century indicated that the control of fire developed more than 500,000 years ago. More recent evidence uncovered in Kenya pushes the date even farther back, to 1.4 million years. But Annaud, an armchair anthropologist who studied the subject in college, insisted that the ability to make fire came and went throughout prehistory, with fiery renaissances alternating with chilly dark ages. "No one knows when man mastered the making of fire. We had to make a guess. Making fire was probably discovered and forgotten and rediscovered many times. Some [primitive] people in the 19th century did not know how to make fire," Annaud said.

The director explained that he chose 80,000 B.C. because the extinct Neanderthal species was still alive at the time, and the much less evolved Neanderthals in the film make good, knuckle-dragging bad guys who steal the Cro-Magnon Ulam's fire and launch the movie's quest.

Doug Feldman, an assistant professor of anthropology at John Jay College of Criminal Justice, felt the Neanderthals got a bad rap in the film, although he undercut his argument by misidentifying the Cro-Magnon Ulam tribe as Neanderthals. The real Neanderthals, according to Dr. Feldman, were not the fur-covered simian villains of *Quest for Fire*. That misconception has come down to us from the writings of French paleontologist Marcellin Boule, who in 1913 examined a Neanderthal skeleton and deduced the species consisted of slouching, waddling brutes with chimp-like behavior, which is the way *Quest for Fire* depicts them, with larceny thrown in. Later scientists realized that Boule's Neanderthal suffered from a severe form of arthritis that caused the creature's deformities.

Neanderthals, Feldman said, "weren't all that different from men and women today." They walked erect, didn't slouch, didn't use their sense of smell to find animals as they do in the film, and they hunted rather than ran in terror from tasty prey like woolly mammoths. And in Feldman's idealized view of Neanderthals—as noble savages with a body waxing problem—they would have been more likely to borrow fire from a friendly tribe next door rather than steal it.

Annaud and screenwriter Gerard Brach relied on so-called "experts," research, and guesswork to create a prehistoric world that looked believable. They hired zoologist and behavioral theorist Desmond Morris, author of *The Naked Ape*, to create a system of gestures that modern audiences could understand but would not appear contemporary. Novelist-linguist Anthony Burgess (who created an Anglo-Russian dialect for his novel *A Clockwork Orange*) invented a vocabulary of 100 words for the film based on Indo-European, the mother of Western tongues, which may have been spoken 80,000 years ago.

In his quest for authenticity, Annaud also became a casting tyrant and insisted that all the actors have small chins and bent foreheads, which the film's makeup artist, Chris Thicker, justified by saying, "You can always build but you can't cut a forehead." Professional wrestlers, including one who weighed 545 pounds, got the job of playing the bigger, less evolved Neanderthals.

No one complained about the film's imagined re-creation of the discovery of making fire because it was based on the stick-drill method used by the Tasadays, a Stone Age tribe that came to light in the Philippines in the 1970s.

But critics did complain about *Quest for Fire*'s R-rated violence, and they weren't the usual opponents like right wingers or Joe Lieberman-type centrists. Dr. Gloria Levitas, an anthropologist at Queens College of the City University of New York, was "astonished" by the characters' brutal behavior, which was inspired by Robert Ardrey's 1960s book, *African Genesis*. Ardrey hypothesized that early man was a killer ape. "People were violent then, but it is incorrect to give the impression of utter mayhem between tribes of people. They were as likely to engage in avoidance behavior as confrontation. Mostly they ran away from conflict," Levitas said. But avoidance doesn't provide screen drama.

Quest for Fire's Kzamm cannibals caught the most flak. Most anthropologists agree that cannibalism was a creation of Dead White European Males, who used the accusation to promote the stereotype of aboriginal peoples as less-than-human flesh-eaters of color who deserved to be colonized by superior white people.

The woman rescued from the cannibals by the Cro-Magnon good guys belongs to a more advanced tribe that not only knows how to make fire but has discovered the joys of face-to-face sex, otherwise known as the missionary position, which she shares with one of her lucky rescuers. Dr. Helen E. Fisher, an anthropologist at the New School for Social Research in New York, said people were having face-to-face sex as far back as four million years ago, as soon as early hominids began walking on hind legs—an obvious prerequisite for the missionary position.

Dr. Feldman of John Jay College said, "As a science fantasy, *Quest for Fire* is a top-notch thriller, but . . . as an anthropological statement, it's a dismal failure." The anthropologist said he dreaded the inevitable sequel, *Quest for the Wheel*.

Director Annaud agreed with Feldman's assessment that his film was more fantasy than anthropology, but naturally disagreed with his criticism of it. "Prehistory is a domain as unknown as the galaxies," he said. "No one objects to extrapolating from our meager knowledge of the future. Why not do this with regard to the past? Intelligent speculation, backed by research, may lead us to the truth."

Or at the very least, a reliable source of fire.

The Ten Commandments (1956)

Directed by Cecil B. DeMille
Written by J. H. Ingraham, A. E. Southon

CAST

Charlton Heston (Moses)
Yul Brynner (Pharaoh Ramses)
Anne Baxter (Nefretiri)
Edward G. Robinson (Dathan)
Yvonne De Carlo (Sephora)
Debra Paget (Lilia)
John Derek (Joshua)
Cedric Hardwicke (Sethi)
Nina Foch (Bithia)
Martha Scott (Yochabel)
Judith Anderson (Memnet)

Vincent Price (Baka)
John Carradine (Aaron)

The Ten Commandments may be one of the best researched movies in the history of the industry, yet it remains largely a work of fiction because its many sources ranged from the questionable to the worthless. In the opening scene, which must be the first biblical epic to include a movie director's office, DeMille crows that his researchers relied on the historical accounts of Philo, Josephus, Eusebius, and the Jewish Midrash, a collection of interpretative studies of the Bible. What DeMille fails to mention is that Philo and the others all lived more than a millennium after the events in the Bible's Book of Exodus, on which the movie is primarily based. He also omits other, less profound sources for the film listed in the credits, including romance novels like Dorothy Clarke Wilson's *Prince of Egypt*, J. H. Ingraham's *Pillar of Fire*, and A. E. Southon's *On Eagle's Wings*.

Moses (Charlton Heston) has his hands full in *The Ten Commandments* trying to get the people of Israel to follow some simple rules and regulations.

The events and characters described in the Book of Exodus are not corroborated by any other contemporary records. The closest reference is a stone tablet dating from the reign of Merneptah, the son of the Egyptian Pharaoh Ramses II, which suggests that around 1215 B.C. the people of Israel settled in Canaan, which became the homeland of the Hebrew people. DeMille accurately sets the story of *The Ten Commandments* in the reign of Ramses II, which would be consistent with the time frame of Merneptah's stone tablet, or stela. Contemporary, nonbiblical documents also show that Ramses' father, Seti I, made extensive use of forced labor to build his treasure city of Avaris, which is consistent with DeMille's depiction, however overwrought, of long-suffering Hebrew construction workers in Egypt. Other Egyptian records mention a group named "Apiru," an approximation of "ivri," the Hebrew word for "Hebrew," were used to build the Pharaoh's treasure cities.

The Bible undramatically gives Moses only one love interest, his wife, the Midianite Sephora. Relying on romance novels rather scripture, DeMille injects a totally fictitious relationship between Moses and Ramses' future wife, Nefretiri, who first loves Moses, then vows revenge after he spurns her for a higher calling—leading his people out of Egyptian bondage to the Promised Land. Historical records indicate Nefretiri was one of Ramses' wives, but a romantic triangle involving them and Moses owes everything to DeMille's reliance on romance novels and nothing to biblical or contemporary sources.

DeMille ignored the Bible when it said that Pharaoh died when Moses closed the Red Sea after parting it to allow the Hebrews to escape. In the film, Pharaoh, played by Yul Brynner, survives—a strange development in a melodrama, where the bad guy usually dies at the end.

The director also gives Moses (Charlton Heston) spurious authorship of the first five books of the Bible, the Pentateuch, based on Jewish and Christian tradition, even though the Bible makes no mention of Moses' contribution to those books. His authorship is implied in the film when Moses, just before his death, hands the five scrolls of the Pentateuch to his brother Joshua for safekeeping. (In the film, Joshua accompanies his brother on the flight from Egypt. In the Bible, he appears later.)

What *The Ten Commandments* lacked in accuracy, it made up for with spectacle. Twelve thousand extras and fifteen thousand animals at one point in the film covered a three-mile area, and the director had to issue commands standing on a crane, using a public address system.

James Thurber said of DeMille's lavish production, "It makes you realize what God could have done if He'd had the money."

The Last Temptation of Christ
(1988)

Directed by Martin Scorsese
Written by Paul Schrader, Nikos Kazantzakis (novel)

CAST

Willem Dafoe (Jesus)
Harvey Keitel (Judas)
Paul Greco (Zealot)
Steve Shill (Centurion)
Verna Bloom (Mary, Mother of Jesus)
Barbara Hershey (Mary Magdalene)

Not since Vanessa Redgrave appeared to fellate a crucified Christ during a sacrilegious fantasy sequence in *The Devils* in 1970 has a film raised the hackles of devout Christians as much as *The Last Temptation of Christ* did in 1988. The opening disclaimer that it was *not* based on the Gospels did not mollify the Christian fundamentalists who picketed theaters and claimed that the production was a conspiracy of Jewish studio executives—in particular Universal chairman Lew Wasserman—whose home was also picketed. Blockbuster Video refused to stock the film when it came out on VHS, and South Africa banned it outright. Italy brought criminal charges against the film's director, Martin Scorsese, who stood trial and was acquitted on obscenity and blasphemy charges. An unsuccessful lawsuit that attempted to ban the film in Pennsylvania went all the way to the U.S. Supreme Court.

So what about *The Last Temptation of Christ* generated so much wrath? There was so much to object to, where to begin? For starters, Paul Schrader's script closely follows the novel by Nikos Kazantzakis, whose Jesus is a modern hero torn between earthly desires and his divine mission. Schrader wanted to avoid famous lines from the Bible, and the modern day vernacular he substituted enraged fundamentalists as being disrespectful or worse. Scorsese not only defended the use of contemporary language, but promoted it, saying, *"The Last Temptation of Christ* will push the concept of Jesus into the 21st century."

Scorsese's Jesus is a man racked by self-doubt. Before the Sermon on the Mount, he obsesses, "What if I say the wrong thing?" He begins the sermon with a stumbling apology, which one critic said made Jesus sound like a Method actor: "Umm, uh, I'm sorry. I'm going to tell you a story. . . ."

In one of many fantasy sequences, Jesus says, "I give my heart to you, [Mary Magdalene]," then literally pulls his heart out of his body. He rejects his mother, Mary, saying, "I don't have a mother. I have a father. In heaven." Instead of the Bible's famous line Jesus used to stop an adulterous woman from being stoned ("Let he among you who is without sin cast the first stone. . . ."), he says in the film, "Who has never sinned here?" In another fantasy sequence, naked women shimmy around St. John the Baptist. In the film, the young Jesus is a collaborationist who uses his carpentry skills to build crosses for Roman crucifixions. Jesus suffers convulsive headaches as he wrestles with the decision to accept his role as the redeemer who must die for our sins. "I lied, I am afraid. Lucifer is inside me!" Jesus exclaims. Evangelical critics complained that Scorsese's Jesus was a "wimp."

Other biblical figures also get a makeover. When Jesus brings Lazarus back from the dead, an observer asks him to compare being alive to being dead, and he replies, "I was a little surprised. There isn't that much difference." Before performing Lazarus' resurrection, Jesus appears afraid to enter the dead man's tomb until Lazarus' arms protrude from the entrance and drag him in. Instead of a glorious apparition, Lazarus is a smelly, half-rotting corpse of a man. The film's Judas is a hero, not the traitor who betrays Christ to the Romans for thirty pieces of silver. One scene shows the two men asleep under a tree in each other's arms, leaving the viewer to decide if their nap is platonic or homoerotic. With Jesus' prodding, a reluctant Judas turns him in so he can fulfill his mission on the cross. Judas insists this act is tougher than Jesus' death. As for Jesus' work making crosses for the Romans, Judas yells at him, "You're a coward! You're a disgrace!" Critics and the faithful lambasted Harvey Keitel's Judas for speaking with a Bronx accent and acting like a Mafia wiseguy. ("The other day, you said, someone hits you, you turn the other cheek. I didn't like that," Judas says in reproach.) Judas sports a fake bulbous nose and an ill-fitting red wig. When a lion approaches Jesus during his temptation in the desert, the animal speaks with Harvey Keitel's voice and asks, "Don't you rekonnize me?" These 20th century intrusions and revisions irritated believers who consider the Bible a literal revelation of God's word. But the biggest offense that sent the faithful to the picket lines was a fantasy sequence more ribald than Redgrave's wet dream sequence in *The Devils*, re-creating the most iconic moment in Christ's life, his crucifixion.

Jesus' last temptation occurs on the cross, when Lucifer in the form of a beautiful young female angel offers to get him off the hook and off the cross. Jesus accepts the offer, escapes crucifixion, and marries his long-time love, Mary Magdalene. Although discreetly shot from a distance, a scene showing Jesus making love to his wife caused the most protest. But the alleged blasphemy didn't stop with Jesus setting up house with a former prostitute. After bearing several of Jesus' children, Mary Magdalene dies, and Jesus welcomes Lazarus' sisters, Mary and Martha, into his bed! The satanic angel removes any guilty qualms about this by telling Jesus, "All women are as one."

Jesus grows old and happy. On his deathbed, Judas reappears, scolding him for forsaking his mission and revealing that the flaxen-haired angel is really Lucifer. Jesus then rejects his happy retirement and returns to the cross.

Despite this redeeming act of piety, the Christian right was not charmed, and a fundamentalist preacher from Tupelo, Mississippi, the Reverend Donald Wildomon, called for a national boycott of the film, the studio that produced it, and the studio's other enterprises and products. The boycott got ugly when some picketers carried placards that included anti-Semitic slurs against the Jewish executives at Universal, which bankrolled the film after a terrified Paramount pulled the plug during pre-production. (The script was such a hot potato, Sylvester Stallone, Robert De Niro, Eric Roberts, and others turned down the title role.)

Not everyone in the religious community found the film objectionable. A Catholic bishop, Anthony Bosco of Greensburg, Pennsylvania, decried the picketers because they only brought the film more publicity. Indeed they did. The $7 million art film seemed to prove Henry Ford's belief that there is no such thing as bad publicity. The public outcry stimulated public interest, and when huge lines formed outside theaters on opening day, they were ticket buyers, not picketers. On only nine screens, *The Last Temptation of Christ* grossed a whopping $400,000 during its opening weekend as the more curious than devout flocked to see for themselves what all the brouhaha had been about. However, mixed to poisonous reviews and word of mouth soon nailed the picture, which disappeared from theaters after three months with a total gross of only $8 million, barely enough to cover the cost of making it. While condemning the film for showing Jesus capable of sin, Bishop Bosco liked the ending that had infuriated his peers. "The key concept, however, is that despite his struggle with the thought of crucifixion, Christ ultimately rejects the temptation and freely accepts his death on the cross in order to redeem humanity," Bosco said. But despite his approval of its message, he still advised his flock to skip the movie. "The sex in this dream sequence is probably rather subdued by modern day film standards but would probably be considered objectionable by many, even if the Christ-figure were not involved," Bosco wrote in a letter to fellow bishops. "Is the film blasphemous? That is a judgment call" the Bishop refused to make.

Liberal Protestants defended the film. The Reverend Charles Bergstrom, a Lutheran and former chairman of the People for the American Way, said, "I was not offended in any way Scripture was used and applied. Obviously, a lot of imagination about what might have been done and said was used, but sermons in church also do that." The Episcopal Bishop of New York, the Reverend Paul Moore, was one of the few in the religious community who gave the film two thumbs up and recommended it to his congregation. "The movie is artistically excellent and theologically sound," Moore said after Universal screened the film for religious leaders. Fundamentalist leaders declined the studio's screening invitation, and much of their protests were based on earlier drafts of the screenplay, which contained lines that didn't make it into the movie, such as Jesus saying to Mary Magdalene, "God sleeps between your legs." (In one draft, Jesus also blames himself for Mary Magdalene becoming a prostitute because he called off their engagement.)

Overwhelmed by the controversy, the director reiterated the film's opening disclaimer: "It's not the literal truth of the Bible. It's a work of fiction." Scorsese defended his all too human hero, saying, "If He's God, when He had temptation brought in front of him, it was easy—He was God, it was easy to reject it. But if He has the human foibles, if He has all the parts of human nature that we have, then it was just as tough for Him as it is for us.

"I didn't want a Christ who glows in the dark."

Gladiator (2000)

Directed by Ridley Scott
Written by David H. Franzoni

CAST

Russell Crowe (Maximus Decimus Meridius)
Joaquin Phoenix (Commodus)
Connie Nielson (Lucilla)
Oliver Reed (Proximo)
Richard Harris (Marcus Aurelius)
Derek Jacobi (Gracchus)

The box-office success of *Gladiator*, with a $184 million gross in the U.S. alone, proves that moviegoers love it when Hollywood makes a spectacle of itself. The archetypes of the biblical and ancient era epics are as classic and compelling as the American Western's good guys in white and bad boys in black, except the epic hero is usually either a noble gladiator or a stoic general, while the decadent emperor twirls a toga instead of a mustache.

Fifteen hundred years after a pious Christian emperor officially banned them, the Roman games still pack 'em in at the multiplex. The creators of *Gladiator* touched a national nerve with a 2,000-year-old story of blood and guts and really hungry animals. But for a change, Hollywood actually toned down the nasty nature of the villain. One historian said of the sixteen-year-old Emperor Commodus played by Joaquin Phoenix in *Gladiator*, "Commodus was one of the few Roman emperors of whom nothing good can be said." Unlike the Roman spectacles of Cecil B. DeMille, which condemned ancient debauchery by showing in leering detail just how debauched those terrible Romans were, *Gladiator*'s emperor is virtually celibate, except for some light petting with his grossed out sister, Lucilla, played with by Connie Nielsen with what looks like a permanent migraine. Far from being celibate, the real Commodus went way beyond incest and was an equal opportunity pervert, with two harems comprising 300 boys and girls each. In an unusual departure from wardrobe-as-character, the good guy, the title character Maximus (Aussie actor Russell Crowe), wears black, while Phoenix' epicene emperor looks positively virginal in one white ensemble after another. Also accurate and something you haven't seen in other Roman epics, women duke it out in the arena, an innovation introduced by that feminist madman Nero. In *Gladiator*, the ladies are buff, chariot-chauffeured-Diana-type huntresses who dispatch male adversaries with bow and arrow.

For the sake of dramatic economy, Commodus fights only once in the film, with fatal results. The real emperor fancied himself a jock and a killer and appeared in the arena 735 times, bankrupting the treasury of Rome by charging it 25,000 pieces of silver per title bout. Unlike in the film, where he loses his one and only match, his real-life adversaries were so intimidated to be fighting a "living god" that they always threw the fight, which may explain Commodus' 735 and 0 record. The Jewish politician Herodian cynically explained the emperor's impressive fight card: "In his gladiatorial combats, he defeated his opponents with ease, and he did no more than wound them, since they all submitted to him, but only because they knew he was the emperor, *not* because he was truly a gladiator."

Sometimes to make absolutely certain he won—or maybe to pump up his win-loss ratio—Commodus tossed handicapped victims into the arena, arming these paraplegics with sponges that were painted to resemble rocks, then shot arrows at them. Commodus also used blood the way others employ cologne. He liked to rub the blood of his victims on his clothes and hair. One historian wrote, "Never did he appear in public without being stained with blood." *Gladiator* omitted the emperor's signature toilette, perhaps feeling it was too ghastly to be credible.

The emperor met a more prosaic end than the creative ones he concocted for his victims. Commodus was strangled in his bathtub by his best friend, a professional wrestler named Narcissus. In *Gladiator*, Maximus guts Commodus like a fat flounder in the arena, literally hoisting the emperor on his own petard, a more dramatic end than perishing in a bathtub, which is not nearly as cinematic as being stabbed in the neck in the arena as thousands of members of the Screen Extras Guild feign bloodlust for their $75 per diem.

For all its realistic touches, like a computer generated Colosseum that for the first time in film history depicts the arena as a four-story behemoth and not the rotting, two-story ruin it is today, *Gladiator* bows to modern sensibilities in an effort to attract a contemporary audience. *The Wall Street Journal* reported that director Ridley Scott treats the *mano a mano* bouts in the Colosseum like "World Wrestling Federation" extravaganzas—only with better hair and makeup. Better dialogue too.

The Roman historian Dion Cassius claimed Commodus poisoned his father with wine, the wise and maxim-quoting philosopher-emperor Marcus Aurelius. To more dramatic effect, in *Gladiator* Commodus clutches his father to his breast in what seems like a filial touch that turns into fatal asphyxiation, drawing him to his bosom in a smothering embrace. Modern historians speculate that the aging Marcus Aurelius may have died of the plague, which was endemic in Rome at the time. Ancient historians were more polemicists than reporters and loved a dramatic fiction over a literal yawn as much as their cinematic heirs two millennia later, so they went with the poisoned wine conspiracy theory.

To play the muscular title character, Method actor Russell Crowe found it hard to lose the 35 pounds he had gained to play the zaftig whistle-blower for his Oscar-nominated performance in *The Insider*. But he managed to drop the weight and morph his body into something the pre-gubernatorial Jesse "The Body" Ventura might have felt proud to display in the ring. But Crowe didn't want the verisimilitude to stop with chiseled pecs and baseball-shaped biceps. The back story revealed that his Roman general Maximus hailed from Iberia, today's Spain, and Crowe wanted to play Maximus with a Spanish accent. "Like Antonio Banderas only with *better* elocution," he said. Director Ridley Scott overruled his star and insisted on a linguistically incorrect Old Vic shtik, or as the hard-drinking Crowe described the *lingua antiqua* he ended up using—"the Royal Shakespeare Company after a few pints."

The Fall of the Roman Empire (1964)

Directed by Anthony Mann
Written by Ben Barzman, Basilio Franchina

CAST

Sophia Loren (Lucilla)
Stephen Boyd (Livius)
Alec Guinness (Marcus Aurelius)
James Mason (Timonides)
Christopher Plummer (Commodus)
Anthony Quayle (Verulus)
John Ireland (Ballomar)
Omar Sharif (Sohamus)
Mel Ferrer (Cleander)
Eric Porter (Julianus)

With its 1960s bouffant hairdos, troweled-on mascara, and permed patricians, *The Fall of the Roman Empire* looks like *Gladiator*'s tacky twin and covers the same time period. Without computers to create a digitized Rome, but with an inflation-adjusted budget even bigger than *Gladiator*'s, the production built an entire Roman Forum from scratch, with no fusty ruins anachronistically sitting in for structures that would have been in mint condition at the time. (People who keep track of such

Lucilla (Sophia Loren) nurses her dying father, the Emperor Marcus Aurelius (Alec Guinness), while her boyfriend Livius (Stephen Boyd) nurses really bad razor burn in *The Fall of the Roman Empire*.

things say the Forum set was the biggest ever constructed, and *The Fall of the Roman Empire* also holds the record for most extras.)

As if the story of the saintly Marcus Aurelius and his psycho heir Commodus didn't have enough inherent drama, and just as *Gladiator* felt compelled to interject a fictional character, Maximus, *The Fall of the Roman Empire* revolves around a fictional rival to Commodus' throne, Livius (Stephen Boyd), and a troubled romance between Livius and Commodus' real life sister, Lucilla, played like a pagan saint by a perpetually tearful Sophia Loren, who should have gone easy on the glycerin eyedrops.

While Livius' and Commodus' (Christopher Plummer) curly hairdos look just like classic Roman statues' coifs, the director bowed to 1960s tastes when he allowed one of the most beautiful women in the movies, Loren, to look as though she just stepped

Statue of Marcus Aurelius Antoninus, Roman Emperor (121-180 A.D.). *Courtesy of The Library of Congress.*

off the cover of *Vogue* for a location shoot in ancient Rome. The slavish close-ups of her watery eyes exacerbate the modern look of tweezed eyebrows and mascara so heavily applied it almost manages to obscure Loren's enormous doe eyes.

Loren's Lucilla is a chaste romantic who only has eyes for the unavailable Livius (he's too busy fighting Commodus' inept rule to spend quality time with her), but the real Lucilla resembled another famous Roman temptress, the Empress Messalina, who like Lucilla had a yen for group sex that rivaled Clara Bow's.

As in *Gladiator*, Commodus kills his father, Marcus Aurelius (Alec Guinness), although in this go-round he uses poison, not asphyxiation. The historical jury is still out on whether Marcus Aurelius died of natural causes like the plague or was murdered, although the identity of his possible murderer has never been established except by tabloid historians like Dion Cassius, who poisoned his account of imperial Rome because he preferred the *ancien regime* of the Roman Republic.

EUROPEAN HISTORY

Braveheart
(1995)

Directed by Mel Gibson
Written by Randall Wallace

CAST

Mel Gibson (William Wallace)
Patrick McGoohan (King Edward I)
Sophie Marceau (Princess Isabelle)
Peter Hanly (Prince Edward)
James Robinson II (Young William)
Sean Lawlor (Malcolm Wallace)
Sandy Nelson (John Wallace)

If director/star Mel Gibson and screenwriter Randall Wallace played fast and loose with William Wallace's life in *Braveheart*, they might be excused because so few documented facts about the warrior who briefly united Scotland against English invaders in the 13th and 14th centuries exist.

Much of the film's story is based on an epic poem written by a minstrel called Blind Harry. Harry was not only blind, but not a great source for Wallace's life, since the minstrel poet lived almost three hundred years after the legendary hero.

Little is known of the historical Wallace. Born the son of a Scottish knight, Sir Malcolm Wallace, a minor member of the gentry, William made his first recorded appearance in history after Edward I of England deposed the Scottish king John Balliol and made himself king of the Scots in 1296. A year later, Wallace and 30 followers rose up in revolt, burned the town of Lanark and killed the English sheriff.

Wallace entered legend when he defeated a far larger English army under the command of the Earl of Surrey at Forth, Scotland, in 1297. Later that year, he invaded Northern England, but neglected to occupy the forts he decimated, then returned to Scotland where he was knighted and named Guardian of the Kingdom and regent in Balliol's absence.

Edward I had been campaigning in France when he learned of Wallace's victories and rushed back to England. His superior force of archers and cavalry easily beat Wallace's primitive spear chuckers at the Battle of Falkirk in Scotland. Wallace's reputation as a warrior was ruined, and he spent the rest of his life fighting small guerilla skirmishes with the English until his capture near Glasgow in 1305. He was brought to London, tried for treason despite his valid argument that he had never sworn allegiance to Edward I, and was executed. The manner of his execution was ghoulish but typical of the times. He was hanged, but cut down before he died, then disemboweled with his organs burned in front of him, castrated, then in what by that point must have seemed like an act of mercy, beheaded.

To this bare-bones record of bravery and butchery, the director and screenwriter injected fictional romances and a homophobic subplot that had gay activists screaming about the portrayal of Edward's son as a screaming queen.

The film portrays Gibson's Wallace as a shaggy, war-painted barbarian when in reality he was a member of the aristocracy who rose to rule Scotland for a brief time. According to historian David Reid of the State University of New York at Stony Brook, Gibson also got the makeup and home furnishings wrong. Like Medieval Mad Maxes, Mel and his boys wear blue face and body warpaint, *de rigueur* in the British Isles of Julius Caesar but *passé* in 13th century Scotland. Professor Reid, a Scottish emigrant, says, "They had 13th century Scots dressing up as Britons of the 1st century B.C.! Julius Caesar described their blue warpaint in *The Gallic Wars*."

Reid also says the film's architecture seems to have come from some time machine, housing the Scots in cozy, fireplace-furnished "crofts," or Highland cottages, circa the 18th not 13th century. Wallace's contemporaries would have lived in "'black houses,' without fireplaces, just holes in the roof for smoke to get out of," Reid says.

Braveheart is also a revenge movie, with Gibson as a Celtic Rambo who begins his rebellion against the English for personal rather than patriotic reasons. It's only after his wife is raped and murdered by an English soldier (though there's no record of this) that he decides to make war on the English.

The other romance in the film contains a glaring anachronism, although it's easy to see why the screenwriter injected the fictional affair between Wallace and the Princess of Wales, since among other things it allows Wallace, even in defeat, to have the last word, so to speak, in the war between England and Scotland.

One critic complained about the plot invention that has Edward I employ his daughter-in-law, Isabelle, the French-born Princess of Wales, as go-between in his negotiations with Wallace. Historians note that a woman in 13th century Europe would never have been used as an emissary in an era when such duties were handled by men. Madame Ambassador would have to wait for the advent of Clare Boothe Luce.

Gibson defended the historical accuracy of his film, which won him a best director Oscar and *Braveheart* four more, including best film. "I would say in broad strokes it's factual," Gibson said. "But I don't think, for example, Wallace fathered Edward III, but it's feasible." No, actually, it's not. The real Princess Isabelle was a child of six and lived in France at the time the film has her relaying messages between her father-in-law and her lover.

During one of these fictional missions, Isabelle falls in love with Wallace and becomes pregnant with his child. In the film's most gripping scene, the villainous Edward I, paralyzed and speechless after a stroke, lies impotent in bed while Isabelle whispers in his ear that Wallace's son, not Edward's, will one day rule England. The immobilized king, whom the film has portrayed as a genocidal psychopath, can only grunt and twitch in fury at the news of his heir's true paternity.

While historians quibbled about fictional additions like those, gay activists condemned the depiction of another character, Edward I's son, whose portrayal was based on fact. The future Edward II, who was indeed homosexual, was eventually disemboweled by homophobic courtiers. Although not depicted in the film because it took place after *Braveheart*'s story ends, the murder had an ironic symbolism that focused on the offending part of the king's anatomy. In what must be history's most grotesque example of *lèse majesté,* the assassins rammed a red-hot poker up the king's anus so there would be no physical evidence of foul play. Contemporary accounts by viewers of the king's open casket describe a face transfigured by indescribable pain.

That's one bit of historical trivia we won't see re-created in a film unless Pasolini comes back from the grave.

The filmmakers take the historical fact of Edward's homosexuality and turn him into an effeminate, feckless youth and the butt of much humor. Worse, in a scene played for laughs, Edward I, who despises his son's sexual orientation and homosexual hangers-on, throws his son's male lover out the window to his death. There is no historical record of such a royal defenestration.

Long before *Braveheart* made it into movie theaters, Mel Gibson was the gay community's *bête noire* for homophobic statements he allegedly made in an interview with a Spanish publication. The film only worsened his relationship with gay activists, who demonstrated outside theaters in nine cities, including Los Angeles and New York.

"The Edward II character in *Braveheart* is a throwback to the classic celluloid 'queer' played for laughs as a simpering weakling," Ellen Carton, executive director of GLAAD (the Gay & Lesbian Alliance Against Defamation), said in calling for the demonstrations. "The film's Edward II provides excessive comic relief; he's shown wearing a dress and lipstick and the audience is cued to laugh every time he appears with his male lover. As if that weren't offensive enough, in an entirely unnecessary [and invented] scene, Edward's father casts the male companion out of a window to his death to the audience's applause."

It didn't mollify gay critics that the hero is eventually disemboweled as Edward would later be, and the depiction of his grisly death elicited derision for its unlikelihood. The *Los Angeles Reader*'s film critic, Andy Klein, complained that no one could behave so heroically while having his intestines scooped out: "Wallace, in mid-disembowelment, cries out 'Freedom!' loud enough for the mob's back row to hear. The idea that any disembowelee, even a stalwart fellow like Wallace, could yell at the top of his lungs, even as his entrails are being ripped pell-mell from his thorax, is simply too much." One aspect of Wallace's execution *was* too much for the squeamish director, who didn't even hint at, much less show, the portion of the execution that included castration. Ouch!

The Passion of Joan of Arc
(1928)

Directed by Carl Theodor Dreyer
Written by Joseph Delteil, Carl Theodor Dreyer

CAST

Maria Falconetti (Jeanne d'Arc)
Eugene Silvain (Eveque Pierre Cauchon)
Antonin Artaud (Jean Massieu)
Michel Simon (Judge Jean Lemaitre)
Maurice Schutz (Nicolas Loyseleur)

Joan of Arc
(1948)

Directed by Victor Fleming
Written by Maxwell Anderson, Andrew Solt

CAST

Ingrid Bergman (Joan of Arc)
Jose Ferrer (Dauphin, Charles V)
Francis L. Sullivan (Pierre Cauchon)
J. Carrol Naish (Count John of Luxembourg)
Ward Bond (La Hire)
Shepperd Strudwick (Father Jean Massieu)
Gene Lockhart (Georges la Tremouille)
Leif Erickson (Jean Dunois)
Cecil Kellaway (Jean Le Maistre)

Saint Joan
(1957)

Directed by Otto Preminger
Written by Graham Greene, George Bernard Shaw (play)

CAST

Jean Seberg (Saint Joan)
Richard Widmark (The Dauphin)
Richard Todd (Dunois)
John Gielgud (Warwick)
Felix Aylmer (Inquisitor)
Archie Duncan (Robert de Baudricourt)
Harry Andrews (John de Stogumber)

The Messenger: The Story of Joan of Arc (1999)

Directed by Luc Besson
Written by Luc Besson, Andrew Birkin

CAST

Milla Jovovich (Joan of Arc)
Dustin Hoffman (The Conscience)
Faye Dunaway (Yolande D'Aragon)
John Malkovich (Charles VII)
Tcheky Karyo (Dunois)
Vincent Cassel (Gilles de Rais)
Pascal Gregory (The Duke of Alencon)
Richard Ridings (La Hire)
Desmond Harrington (Aulon)
Timothy West (Cauchon)

The true story of Joan of Arc, an illiterate teenage peasant who heard voices from God and followed their counsel to successfully lead the armies of France against the English for a time, begs for cinematic treatment, and there have been at least four screen depictions of her life. Despite the inherent drama in the historical story of Joan, including a built-in fiery climax, moviemakers have felt compelled to juice up her tale by fictionalizing a life that was stranger than fiction.

Some critics felt Ingrid Bergman, at thirty-three, was a bit long in the tooth to play the nineteen-year-old title hero-ine of *Joan of Arc*. Here she proves the wisdom of always wearing full body armor and makeup before going into battle.

The most recent rendering of history's most famous burn victim, *The Messenger: The Story of Joan of Arc* (1999), deserves points for providing a psychological context to better understand her life, even though the context was made from whole cloth. Director Luc Besson embroiders the life of the saint (played by his then girlfriend, supermodel Milla Jovovich), but the resulting tapestry is a brilliant case study of what makes Joan run.

In Besson's retelling, English soldiers rampage through Joan's hometown of Dom-remy. She returns home from church and finds her older sister, Catherine, about to hide in the cupboard. Instead, Catherine stuffs her younger sibling inside, closes the cup-board door, then stands guard as three English soldiers enter. Two of the English goons help themselves to the family's dinner, while a third—filthy, leering—pins Catherine's body to the cupboard with his sword, then rapes her corpse. Inside, Joan narrowly misses being impaled on the sword herself. The youngster watches the rapist's contorted face through cracks in the cupboard door, while the other soldiers watch. When the soldier finishes his necrophiliac act, he pulls up his fly and says to his comrades, "Your turn."

While the horrific scene gives a sophisticated, 20th century psychological explanation for Joan's later zealotry in driving the English from her country, there is no record that she had any siblings.

The rest of the film treats Joan's exertions against the English invaders as symptoms of post-traumatic stress disorder rather than the promptings of Saints Margaret, Catherine, and Michael, who appeared to her in what may have been hallucinations caused by epilepsy and told her to whip British butt.

The facts and myths surrounding Joan also provided a delectable vehicle for Victor Fleming, a director who specialized in epics like *Gone With the Wind*. Fleming valiantly attempted to provide a rational explanation for the supernatural apocrypha attributed to the toughest—and first—female G.I. in history. Strangely, for all the director's attempts at verisimilitude, he cast an over-the-hill superstar, Ingrid Bergman, then 33, in the title role of his 1948 production, *Joan of Arc*.

In the film, when Joan tries to gain access to a military commander who can lead her to the Dauphin, France's uncrowned king, the hens in the courtyard stop laying eggs until she gets her way. But the director suggests the incident may have been a coincidence rather than a miracle.

When Joan is denied an audience with the Dauphin, she predicts the soldier who bars her way will die soon—and he drops dead on the spot! The director also stages this "miracle" so it appears that the soldier may have died of natural causes.

As though the kangaroo court that sent her to the stake didn't contain enough inherent drama, Fleming felt compelled to tweak the trial with an ahistorical conflict. One of her judges in the film excuses himself from the proceedings because of procedural and legal flaws in the charges against Joan. The jurist is arrested by the Bishop of Beauvais, England's point man in France and the worst French collaborationist until Petain, for refusing to preside over the trial. Perhaps because of its notoriety, the transcripts of Joan's trial have been preserved over the centuries, and contemporary documents show no evidence that any of the judges objected to the corrupt nature of the proceedings.

Taking a slightly different tack, Otto Preminger's glossy production, *Saint Joan* (1957), remained remarkably faithful to the 1923 classic play by George Bernard Shaw. Joan's alleged miracles are debunked and explained in the film. But Shaw, with Preminger following his lead, couldn't resist creating a whole new mythology for one of history's most famous Catholics, namely that the saint was a proto-Protestant who anticipated Luther's doctrine that the faithful could speak directly to God (Joan's voices), which was a burning offense in her day and in Luther's. In both the play and film, Joan's Lutheranesque speeches during her trial were all fabricated by Shaw, who ignored the extant transcripts of the proceedings.

A renowned troublemaker who won the Nobel Prize for literature in 1925 in part because of his masterpiece, *Saint Joan*, the crowning achievement of his long career, Shaw couldn't resist the ironic resonance of turning Joan into a closet Protestant since his play premiered a few years after the Catholic Church canonized her.

Half a millennium after Joan frustrated England's colonizing efforts in France, the British were still so ticked off at the saint that authorities in Britain banned the showing of what is considered by critics the most artistic rendering of her life, the 1928 French film *The Passion of Joan of Arc*, which starred the famous stage actress Renée Falconetti in the title role, which was also her only screen performance. (Legend has it that after enduring Joan's "passion" in a series of tight close-ups that were praised for their cinematic innovation, Mlle. Falconetti had a nervous breakdown and vowed never to appear in front of the cameras again, a promise she kept.)

The movie, which *New Yorker* film critic Pauline Kael called "one of the greatest of all movies. Falconetti's Joan may be the finest performance ever recorded on film," was also a major box-office dud, or in *Variety's* acid assessment, "isn't worth a dollar to any commercial picture theatre in the U.S."

The film's poor reception by the public may have resulted from avant-garde director Carl Dreyer's curious decision to focus on the last day of Joan's life with an endless series of close-ups of Falconetti's tormented face as sadistic English inquisitors grill her in five interrogation scenes, which may explain the British ban, which was lifted two years after the film's release in France.

History buffs may cavil that the director missed all the drama leading up to her last fiery day on earth, but French theater fans got to see every pore on the star's beautiful,

Saint Joan of Arc (1412–1431), *Courtesy of the Library of Congress.*

ravaged face. Despite the film's less than two-hour running time, the pathological use of the camera eventually seems more cruel than Joan's interrogators—and after 100 minutes, ultimately tedious to everyone but voyeurs who shared Dreyer's passion for Joan of Arc.

Christopher Columbus (1949)

Directed by David MacDonald
Written by Muriel Box, Sydney Box

CAST

Frederic March (Christopher Columbus)
Florence Eldridge (Queen Isabella)
Francis L. Sullivan (Francisco de Bobadilla)
Kathleen Ryan (Beatriz)
Derek Bond (Diego de Arana)
Nora Swinburne (Joanna de Torres)

Christopher Columbus (1985)

Directed by Alberto Lattuada
Written by Adriano Bolzoni, Laurence Heath

CAST

Gabriel Byrne (Christopher Columbus)
Faye Dunaway (Queen Isabella)
Nicol Williamson (King Ferdinand)

Max von Sydow (King John of Portugal)

Oliver Reed (Martin Pinzon)

Christopher Columbus: The Discovery (1992)

Directed by John Glen

Written by John Briley, Mario Puzo (story)

CAST

Marlon Brando (Tomas de Torquemada)

Tom Selleck (King Ferdinand)

Georges Corraface (Christopher Columbus)

Rachel Ward (Queen Isabella)

Robert Davi (Martin Pinzon)

Catherine Zeta-Jones (Beatriz)

1492: Conquest of Paradise (1992)

Directed by Ridley Scott

Written by Roselyne Bosch

CAST

Gerard Depardieu (Columbus)

Armand Assante (Sanchez)

Sigourney Weaver (Queen Isabel)

Loren Dean (Older Fernando)

Angela Molina (Beatriz)

Fernando Rey (Marchena)

Michael Wincott (Moxica)

Tcheky Karyo (Pinzon)

1949's *Christopher Columbus* (with Frederic March as the Italian conquistador) is considered to be the most accurate film portrayal of the famous explorer and genocidal maniac.

The controversy surrounding Columbus' discovery of the New World, not to mention all the mythology that has been added to it, has long tempted Hollywood, which has produced four films about the Italian explorer's life and exploits.

Ironically, the first film, eponymously titled and produced in 1949 without the benefit of today's special effects, remains the most accurate portrayal of Columbus. Frederic March gives a multi-dimensional, warts and all portrayal that coincides with the historical record that Columbus was obnoxious, cranky, sanctimonious, determined, quick to anger, and an all around pain in neck. Unlike later casting, Frederic March even resembles physical descriptions of Columbus, although no contemporary portrait of one of the most pivotal figures in history has come down to us.

More recent films on Columbus have presented a distorted picture of the explorer because they used as primary source material an unreliable source: a whitewashed, mythologized biography written by Columbus' illegitimate son, Hernando, that borders on hagiography.

1985's *Christopher Columbus*, with Irish (!) actor Gabriel Byrne (much too handsome for the title role), dramatizes the clichés of Columbus' voyages, which have the further misfortune of being mostly myth, like his son's biography. Columbus did not, as every schoolchild learns and this film repeats, recruit his crew from the jails of Seville. Only three of the sailors on his maiden voyage were ex-criminals.

The real Columbus promoted enslaving the indigenous people he found on his voyages, but to maintain his heroic character, Byrne's Columbus is anti-slavery and King Ferdinand and Queen Isabella are indicted as supporters of the "peculiar institution." In reality, both rulers condemned Columbus for the practice. In keeping with its anti-Eurocentric, multicultural bias, the film claims the Catholic Church also encouraged slavery despite the fact that the Pope at the time, Paul III, issued the encyclical *Sublimis Deus*, forbidding any mistreatment of the Indians, especially enslavement.

Two films were released in 1992 to celebrate the quincentenary of Columbus' voyage to the new world.

What can you say about a film (*Christopher Columbus: The Discovery*) that was made by the producer of *Superman* and co-written by the author of *The Godfather*, a movie that casts TV's Magnum P.I., Tom Selleck, as King Ferdinand, who, with his wife, Isabella (gorgeous former fashion model Rachel Ward risibly miscast as the dumpy monarch), finances Columbus' trips. The word "docudrama" does not come to mind, nor does it appear on the screen. In addition to the bizarre casting, which includes Marlon Brando still relying on The Method to portray the sadistic Spanish inquisitor Torquemada, the screenwriters, among them John Briley (*Gandhi*) and Mario Puzo (*The Godfather*), add unnecessary bits of fictionalized drama to a story that contained plenty of genuine historical thrills.

To liven things up on the voyage, the film has one mutinous sailor murdered and another devoured by sharks. During the real trip, no one died on Columbus' watch.

Queen Isabella was a pious fanatic who expelled the Jews and the Moors from her kingdom, including many of her advisers who were Jewish. In the film, Columbus op-

Columbus (Gerard Depardieu) convinces Queen Isabella (Sigourney Weaver) and King Ferdinand of Spain (Fernando Garcia Rimada) that the world isn't flat in *1492: Conquest of Paradise*, although most educated Europeans of the time already knew that.

poses the Queen's anti-Semitism, although there is no historical record that he championed the Jewish cause in Spain. The film attributes its hero's pro-Semitism to his fictional friendship with a Jewish mapmaker.

The production curiously fails to take advantage of one well-known fact about Columbus' life that would have added pathos and irony to the story. After mismanaging the lands he discovered in America, Columbus was sent home to Spain in chains and died in disgrace. In the film, Columbus dies a royal favorite, honored by Ferdinand and Isabella.

More bizarre casting afflicts *1492: Conquest of Paradise*. The short, fat Queen of Spain is played by the Amazonian star of *Alien*, Sigourney Weaver. Her Isabella is a flirtatious charmer who wears skimpy designer gowns in the dead of winter. Ferdinand of Aragon, who ruled Spain jointly with his wife and inspired Machiavelli's wheeler-dealer *The Prince*, is reduced to something less than a cameo and doesn't utter a single word in the film.

The villains here are academe—the faculty of the University of Salamanca, which opposes Columbus' voyage because they believe the earth is flat. Actually, all educated Europeans by the end of the 15th century realized the world was round, and university scholars correctly maintained that Columbus had underestimated the distance to what he thought was China by thousands of miles. The University was at the cutting edge of cartography and renowned throughout Europe for its scholarship. The academics were not the backward dolts portrayed in the film and designed to heighten Columbus' wisdom and innovative thinking by contrast.

Born in Genoa, Columbus spoke Castilian Spanish (*castellano*) with an Italian-Portuguese accent, developed during the years he spent at the court of Portugal unsuccessfully trying to gain funding for his trip. He married the daughter of minor Portuguese nobility, who provided him with an introduction to Spain's rulers. Depardieu's Columbus speaks with an impenetrable French accent that should be accompanied with subtitles.

In the film, Columbus is betrayed by a single individual, an aristocrat named Adrian Moxica, who accompanies him on his second voyage to the New World and bad-mouths him to the queen on their return. The real Columbus was an incompetent administrator and not just the courtier Moxica, but other members of Columbus' entourage, including ill-treated colonists and Dominican friars who condemned his enslavement of Native Americans, provided the damaging information that led to Columbus' trip back to Spain in shackles.

As if the chains and other indignities weren't enough to enlist our sympathies, the film inaccurately claims that Columbus was all but forgotten until his son's skewed biography revived his name. In fact, 16th century chronicles are filled with Columbus' exploits and praise for his accomplishments.

Christopher Columbus, reputed discoverer of America (1451–1506). *Courtesy of the Library of Congress.*

The Private Life of Henry VIII (1933)

Directed by Alexander Korda
Written by Arthur Wimperis, Lajos Biro (story)

CAST

Charles Laughton (King Henry VIII)
Franklin Dyall (Thomas Cromwell)
Laurence Hanray (Archbishop Thomas Cranmer)
Merle Oberon (Anne Boleyn)
Wendy Barrie (Jane Seymour)
Elsa Lanchester (Anne of Cleves)

Robert Shaw's King Henry VIII is a cuddly psychopath in *A Man for All Seasons*.

Binnie Barnes (Catherine Howard)
Everley Gregg (Catherine Parr)

A Man for All Seasons
(1966)

Directed by Fred Zinnemann
Written by Robert Bolt

CAST

Paul Scofield (Sir Thomas More)
Wendy Hiller (Alice More)
Leo McKern (Thomas Cromwell)

Sir Thomas More (Paul Scofield) is *A Man for All Seasons*, a martyred saint who goes to the scaffold rather than betray his Catholic faith. The real More was a bigot and zealot who felt all Protestants should be burned alive. (Susannah York plays his daughter.)

Sir Thomas More (1478–1535). *Copyright © J. F. Gleeson, courtesy of the Library of Congress.*

Robert Shaw (King Henry VIII)
Orson Welles (Cardinal Wolsey)
Susannah York (Margaret More)
Nigel Davenport (The Duke of Norfolk)
John Hurt (Richard Rich)
Corin Redgrave (William Roper)
Cyril Luckham (Archbishop Cranmer)

Anne of the Thousand Days (1969)

Directed by Charles Jarrott
Written by Bridget Boland, Maxwell Anderson (play)

CAST

Richard Burton (King Henry VIII)
Genevieve Bujold (Anne Boleyn)
Irene Papas (Catherine of Aragon)
Anthony Quayle (Cardinal Wolsey)
John Colicos (Thomas Cromwell)
Michael Hordern (Thomas Boleyn)
Katharine Blake (Elizabeth Boleyn)
Peter Jeffrey (Duke of Norfolk)
Joseph O'Connor (Archbishop Fisher)
William Squire (Thomas More)

The Six Wives of Henry VIII (TV miniseries) (1971)

Directed by Naomi Capon, John Glenister
Written by Beverley Cross, Nick McCarty, Jean Morris, John Prebble, Rosemary Anne Sisson, Ian Thorne

Henry VIII (Richard Burton) flirts with his second wife (Genevieve Bujold, in the title role) in iambic pentameter in *Anne of the Thousand Days*.

CAST

Keith Michell (Henry VIII)

Annette Crosbie (Catherine of Aragon)

Dorothy Tutin (Anne Boleyn)

Anne Stallybrass (Jane Seymour)

Elvi Hale (Anne of Cleves)

Angela Pleasence (Catherine Howard)

Rosalie Crutchley (Catherine Parr)

John Baskcomb (Cardinal Wolsey)

Bernard Hepton (Archbishop Thomas Cranmer)

Wolfe Morris (Thomas Cromwell)

Jo Kendall (Princess Mary)

Edward Atienza (Eustache Chapuys)

Sheila Burrell (Lady Rochford)

Michael Osborne (Mark Smeaton)

Ronald Adam (Cardinal Campeggio)

Carry On Henry
(1971)

Directed by Gerald Thomas
Written by Talbot Rothwell

CAST

Sid James (King Henry VIII)

Kenneth Williams (Thomas Cromwell)

Joan Sims (Queen Marie of Normandy)

Terry Scott (Cardinal Wolsey)

Peter Gilmore (Francis, King of France)

Gertan Klauber (Bidet)

Bill Maynard (Guy Fawkes)

Leon Greene (Torturer)

David Prowse (Torturer)

Monika Dietrich (Katherine Howard)

Patsy Rowlands (Queen)

Jane Cardew (Henry's Second Wife)

Henry VIII and His Six Wives
(1973)

Directed by Waris Hussein
Written by Ian Thorne

CAST

Keith Michell (Henry VIII)
Donald Pleasence (Thomas Cromwell)
Charlotte Rampling (Anne Boleyn)
Jane Asher (Jane Seymour)
Frances Cuka (Katherine of Aragon)
Lynne Frederick (Catherine Howard)
Jenny Bos (Anne of Cleves)
Barbara Leigh-Hunt (Catherine Parr)
Michael Gough (Norfolk)
Brian Blessed (Suffolk)

Keith Mitchell is a lady-killer (literally) in *Henry VIII and His Six Wives* with Jane Asher as his third missus, Jane Seymour.

Michael Goodliffe (Thomas More)
Bernard Hepton (Cranmer)
Garfield Morgan (Cardiner)
John Bryans (Wolsey)

Crossed Swords
(1978)

Directed by Richard Fleischer
Written by Berta Dominguez, George MacDonald Fraser, Pierre Spengler, Mark
   Twain (novel)

CAST

Oliver Reed (Miles Hendon)
Raquel Welch (Edith)
Charlton Heston (King Henry VIII)
Mark Lester (Edward/Tom)
Ernest Borgnine (John Canty)
George C. Scott (The Ruffler)
Rex Harrison (Duke of Norfolk)
Richard Hurndall (Cranmer)

Hollywood loves larger-than-life figures. Their size, whether emotional or physi-cal, makes a perfect fit with the big screen. So it's no surprise that a mountain of a man like Henry VIII (six-foot-three, a giant in those days) has been the subject of so many films for three-quarters of a century.

The 16th century English monarch's screen life began in 1933 with Charles Laughton playing the title role in *The Private Life of Henry VIII*, a British produc-tion. The film was the first screen portrayal of Henry, and most critics say that it was also the worst in terms of accuracy. Despite critical complaints that Laughton played the aging king like a caricature and a buffoon, Laughton's over-the-top performance won him a best actor Oscar, and the movie was the languishing British film industry's first international hit.

Laughton's Henry drools and belches in public and throws chicken bones over his shoulder, something the real Henry, a Renaissance *gallant* whose manners, in public at least, were impeccable, would never have done. There is, however, some historical justification for Laughton's acting excesses. The film captures the king in his last years, when he was not only in his dotage, but possibly dying of the third stage of syphilis, which would account for Laughton's drooling imbecility. (Historians still can't agree on what actually killed the king in 1547, with forensic scientists arguing for everything from tuberculosis, heart and renal failure, sinusitis, and morbid obesity to brain damage after one too many jousts. The famous portrait by Hans Holbein of the grossly overweight king suggests complications of obesity as the cause of death.)

There have been at least five other screen Henrys, in either leading or supporting roles, but even in the latter, the plus-size ruler manages to grab center stage whenever he appears.

There was a veritable outbreak of movies on Henry in the 1960s and 1970s, with diverse portraits ranging from a stately movie based on a play written in verse (*Anne of the Thousand Days*) to a 1971 farce (*Carry On Henry*) that made Laughton's drooler seem like a venerable statesman by comparison. Henry had a supporting but major role in the best screen portrayal of him, Robert Shaw's in *A Man for All Seasons*. Charlton Heston revived the Henry-as-Slob myth in 1978's *Crossed Swords*, based on Mark Twain's novel *The Prince and the Pauper*, although the fairy tale accurately depicted the king's death throes, when he muttered, "Monks, monks, monks"—his final words on the victims whose monasteries and wealth he had expropriated with a guilt that only appeared on his deathbed.

Keith Michell, who played Henry in a six-part British miniseries (*The Six Wives of Henry VIII*) and later reprised the role in a 1973 feature film (*Henry and His Six Wives*), which recast the miniseries' wives with younger, more photogenic actresses, had the toughest job since his performance covered most of the king's life, from idealistic (and svelte) youth to lady-killer (literally) to the living, rotting corpse Henry became with a foul-smelling ulcer on his leg that would not heal and made favor-seeking courtiers faint from the odor.

Anne of a Thousand Days saddled its Henry, Richard Burton, with the difficult task of speaking his lines in iambic pentameter, based on the play by Maxwell Anderson.

Burton was a megastar by then, a co-star in the international tour of the Liz and Dick show, and it may have been vanity and star clout that resulted in a Henry who was much too thin to play the corpulent, middle-aged monarch. If you don't count Laughton's clown, this soap opera look at the king's wooing, bedding, and beheading of second wife Anne Boleyn is probably the least accurate historically. While Henry did have an affair with Anne's older sister Mary, in the film Mary also conceives a child by Henry, who then abandons her to the shame of unwed motherhood. The real Mary was never impregnated by her royal lover. The film's Anne Boleyn—Genevieve Bujold looking amazingly like contemporary paintings of the luckless queen—is a big tease in the film, rejecting Henry's advances at first. In real life, Anne, like every other woman in England, was more than eager to hop into bed with a man who was famous for showering honors and titles on the relatives of every woman he took a fancy to. (Anne's father, a commoner, was elevated to an earldom after Henry fell for his daughter.) The King last saw his second wife at a May Day tournament, after which he sent her to the Tower to be tried on trumped up charges of adultery and witchcraft. For high drama, Henry appears at the trial (he stayed away in real life) and intimidates witnesses into offering false testimony against his wife. The film Henry also offers to let Anne keep her head if she agrees to an annulment of the marriage, a life-saving proposal that the real Henry never tendered to a woman he had come to loathe for her radical Protestantism and jealous rages prompted by his extramarital flings.

Henry necessarily plays the villain in the best film about the period, *A Man for All Seasons*, since he sends the saintly Sir Thomas More (best actor Oscar winner Paul Scofield) to the scaffold for opposing the king's break with Rome. To inflate Henry's villainy and boost More's saint appeal, the film soft-pedals the fact that More was a bigoted, born-again Catholic who wrote hundreds of pages of polemical tracts demanding the death of Protestants, preferably by being burned alive. More displayed his bloodlust in more than one tract, none of which made it into the screenplay, which seemed intent on canonizing him a second time after the Pope made him a saint in 1935. "The author showeth his opinion concerning the burning of heretics, and that it is lawful, necessary, and well done," More wrote. In another tract, he demanded that Martin Luther and other "heretics" be incinerated. (More enjoyed a

Henry VIII (1509–1547), engraved by T. A. Dean.
Courtesy of the Library of Congress.

kinder execution by beheading, normally reserved for the noble-born, which More was not.) Henry never persecuted Catholics as viciously as More would have hounded Protestants had he been king rather than the king's chancellor, the Renaissance equivalent of Prime Minister.

Sadly for history buffs, all of the film bios of Henry VIII ignore or only briefly touch upon the fascinating political events of his reign: the Reformation in England, the dissolution of the monasteries, and the King's ill-fated use of Parliament to enact legislation that not only allowed Henry to dispose of wives and the Catholic Church, but turned the legislative body into a powerful political organ that would eventually usurp all the monarchy's power and behead a reactionary monarch (Charles I) to boot.

It's understandable, however, that films about Henry subordinated the king's public life to his private one, since the latter contained more real life drama than many of the soap operatic depictions of it on the big screen.

Elizabeth
(1998)

Directed by Shekhar Kapur
Written by Michael Hirst

CAST

Cate Blanchett (Elizabeth I)

Kathy Burke (Queen Mary I)

Joseph Fiennes (Robert Dudley, Earl of Leicester)

Emily Mortimer (Kat Ashley)

Christopher Eccleston (Duke of Norfolk)

Geoffrey Rush (Sir Francis Walsingham)

Richard Attenborough (Sir William Cecil, Lord Burghley)

Fanny Ardant (Mary of Guise)

Vincent Cassel (Duc d'Anjou)

John Gielgud (Pope Paul IV)

Elizabeth, the 1998 film about the great 16th century monarch, takes the old Oscar Levant joke that he knew Doris Day *before* she was a virgin and applies it literally to the life of England's Virgin Queen.

Elizabeth is a royal version of the *Bildungsroman*, a fancy German term for a novel about the spiritual and intellectual development of the protagonist. The film charts the emotional evolution of Queen Elizabeth I from lusty youth to born-again virgin. Using both Madonnas as role models, the screenwriter, Michael Hirst, has the Tudor vixen turned celibate proclaim at film's end, "I have *become* a virgin."

During this unusual transformation on screen, many critics felt history had been abandoned in favor of modern day soap opera and gangster flicks. Indian director Shekhar Kapur admitted he wasn't making a documentary. "I had to make a choice: whether I wanted the details of history or the emotions and essence of history to prevail." Emotion in the form of outrageous anachronism won out over historical accuracy, detractors scoffed. Or as the *New York Times* said, "This is indeed historical drama for anyone whose idea of history is back issues of *Vogue*"—although the *Times'* Janet Maslin might have added that this version of history also contained bits of *Dynasty, Dallas*, and the *Godfather* trilogy.

Britain's *Majesty* magazine, which reports on present-day royals with the thoroughness of a biologist examining a paramecium under a microscope, found a lot to complain about in this depiction of a Renaissance royal. *Elizabeth* even got the opening shot wrong, according to *Majesty*. The chilling sequence shows three Protestant martyrs being burned at the stake by the Catholic bigot "Bloody Mary" Tudor, Elizabeth's older half-sister. The film correctly identifies two of the burn victims as Bishops Latimer and Ridley, but who is the unnamed female bound to the stake with them? No such woman joined their (former) Excellencies on the pyre. (The date of the execution is also off by a year, fastidious *Majesty* noted.)

Then there's the supporting cast, which needs to take a look at the DOB on their driver's licenses. Elizabeth is 25 at the beginning of her reign (right) and her chief minister, William Cecil, is a venerable old sage (wrong). The real Cecil, later Lord Burleigh, was roughly the same age as his sovereign and lived long enough to counsel her through much of her reign. Maybe Cecil was turned into a white-bearded pensioner so a great older actor like Lord Richard Attenborough could play him. In a reversal of this premature aging process, Elizabeth's favorite lady-in-waiting, Kat Ashley, is transformed into the Queen's girlish contemporary when she had in fact been the pre-queen princess' governess. Elizabeth's spymaster, Sir Francis Walsingham, was also only 25 at the time of his sovereign's ascension to the throne, but here he's played by the middle-aged Oscar winner Geoffrey Rush (*Shine*). Walsingham was a strict Puritan who would never have committed murder or romanced the Queen Regent of Scotland, as he does in the film. And his Scottish inamorata, Mary of Guise, was a pious Catholic who would never have had sex outside marriage period—and especially not with a Protestant—and worse, a Puritan like Walsingham.

Elizabeth's biggest historical stretch has the virgin princess, then queen, engaged in a rapturous affair with Robert Dudley, whose prowess in and out of bed she rewarded with the title of Earl of Leicester. *Majesty* magazine, which treats 21st century royals with as much prim discretion as it would like films to treat their 16th century counterpart, says it's unlikely the queen and her earl ever went all the way, although other historians beg to differ, as did director Kapur, who insisted, "She had at least three very well documented relationships. She made a declaration of virginity as a political statement."

Regardless of the truth, an Elizabeth without love would be like Maui without sunshine. OK, it does rain in Hawaii, but that's not the popular image of the state. The real Elizabeth probably lies somewhere in between: a horny youngster who forced herself to give up men in order not to dilute her power with a self-aggrandizing consort or lover. Whether or not Dudley bedded his Queen, he certainly did not, as Joseph Fiennes' Dudley does in the film, betray her. As if their illicit affair didn't have enough soap, Dudley is shown plotting against the Queen, despite the record that shows he was a faithful, besotted lover and subject until his death. And despite her own apparent infatuation with Dudley, had he plotted against Elizabeth, one of earliest practitioners of *Realpolitik*, who put affairs of state above those of the heart, she would have ordered her lover's execution at the first whiff of treason without hesitation or regret, as she did with two other powerful aristocrats who tried to take her throne away, the Duke of Norfolk and the boy toy of her final years, the Earl of Essex. The biggest loser may be Elizabeth's French suitor, the Duc d'Alencon, historically heterosexual but a drag queen with a harem of boys and girls in the film. The transgendered rendering, however, does allow a terrific scene where Elizabeth decides to call the marriage off when she discovers the Duc reveling with his minions and wearing a more fetching frock than hers. You don't have to be a film buff to notice that the penultimate montage, a series of assassinations/executions that wipe out Elizabeth's adversaries, was an *homage* bordering on plagiarism of the alternating baptism/mob hits in *The Godfather* except that this Elizabeth is more amoral and ruthless than Don Corleone.

The film's costume designer, Alexandra Byrne, wouldn't disagree with the *New York Times'* dismissal of *Elizabeth* as history as interpreted by *Vogue*. Instead of Holbein, Byrne said she took her inspiration from French couturier Christian Lacroix, inventor of the 1980s "poof" dress. Byrne embraced anachronism for the sake of character. Elizabethan ladies of the court wore rigid corsets stiffened with pieces of wood that made them ramrod straight. Elizabeth and her ladies in the film wear soft and curved corsets that wouldn't make the royal scene for another three centuries. But in the final sequence, when Elizabeth desexualizes herself with a boyish haircut hidden under a fright wig and white pancake makeup that heighten her androgyny (actually, she wore clown-like makeup to hide horrible smallpox scars), the self-proclaimed Virgin Queen wears the historically correct wood-supported corsets in keeping with her new, strait-laced persona. To underscore her virginity, she also wears a chalk-white gown, a color the colorful monarch eschewed.

Critics even carped about Elizabeth's score, which included riffs from 19th century orchestral composer Edward Elgar and the final scene's *Requiem* by 18th century Mozart. Music professor Ross Duffin of Case Western Reserve University said composer David Hirschfelder made "a mess of the music." Hirschfelder offered several justifications for the musical century-hopping, the most cogent being the director made me do it. "Shekhar made it very clear to me right from our first meeting that he didn't want to limit the palette of the score to the sound of Elizabethan music," which is primitive, saddled with limited harmonic language, and played with tinny instruments lacking the rich sound of late 18th century and later symphonic music. Professor Duffin also complained that the film's choreographer turned the Elizabethan *La Volta* into a sexy dance that looked more like a tango. The *New York Times* was even crueler and felt the *La Volta* sequence looked as though it had been lifted from the dance floor of *Saturday Night Fever.*

Director Kapur dismissed all these historical fact checkers by suggesting he was going for *pentimento*, not bio: "We took the icon, and went behind the icon," Kapur said.

Shakespeare in Love (1998)

Directed by John Madden
Written by Marc Norman, Tom Stoppard

CAST

Joseph Fiennes (William Shakespeare)
Gwyneth Paltrow (Viola De Lesseps)

Geoffrey Rush (Philip Henslowe)
Steven Beard (Makepeace, the Preacher)
Simon Callow (Tilney, Master of the Revels)
Judi Dench (Queen Elizabeth)
Joe Roberts (John Webster)
Ben Affleck (Ned Alleyn)

Despite the fact that William Shakespeare's plays have been scrutinized and lionized by scholars and theater-lovers for 400 years, very little is known about the man who wrote them. There are records of his real estate transactions, minor lawsuits, and a curious will that bequeathed his second-best bed to his long-ignored wife, Anne Hathaway. We also know that he wrote two plays a year for his theater company, had a handsome income, invested prudently and retired to his hometown of Stratford-upon-Avon, where he bought one of the finest homes in town. The historical Shakespeare, Harvard professor Stephen Greenblatt wrote, is "a major yawn" and not the stuff that dreams—or movies—are made of.

This lacuna of historical information proved invaluable for screenwriters Marc Norman and Tom Stoppard, who had free rein to invent just about anything they wanted while writing *Shakespeare in Love*.

Despite the paucity of biographical data on Shakespeare, the writers injected a lot of what little information exists into the script. Real and fictional characters populate the lively (and filthy) world of 1590s London, during the zenith of the Renaissance. The heroine Viola de Lesseps is fictional, as is her obnoxious fiancé, the Earl of Wessex, but many of the other players existed. Philip Henslowe, the perpetually out of pocket impresario, was the actual owner of the Rose Theatre in which the premiere of *Romeo and Juliet*, the film's centerpiece, takes place. Sir Edmund Tilney, who threatens to close down Shakespeare's racy production about the two star-crossed lovers, was Queen Elizabeth's Master of the Revels, a misnomer since his real job was censor, although unlike in the film, he was more obsessed with treason against his mistress than R-rated romances on the Elizabethan stage. Richard Burbage was the equivalent of a matinee idol of his day and Shakespeare's leading man and partner. Elizabeth I was England's greatest monarch, but not the five-foot-zero shrimp the actress Judi Dench, who plays her, was. Makepeace is a composite of the Puritanical preachers who half a century later would succeed in shuttering theaters throughout England during Cromwell's rule. Alhtough Ben Affleck's role as Ned Alleyn might seem to have been created out of whole cloth to give Gwyneth Paltrow quality time with her then-boyfriend, Alleyn was a matinee idol of the time who became famous for starring in plays by Shakespeare's rival, Christopher Marlowe, who also has a cameo in the film. We seem to know more about Alleyn than Shakespeare. In the film, leading man Alleyn is seduced into taking the supporting role of Mercutio when he's falsely told that the title of *Romeo and Juliet* will be *Mercutio*. John Webster, the street urchin who loves Shakespeare's gory tragedy *Titus Andronicus* and is always calling for more gore, would grow up to be the equivalent of a slasher movie director and author of the bloodiest plays of the era, including *The Duchess of Malfi*.

One of the main plot twists of the film, the evil Earl of Wessex' plan to take his unwilling bride, Viola, across the ocean to his tobacco plantation in Virginia, couldn't have happened because Virginia didn't exist at the time. (Running off with her to Ibiza would have been more historically accurate and scenic, but would have lacked the aching finality of her permanent removal to the New World.)

Tom Stoppard, probably the greatest living playwright in England, rewrote Marc Norman's (*Cutthroat Island, Waterworld*) unproducible script and turned it into Oscar's best picture of 1998. Stoppard has made a career out of injecting modern elements into historical plays like *Rosencratz and Guildenstern Are Dead* and *Travesties*. Stoppard's affinity for anachronisms also suffuses his draft of *Shakespeare in Love*. His neurotic bard suffers from the very modern and probably eternal problem of writer's block, and before finding Viola as the muse who inspires his *Romeo and Juliet*, the Bard visits the Elizabethan equivalent of a psychiatrist, who times their one-hour sessions with an hourglass. Then there's the chatty boatman, who seems more like a combination of New York cabbie and a struggling writer with a lousy day job rowing boats but the ambition to be a playwright with a script he tries to pitch to Shakespeare. Although her appearance provides a sparkling denouement in the film, the real Queen Elizabeth would not have attended the premiere of *Romeo and Juliet* in a filthy London theater. When it came to the theatrical productions, the monarch ordered in, inviting acting troupes to play "the palace" at one of her many residences. As a marriageable and marketable virgin, the daughter of a wealthy merchant like Viola would never have been unsupervised to the extent that she is able to have a clandestine affair with a low class writer like the struggling Will Shakespeare . . . and definitely not under her father's roof. The film accurately portrays the fact that women were not allowed to appear on the stage in the 16th century and so the female roles were all played by men in drag. Viola would never have gotten away with impersonating a man in order to act in the theater, and she doesn't get away with it in the film either. After enjoying the premiere of *Romeo and Juliet*, the Queen tells Shakespeare to write another audience-pleaser in time for the Elizabethan holiday known as Twelfth Night, which suggests that that's how Shakespeare's next play, *Twelfth Night*, came about, when in reality five years separated the two plays.

The screenwriters did get the chronology of two Shakespearean plays correct, with the mediocre *Two Gentlemen of Verona* followed by the playwright's tragic masterpiece *Romeo and Juliet*. So what turned a hack into a poet? As with almost all of Shakespeare's life, there is no way of knowing, but the writers use this historical gap to hypothesize that a beautiful woman like Viola, whose love he could never have completely, inspired the creation of a star-crossed romance that would also never prosper.

Viola was definitely not the muse who inspired the real Shakespeare to write his most famous sonnet, "Shall I Compare Thee to a Summer's Day?" After suffering monumental writer's block in the film, Will is cured after a night of lovemaking with Viola and runs home, unblocked, to write Sonnet No. 18. Most literary scholars agree, however, that Sonnets No. 18 through 126 were addressed to a fair-haired wealthy young man, whom Shakespeare ambiguously called "the master mistress of my passion." When Harvard professor Stephen Greenblatt suggested to screenwriter Marc Norman that he write a drama about Shakespeare's affair with Christopher Marlowe, which would lead to Marlowe's murder, Norman said no studio would finance a big budget costume drama about a homosexual affair.

The most clever fabrications in *Shakespeare in Love* show the cast using famous phrases from his plays in their offstage dialogue. When Viola auditions for a play disguised as a man, she hopes to charm the playwright by using Valentine's soliloquy "if Silvia be not seen" from his *Two Gentlemen of Verona*. When Shakespeare bellies up to the bar in a tavern and says, "Give me to drink mandragora," he's quoting Cleopatra in his *Antony and Cleopatra*. When the theater censor Makepeace screams, "A plague on both your houses," he's referring to Shakespeare's two theaters, but the inside joke is that the curse came from *Romeo and Juliet*.

In a tsk-tsk editorial in the *Times of London*, high school English teacher Susan Elkin clucked that "from an Eng Lit point of view, *Shakespeare in Love* should probably come with a strong health warning," and Stoppard conceded that the film took a "completely irreverent attitude toward history." But Harvard's Greenblatt guessed that the Bard would have been delighted with the film's pick-and-choose sampling of twisted history. "Shakespeare would probably have understood the canniness that led screenwriters to fiddle with the facts," Greenblatt said. "After all, he himself did so spectacularly in his historical plays," which distorted the lives of past English monarchs (Richard III bad, Henry VIII good!) to please the English monarch of his day. The screenwriters of *Shakespeare in Love* had to please an even more imperious audience, American moviegoers.

The Madness of King George (1994)

Directed by Nicholas Hytner
Written by Alan Bennett

CAST

Nigel Hawthorne (George III)
Helen Mirren (Queen Charlotte)
Ian Holm (Dr. Willis)
Rupert Everett (Prince of Wales)
Amanda Donohoe (Lady Pembroke)
Julian Wadham (Pitt)
Jim Carter (Fox)

Queen Charlotte (Helen Mirren) copes with mental illness (her husband's) in *The Madness of King George*, with Nigel Hawthorne as the deranged monarch.

No one embodies the claim that history is written by the victors better than King George III. As the nominal leader of the losing side in the American Revolution, the king has long been the poster *roi* for tyranny on this side of the Atlantic, although knowledgeable folks realize that Parliament, not the king, held the reins of power and lost the colonies. The British, however, fondly recall the king as the country-loving "Farmer George," a man who adored his 13 children (except his eldest son, an indolent, alcoholic womanizer) and ended his days as a sad figure, haunting the halls of his weekend getaway, Windsor Castle, blind and demented—anything but the demon of American mythology peddled as history.

A film called *The Madness of King George* can be forgiven for only focusing on the title character's mental illness in its portrayal of the life of the far from merrie monarch, but in doing so, many other fascinating elements of his long life get short shrift or aren't explored at all.

Although the king reigned for 60 years, from 1760 to 1820, the film (which in Britain was called *The Madness of King George III*; the American distributors deleted the Roman numerals, fearing that audiences ignorant of history would think the movie was a sequel and they had missed the first two installments) deals with only a short period in his life, several months in the winter of 1788–1789, the period when symptoms of his madness first surfaced. It was a dramatic time and a dramatic choice for the film's focus, but it leaves the viewer with a limited view of the vast panorama that made up the unfortunate ruler's life. Indeed, George has another 30 years to live when the final credits roll.

During the brief period of his life the film does examine, a few historical inaccuracies crop up among a production that is otherwise faithful in its depiction of the mad monarch.

The most glaring distortion may be the cause of the king's madness. The film implies that the king was cured of his malady by the innovative methods of a minister turned proto-psychologist, Dr. Willis (Ian Holm), who rejected popular 18th century treatments like placing red-hot glass bowls on patients' backs to burn away the illness. Instead, Willis believed that strong discipline could bring a wayward mind back to sanity. To that end, Dr. Willis orders His Royal Majesty, the King of England, Scotland, Ireland, and Wales, tied to a chair and gagged whenever he displays symptoms of his madness, which include fouling himself, fondling a lady of the court in public, and screaming as he runs down the halls of Windsor Castle. The film ends with this "modern" barbaric treatment curing the king and leaves the unknowledgeable viewer, especially Americans, with the impression that George III was permanently cured and went on to a prosperous life and reign. In the stage version, but not the movie, it was mentioned that the king's illness was physiological not psychological, caused by a hereditary disease called porphyria, a neurological condition that produces skin rashes, stomach pain, and mental disorientation. Victims also produce red, brown, purple, or black urine. The film does refer to the purplish color of the monarch's urine, but as a period piece it cannot offer the modern explanation for its cause. It also implies that Dr. Willis' weird treatments brought about the King's recovery, when the illness in fact resolved itself, although only temporarily, as it resurfaced several more times in the kings' life.

At film's end, a fully recovered king rebuffs his former tormentor, Dr. Willis' condescending aid, and triumphantly enters the House of Commons to forestall a vote that would have replaced him with his son. Left out is the King's real end, which was more pitiful than anything shown in the film. George III had several recurrences of porphyria followed by recovery until finally, in 1811, his madness returned and stayed. By this time he was also blind and probably suffering from Alzheimer's. In that year, Parliament reluctantly agreed to let the much hated Prince of Wales, the king's son, serve as regent until George's death in 1820.

The Prince of Wales, who became George IV on his father's death, is played by Rupert Everett, a strange casting choice since Everett is slender and the gluttonous, alcoholic Prince of Wales was famously obese. To get the actor in character, he wears what is obviously a padded "fat suit." The Prince of Wales' character is also misrepresented. Although he was a womanizer and compulsive gambler perpetually in debt (none of which the film indicates), he was not power mad and did not try to snatch the throne from his father. While father and son did loathe one another, the Prince, as he does in the film, never teamed up with the opposition party in Parliament, the Whigs, to have the king declared incompetent and install his son as regent. Until the 20th century, insanity was believed to be hereditary, and a mad relative in the 18th century was often hidden from view out of shame and the fear of what his condition foreboded for his relatives. The Prince of Wales lived in denial, refusing to believe his father was mad, but he was often brought to tears by his father's pitiable state, which the film does not show. The film does show the leader of the Parliamentary opposition, George Edward Fox, colluding with the prince to remove his father, when the MP actually tried to reconcile father and son. (The famously faithful and abstemious George III objected to his son's fiscal and marital irresponsibility.)

The film's limited scope is frustrating to historians who know how much more drama and riveting elements there were in the king's life not covered by the film.

While not exactly an intellectual, he did respect and promote learning. He paid for the founding of the Royal Academy of Sciences with his own money and granted Rousseau a pension despite the writer's revolutionary leanings. Under the pseudonym "Ralph Robinson of Windsor," he wrote letters to an agricultural journal, which led his subjects to affectionately nickname him "Farmer George." His library contained 70,000 volumes, including works by Shakespeare, Corneille, Dante, as well as first editions of Shakespeare and Caxton and a Gutenberg Bible. Now housed in the British Museum, his collection demonstrates his encyclopedic range of interests in everything from theology to astronomy to agriculture. While his bibulous son squandered his fortune on women and cards, the bibliophile father spent a fifth of his personal income on books.

George III took his royal duties so seriously that he sometimes overstepped constitutional bounds but never lapsed into tyranny. He tried to control Parliament, which exceeded his constitutional authority, and he had to resort to threats to get his way. To kill a Parliamentary bill he opposed, he once sent a message to the House of Lords warning that those who voted for the legislation "were not only not his friends, but that he should consider them his enemies." Such was the prestige of the monarchy that the Lords caved in, the bill failed to pass, and Parliament was forced to dissolve itself. For the increasing number of citizens who felt the king should be a symbol rather than an executor of power, his interference in Parliamentary affairs caused a scandal that lost the Royal family much of the affection the people felt for it.

George's political meddling had even more disastrous consequences when at the turn of the century his illness went into brief remission, and the king killed a bill that would have granted Catholics the right to vote. This reactionary interference would have tragic consequences extending all the way into the next century and climaxing with the Irish rebellion.

For American audiences, the most intriguing and regrettable omission of the film may be George's relationship to the American Revolution. There was some justification for the colonists considering him a tyrant. Even after the war had been clearly lost and the new party in power in Parliament decided to sue for peace, George tried to keep the war going.

The movie might have begun with an ironic note of special interest to Americans. Unaware of the physiological basis for the king's madness, his subjects blamed the first appearance of his mental illness on his frustration and self-recriminations for having lost Britain's vast empire in America.

However, genetics, not politics, caused The Madness of King George.

Charlotte, Queen of Great Britain (1744–1818), drawn by Thomas Frye. *Courtesy of the Library of Congress.*

From Hell
(2001)

Directed by Albert Hughes and Allen Hughes
Written by Terry Hayes and Rafael Yglesias
Based on the graphic novel by Alan Moore and Eddie Campbell

CAST

Johnny Depp (Fred Abberline)

Heather Graham (Mary Kelly)

Ian Holm (Sir William Gull)

Robbie Coltrane (Peter Godley)

Ian Richardson (Sir Charles Warren)

Jason Flemyng (Netley)

Katrin Cartlidge (Dark Annie Chapman)

Terence Harvey (Ben Kidney)

Susan Lynch (Liz Stride)

Paul Rhys (Dr. Ferral)

Joanna Page (Ann Crook)

Mark Dexter (Prince Albert, Duke of Clarence)

During a 10-week period in the fall of 1888, a serial murderer disemboweled five prostitutes in the Whitechapel slums of London's East End, then disappeared and was never caught or identified. The murderer got his name from a fake letter concocted by tabloid journalists and signed "Jack the Ripper." Another letter, which was genuine because it came with the liver of one of his victims, was signed "From Hell," which is also the title of the film co-directed by twin brothers Albert and Allen Hughes, born in Detroit and best known for their film *Menace II Society*, a corrosive drama set in L.A.'s black ghetto.

The Hughes bros, who have said they don't want to be "ghettoized" as black directors, chose another 'hood, the Cockney slums of London, and seem just as at home as if they had turned their artistic attention to South Central Los Angeles or Harlem.

Who was Jack the Ripper? The question still obsesses the British as much as who killed Kennedy continues to attract conspiracy buffs in the U.S.

From Hell finally answers the question. (Don't read any further if you plan to rent the film on video or DVD.)

Johnny Depp (Jude Law was the directors' first choice but he was unavailable) plays the real-life homicide detective Fred Abberline, who investigated the murders. British film critics pointed out that the real Abberline hailed from England's West Country, but Depp gives him a Cockney accent, which a British publication derided as "Mockney."

Similar criticism was leveled against the Irish accent of American actress Heather Graham, who plays the real life prostitute Mary Kelly, an emigrant from Ireland. And unlike Depp's character, the real Abberline was not an opium and absinthe addict and didn't OD, as Depp does at the end of the film. (We told you not to keep reading if you plan to rent *From Hell*.) One of the ahistorical conceits of the film is that during his opium-fueled hallucinations, Abberline has psychic powers that allow him to see details of each murder.

In the film, an unidentified Jack the Ripper makes the unlikely boast, "One day men will look back and say I gave birth to the twentieth century." That gives too much import to the Ripper's legacy, but he did give birth to tabloid journalism. He was, in fact, the first tabloid star. Johnny Depp has said, "Before Jack the Ripper, there were a few hundred newspapers in London. At the height of his murder spree, thousands of additional papers emerged." Jack was the forerunner of the Menendez brothers, O. J., and Elizabeth Taylor's unfortunate infatuation with food.

From Hell accurately reports that whoever Jack the Ripper was, he had a sophisticated knowledge of anatomy, which he demonstrated as he eviscerated his victims, which included the symbolic removal of what one pimp in the film calls "her moneymaker" (i.e. vagina).

The Hughes brothers offer a smorgasbord of red herrings as potential candidates for Jack the Ripper then quickly dispose of or exonerate them: Prince Albert (Mark Dexter), the Duke of Clarence, Queen Victoria's grandson and second in line to the British throne. Nope. The deranged Prince was dying of syphilis, which caused a tremor in his hands that would have made it impossible for him to perform the precise disembowelings. Another candidate is the Queen's personal physician, Dr.

William Gull (Ian Holm), a university surgeon who has had to give up his practice due to a heart condition. Plus he makes an unlikely suspect because he becomes a kindly mentor to the low caste Depp's detective when high society refuses to help him solve the murders. Then there's the creepy Dr. Ferral (Paul Rhys), who despite his aristocratic bearing is as feral as his name and a member of the Freemasons, who also pop up in the film as contenders for Jack and his coachman/aide de camp. The possibility that Queen Victoria herself was directing the carnage to protect her syphilitic grandson is also raised.

So who was the perp? Or at least, who is the Hughes brothers' perp? *Daily Variety* played killjoy and said "much of the steam is taken out of the [film] by a recent book that 99.99% solved the mystery, pinning it on an Irish-American quack who later died in obscurity in the States," without naming the book!

There's lots of steam still left in *From Hell* because the Hughes brothers and screenwriters Terry Hayes and Rafael Yglesias (based on a "graphic novel," a euphemism for comic book, by Alan Moore and Eddie Campbell) come up with the ingenious idea of turning history's most famous whodunit into virtually an "everbody-dunit" by making almost all the red herrings guilty. From the Queen on down, they are all co-conspirators, including her Prime Minister and the Chief of Police (Ian Richardson). Sir William Gull, who seems to miss performing autopsies in front of medical students, somehow overcomes his cardiac problem and actually carries out the murders with the precision of—what else?—a surgeon!

The Sunday Times of London unintentionally paid the filmmakers a compliment when it said, "*From Hell* offers a final solution of its own, one involving a conspiracy between Masons and the monarchy that is so preposterous it would make Oliver Stone [the great JFK conspiracy-weaver] blush." More likely, the "final solution" here might make Stone green with envy rather than red with embarrassment because the Hughes brothers' denouement is so clever and original.

Per the film, Sir William murders five prostitutes because they attended and were witnesses at the wedding of Queen Victoria's heir, Prince Albert, to a prostitute (Joanna Page) in a Catholic Church! The prostitute then gives birth to a baby girl, who is the rightful heiress to a throne in a Protestant country that loathed papists as much as Americans hated Commies in the 1950s.

The Queen is not amused. So she has her granddaughter-in-law seized, silenced with a lobotomy, and incarcerated in a mental institution. The baby, third in line to the throne, is left in the care of Mary Kelly.

But Her Majesty is appalled that Sir William exceeded his orders to dispose of the five witnesses and created a scandal by cutting out their private parts as well.

The Freemasons condemn Sir William for overstepping his bounds and in a neat parallel irony, the surgeon is also lobotomized like the poor wife of Prince Albert, and ends up staring into space just as she does in some corner of Bedlam—or is it hell?

The real life Mary Kelly was also murdered by the Ripper, but this being Hollywood (on the Thames and in Prague, where many exteriors were shot), in the film she is spared and escapes to Ireland with the true heiress to the British throne, the prostitute-princess' daughter.

An original ending and a terrific explanation of who Jack the Ripper was and who pulled his strings and scalpel. But the Hughes are not content to stop here. Using the same conceit in *Sunset Boulevard*, where a corpse (William Holden) serves as narrator, it turns out that the film, which has been told from the point of view of Depp's police detective, has also been narrated by a corpse. Depressed by what he has learned and his inability to expose all the high-born conspirators, Depp's Abberline, unlike the real-life detective, dies at the end of the film, "chasing the dragon," i.e., after taking one too many hits on an opium pipe. Merchant-Ivory might have made this film on drugs.

From Hell ends up in a twist on Shakespeare's a "tale told by a [dead]man, full of sound and fury, signifying," however, a great deal.

Enemy at the Gates
(2001)

Directed by Jean-Jacques Annaud
Written by Jean-Jacques Annaud and Alain Godard

CAST

Joseph Fiennes (Commisar Danilov)
Jude Law (Vassili Zaitsev)
Rachel Weisz (Tania Chernova)
Bob Hoskins (Nikita Khrushchev)
Ed Harris (Major König)
Ron Perlman (Koulikov)

Enemy at the Gates re-creates the siege and battle of Stalingrad, arguably the most important and pivotal clash of World War II. After Hitler broke his non-aggression pact with Stalin in 1941, German troops quickly overran thousands of miles of Russia until the Wehrmacht reached the city of Stalingrad. The city was the prize Hitler wanted most because beyond it lay the oil fields of the Caucasus, which the fuel-starved Wehrmacht desperately needed access to. When the Germans arrived at the "gates," actually the suburbs, of Stalingrad, they appeared invincible after defeating France and Poland in a matter of months. Conquest of the city seemed like a sure thing.

By the time the 180-day siege ended, a quarter million German soldiers had died, another 100,000 had been captured along with their leader, the first German Field Marshall, von Paulus, to become POWs, and the once mighty Wehrmacht was in retreat on its way to final defeat outside Hitler's bunker in Berlin. It was, however, a pyrrhic victory for the Russians, who lost more than one million soldiers and civilians. Amid the wreckage of Stalingrad, which has been compared to the devastation of Hiroshima, only 1,000 civilians remained in a city whose original population was 500,000.

The battle of Stalingrad is a natural for epic treatment and provided real life heroes who seem perfectly camera-ready. Against the backdrop of disease, starvation, millions dead, and even cannibalism, director and co-writer Jean-Jacques Annaud and writer Alain Godard tell the true story of a shepherd from the Urals who is also a crack shot, Vasili Zaitsev (Jude Law). Zaitsev engages in the film's climactic duel with a German sharpshooter, an aristocrat named Major König (Ed Harris). Under the guidance of his grandfather, Zaitsev honed his skills while shooting wolves that attacked his sheep. Like so many epics, this one involves a love triangle among Zaitsev, a female sharpshooter, Tania (Rachel Weisz), and the propaganda officer, Danilov (Joseph Fiennes), who uses his p.r. savvy to turn Zaitsev into a national hero around whom the beleaguered Russian people can rally and take inspiration from. Zaitsev's prowess was so demoralizing to the German war effort, the Nazis brought in their best marksman, König, to rub out this troublesome hero.

The duel and the love triangle come from the 1973 book *Enemy at the Gates*, by the late William Craig, who based his story on primary accounts of the participants, including the memoirs of General Chuikov, commander in chief of Stalingrad's defense.

Significantly, Craig's book is not listed in the credits. There's a good reason for this, according to historian Anthony Beevor, author of *Stalingrad*, another account of the epic clash between fascism and bolshevism. Craig made a big mistake in swallowing the Russian's account of Zaitsev and König's duel as well as the romance among Zaitsev, his personal publicist Danilov, and the beautiful Tania.

Before the Soviet Union imploded, the Russians had long been fed an Orwellian take on history. To paraphrase the American reporter who said never let the truth get in the way of a good story, the Soviet propaganda machine believed never let historical fact get in the way of propaganda that glorifies the Great Patriotic War and its heroes. Or as Beevor said of *Enemy at the Gates*, "It's bad history. Major König never existed. He was an invention of Soviet propaganda specialists."

After picking off 149 German officers in a row, Zaitsev, who did exist, achieved heroic status, and he needed a villain of equal power and prowess with a rifle to make the match an even one. In the film's climactic scene and in Soviet "history" *á la* Orwell, the German and Russian troops temporarily pull back so the best marksmen in Russia and Germany can go *mano a mano* in the brilliantly recreated ruins of Stalingrad. It's *High Noon* with Jude Law's Zaitsev in the Gary Cooper role and Stalin's namesake city standing in for Hadleyville.

"It's a great story, beloved of Soviet propaganda," Beevor said. "General Chuikov, the commander of the army at Stalingrad, recounted it in his memoirs. But there is no trace of it in the relevant reports at the time. The story probably stemmed from a brief battle of wits between Zaitsev and an [unidentified] German sniper, but all the trimmings added subsequently, especially the König figure and love story brought in by Craig, are pure fiction." (Craig believed the love triangle was real, but Beevor insists Craig's only source was a woman he interviewed who claimed to be Zaitsev's lover. Craig's credulity is understandable and forgivable. Major König, a total fabrication, has a memorial of sorts that still exists at the Armed Forces Museum in Moscow. The museum has König's alleged telescopic rifle sight on display with the inscription: "Major König, head of the Berlin Central Snipers School and Olympic shooting champion of 1936." A real gun that was never fired by a fantasy figure in charge of a school that never existed and a gold medalist in an Olympics he never competed in.)

"We have taken a historical event and tried to understand what happened in the hearts of people who lived through it," Annaud said. "We know about some of these characters from the archives and newsreel footage. The rest is open to interpretation." In this case, interpretation sounds more like fabrication.

Despite his willingness to swallow Soviet propaganda whole and spit out a film based on it, the director once again shows he can create the feel and touch, almost the smell, of the past just as he created a believable prehistoric world and Indo-European language in *Quest for Fire* and the squalid milieu of the Dark Ages in his *In the Name of the Rose*. In *Enemy at the Gates*, Annaud gets the big picture right while getting the little picture entirely wrong, according to Beevor.

The Volga River, which flows past Stalingrad (now called Volgograd after Kruschev's posthumous purge of Stalin) was re-created in an open-pit mine in Germany near the Polish border. An abandoned factory in Rudersdorf, Germany, doubles for the spot in bombed-out Stalingrad where Zaitsev and König have their final blowout. The actors waded through mud created by pumping 10,000 gallons of water onto the set. Three thousand extras had to wear 17,000 costumes because the battle scenes often tore their clothes apart. Annaud's meticulousness made the budget balloon to $90 million, a huge amount for a European-financed film.

The actors took marksmanship classes at the British version of the FBI, where it turned out that Rachel Weisz was the best shot, although strangely the film never shows her character, purportedly a crack shot, firing a gun. Filming lasted longer than the real siege.

The advertising slogan for the movie was the fatuous "A single bullet can change history," which implied that the one-on-one shoot-out between Zaitsev and König determined the outcome of the battle of Stalingrad and by implication the outcome of World War II.

While millions, probably hundreds of millions of bullets were expended during the war, a film that purports to be a history of that war fixates on a single bullet that was never fired. That conceit does a disservice to the millions who died from millions of bullets and insults the intelligence of anyone who cares to research and know about the true battle of Stalingrad.

AMERICAN HISTORY

1776
(1972)

Directed by Peter H. Hunt
Written by Peter Stone

CAST

William Daniels (John Adams)
Howard Da Silva (Benjamin Franklin)
Ken Howard (Thomas Jefferson)
John Cullum (Edward Rutledge)
David Ford (John Hancock)
Ron Holgate (Richard Henry Lee)
Blythe Danner (Martha Jefferson)
Virginia Vestoff (Abigail Adams)

1776 was a feel-good movie musical designed to cheer up an America that in 1972, the year of its release, felt bad about itself. The growing guilt about the nation's involvement in the Vietnam War needed an antidote, and an upbeat musical about the founding of the U.S. of A. turned out to be the perfect ticket for a trip away from the My Lai massacre and carpet bombings of Northern Vietnam to an earlier, more noble time when our leaders didn't order illegal burglaries of the opposition party's headquarters.

The nation apparently needed a spoonful of sugar to make the bitter medicine of Vietnam go down, as the Tony-award-winning Broadway musical became a hit film with a sold-out run at New York's Radio City Music Hall. In a production that turns the delegates to the Second Continental Congress, which ratified the Declaration of

1776 reveals the little known fact that Benjamin Franklin (Howard Da Silva, center) loved to sing and dance when he wasn't fomenting rebellion with John Adams (William Daniels, left) and Richard Henry Lee (Ron Holgate).

Independence, into an all-singing, all-dancing cabaret act starring our Founding Fathers, it may be more commendable that the screenwriter managed to get anything right as opposed to criticizing the production for getting a lot of the historical record so wrong.

Despite the feel-good imperative of the project, *1776* did cover the feel-bad issue of slavery, which the Declaration of Independence ignored, as well as the complex maneuvers that rammed ratification of America's most venerated artifact through a querulous group of plutocrats.

What did *1776* do *right* despite the distractions of Founding Fathers who tell bathroom jokes and exclaim G-rated 20th century profanity like "Oh, hell!" and "Goddammit"?

Historians and critics praised the final scenes of the film dramatizing the debate over whether to sever ties with England, in which the delegates came close to scuttling the entire independence movement until Benjamin Franklin, South Carolina's Edward Rutledge, and Delaware's Caesar Rodney all twisted arms to get 12 of the 13 states to agree to independence. (New York abstained because its delegate hadn't been granted voting rights as of July 1776.) Rarely does a film, much less a musical film, explore the intricacies of politics as unusual as those practiced by the disparate signers of the Declaration of Independence, who were slaveowners and abolitionists, country squires and urban merchants.

Most amazingly for a frothy bit of filmmaking, *1776* mentioned the little-known fact that Thomas Jefferson, a slave owner, tried to insert a clause about the evils of slavery into the document he composed and which the Southern delegates managed to excise.

The rest of the film was widely excoriated for being a "sugar-coated, Disneyesque version of American history," according to the *Saturday Review*. Actually, Disney treats its animated characters with more respect. The signers of the Declaration of Independence here are an "early version" of the cast of *"Animal House,"* historian and novelist Thomas Fleming carped. Virginia's Richard Henry Lee was an ascetic Puritan who next to John Adams was the biggest booster of independence from Britain. *1776*'s Lee is a giggling buffoon who has no idea of what he's doing at the Continental Congress until Adams and Franklin tell him, in effect, "It's independence, stupid." Fleming complained that the brilliant New York representative, Lewis Morris, was "depicted as an idiot." James Wilson, a Philadephia lawyer and probably the second-greatest intellect at the gathering after James Madison, "is portrayed as a timid fool," according to Fleming. And New York delegate Robert Livingston, who was smart enough to negotiate the Louisiana Purchase in 1803, acts like an "utter twit."

The story of the signing of the Declaration of Independence was an all-male affair, but to appeal to modern audiences, women were injected into the proceedings with little regard for history. Screenwriter Peter Stone must have been aware that Abigail Adams was a no-show in Philadelphia, so he created a fantasy sequence in which John and his wife belt out a love duet despite the fact that he's in Philly and she's down on the farm in Massachusetts. Poor Martha Jefferson gets an even racier incarnation. The real wife of Thomas Jefferson was so ill at the time she was unable to even write her husband a letter from their Monticello home. In the film, the director not only yanks her out of her sick bed, but instead of employing another fantasy sequence, transports her to a convention she never attended in real life. It gets worse. In *1776* but not in 1776, Jefferson is afflicted with writer's block, but after a night of rejuvenating sex with Martha, the words flow and the document gets committed to calfskin. And worst of all, after sex with her husband, Martha sings a double-entendre-ridden ditty, "He Plays the Violin," in which she's not referring to the stringed instrument but some kind of 18th century G-spot. The *Saturday Review,* with its trademark leftist hysteria, overstated the case against *1776* by calling the patriotic lollapalooza "as much an exploitation film as *Deep Throat* or any other hard-core porno movies" of the time. Not quite. More like PG-13 porn for a Middle America that craved release from the tarnished travesties of the Nixon-Kissinger cabal.

America was more polarized then than now, and burned-out critics were merciless. Even the middle-of-the-road *Life* magazine overstated the case for the prosecutorial press, calling *1776* "one of the worst ideas since George III and his ministers dreamed up the Stamp Act."

The Patriot
(2000)

Directed by Roland Emmerich
Written by Robert Rodat

CAST

Mel Gibson (Benjamin Martin)
Heath Ledger (Gabriel Martin)

Joely Richardson (Charlotte Selton)

Jason Isaacs (Col. William Tavington)

Tcheky Karyo (Jean Villeneuve)

Rene Auberjonois (Rev. Oliver)

Lisa Brenner (Anne Howard)

Tom Wilkinson (Gen. Charles Cornwallis)

Adam Baldwin (Capt. Wilkins)

Gregory Smith (Thomas Martin)

Jay Arlen Jones (Occam)

The fictional American Revolutionary War hero Benjamin Martin, played by Mel Gibson in *The Patriot,* is a composite character based on several real-life figures. Screenwriter Robert Rodat described the stew of originals who went into the making of the protagonist: "Our Benjamin Martin has liberal amounts of Thomas Sumter, Andrew Pickens, Daniel Morgan and even Elijah Clark, as well as Francis Marion."

It may only have been a coincidence that Rodat, who wrote another rousing American war epic, *Saving Private Ryan*, added the name of Francis Marion to the list almost as an afterthought. The real Marion was anything but a hero, and the screenwriter may not have wanted his hero associated with Marion, a South Carolina planter who repeatedly raped his female slaves and hunted Native Americans for sport.

But a lot of Mel Gibson's hero bears striking similarities to Marion, just not the ugly ones. Both Gibson's Martin and Marion served in the French and Indian War, both served in the pre-Revolutionary South Carolina assembly, both were gentleman plantation owners, both employed guerilla tactics against the British, and both used the inaccessible swamps of South Carolina as their base of operations.

Historian Christopher Hibbert says, "Marion was a wily and elusive character, very active in the persecution of Cherokee Indians and not at all the sort of chap who should be celebrated as a hero." But history is recorded by the winning side, and Hibbert adds, "As with most wars, the winner enjoyed a monopoly on allegations of brutality, but the truth is that people like Marion committed atrocities as bad if not worse than those perpetrated by the British." For good measure,

Hibbert, who is British, throws in the "scandal" created when Marion married his cousin.

Screenwriter Rodat, who went through 39 drafts of his script, all approved by the Smithsonian Institution, counters that Gibson's character is more closely based on the more viewer-friendly Thomas Sumter, and many events in the film do parallel those in Sumter's life. Sumter, like *The Patriot*'s Benjamin Martin, had become an ardent pacifist after participating in atrocities during the previous conflict, the French and Indian War. At the beginning of the War of Independence, Sumter, like Martin, was practically a conscientious objector suffering post-traumatic shock disorder from the French and Indian War. Sumter only agreed to fight in the Revolution after the British burned down the cottage to which his family had been sent for safety. (In the film, Martin forgets his pacifism after the British not only burn down his cozy mansion, but also kill his young son in cold blood and take another son away to be hanged as a spy.)

While Martin/Marion was whitewashed, the British were demonized, according to a furious editorial in the *Sunday Times of London*. "Martin was a real-life fighter in the war of independence," the *Times* inaccurately claimed, and "his story has been transformed into a 160-minute polemic against the British."

The *London Express* luridly asserted that *The Patriot* and a host of other American films amount to a "virtual declaration of war on this county by the geographically small but globally incredibly powerful Los Angeles suburb of Hollywood."

Some events in *The Patriot* do demonize the British, but the historical record shows that sometimes their behavior was indeed demonic.

One of the grimmest episodes in the film depicts the evil Col. Tavington (Jason Isaacs) herding a bunch of civilians into their church, then burning the place down. That sounds more like the kind of atrocity committed by the Third Reich, but during the American Revolution, the British and colonists loyal to the mother country did burn several Presbyterian churches. Both the British and the rebels burned buildings with people inside.

The *Sunday Times of London* also took issue with the depiction of Col. Tavington, who the screenwriter conceded was based on Lt. Col. Banastre Tarleton. The *Times* claimed that Tarleton was a "dashing officer loved by his soldiers. He was no bloodthirsty villain." Certainly not someone like the film's Tavington, who not only immolated innocent churchgoers but killed two of Gibson's young sons.

The motive for Tavington's villainy does not square with the historical Tarleton. In the film, Tavington explains that his father has squandered his inheritance, and in order to make his fortune, he will do Lord Cornwallis' dirty work in return for a huge land grant in Ohio, which King George has promised to Cornwallis (along with most of the future Louisiana Purchase) as a reward for winning the war.

Tarleton, on the other hand, had no money worries, and his father was no dissolute wastrel, but the Lord Mayor of Liverpool and a wealthy merchant who made his fortune in the slave trade. And unlike Tavington, Tarleton did not perish in the conflict, but returned to England after the war to become a respected member of Parliament and a scholar who wrote *A History of the Campaigns of 1780 and 1781 in the Southern Provinces of North America*. He was an Oxford graduate to boot.

Ironically, British historian Christopher Hibbert, while decrying the glorification of Marion/Martin, agrees that Tavington's real life model was no poster boy for chivalric warfare. Nicknamed "Bloody Ban" Tarleton, this scholar was no gentleman and "none too scrupulous" in his treatment of the enemy, Hibbert says. That's putting it mildly. According to Hibbert, Tarleton was not only cruel to horses, but he ordered the cold-blooded murder of wounded American soldiers, as Tavington does in the film.

The American historian Kevin Phillips faults the costume designer for outfitting Tavington and his men in trademark redcoat uniforms, when Tarleton's dragoons wore green.

The Patriot managed to stir up almost as much controversy on this side of the Atlantic, only not because of its mustache-twirling depiction of the British but for its presentation of blacks as "happy darkies," gratefully serving "massuh" in the fields of both peace and war.

Spike Lee, whose career as Hollywood's unelected conscience draws more attention than his hitless career as a director, sounded even angrier than the *Sunday Times of London* and the *Express* when he blasted *The Patriot* as "blatant American Hollywood propaganda" and a "complete whitewashing of history."

In the film, Gibson has freed his slaves, who have stayed on to work his fields for wages. (The Smithsonian signed off on that unlikelihood, even though both Francis Marion and Thomas Sumter had not been so kind to their slaves.) "Where are the slaves? Who's picking the cotton?" Lee wanted to know in a letter to the *Hollywood Reporter*.

Screenwriter Rodat countered that he was making a film about the American Revolution, not slavery, hence the dearth of black faces on screen. "While it is true that Washington and Jefferson were slaveholders, many of the founding fathers were not. Benjamin Martin [Mel Gibson] is a back-country South Carolina farmer. In creating this composite character, I chose to make him a man who had freed his slaves. Would it have been better to glorify a slaveholder and racist? In telling Benjamin Martin's story, with the help of historians from the Smithsonian, we sought to have the African-Americans in the film depicted responsibly," Rodat said.

Spike Lee's complaints about the absence of slaves in *The Patriot* suggests he didn't watch the entire film, which would be forgivable, since it ran on for almost three hours. *The Patriot* does have slaves—or at least one slave who joins the rebels in return for the promise of freedom after a year of service against the British. But while giving this character an impressive amount of screen time and several stirring speeches about liberty "for all men," the director erred in placing him in the South Carolina militia, which had a "whites-only" policy based on the fear of arming slaves. Slaves were, however, allowed to serve in the South Carolina navy, safely away at sea and away from the cotton fields.

While the film got its geography wrong, it was accurate in portraying black participation in the war. The film's producer, Dean Devlin, said research proved "that the American Revolution was fought and won by an integrated army, that seven to eight percent of the army was black."

Besides faulting for historical bloopers, many critics on both sides of the Atlantic were horrified by the film's bloodlust, which earned it an R rating and dire warnings that several scenes promoted school and modern militia violence. Because of its vaguely vigilante flavor, one critic subtitled the film, "Rambo Does the Revolution."

In perhaps the most riveting but also the bloodiest scene in the film, Martin arms his sons, aged 10 and 13, and together they ambush and slaughter 20 British soldiers, with Mad Mel repeatedly hacking the final, already dead victim until he's drenched in the soldier's blood. However sanguine, the segment is not unlikely. Because of the boys' background living on the edge of the wilderness, historian Kevin Phillips says, "The boys already would have known how to shoot squirrels and rabbits and could probably have evaded British redcoats in the local woods."

The reasons for most of the historical inaccuracies in *The Patriot* lay where most films' do—on the bottom line. Every commercially successful movie needs a hero to root for, and if Mel Gibson had been a slave owner, his heroic quality would have been seriously undermined. And all action films need a hissable villain, hence the film's portrayal of the British as what the *Sunday Times of London* called "bloodthirsty stormtroopers."

British historian William Rubenstein offers a more sophisticated and less polemical explanation for the fact that Dead White European Males often come off badly in American films—and his argument has nothing to do with the current academic battles that favor multiculturalism over Eurocentrism. "It is more than just dramatic or commercial considerations: the great liberal establishment of Hollywood does all it can to blacken the Western, imperial colonial past, probably because the Americans largely missed out on the spoils," Rubenstein says, apparently forgetting the bonanza of Cuba, Puerto Rico, and the Philippines America won as spoils after the Spanish-American War of 1898.

In one of two articles it published blasting *The Patriot*, the *London Express* theorized that Hollywood's enduring Anglophobia is nothing less than a massive case of psychological projection. "It is easy to explain psychologically why in film after film the British Empire is depicted as genocidal and grossly exploitative, when it fact it was neither. It is because with their own record of killing 12 million American Indians and supporting slavery for four decades after the British abolished it, Americans wish to project their own historical guilt onto someone else."

Amistad
(1997)

Directed by Steven Spielberg
Written by David Franzoni, William Owens (book)

CAST

Morgan Freeman (Theodore Joadson)
Anthony Hopkins (John Quincy Adams)
Matthew McConaughey (Roger Baldwin)
Djimon Hounsou (Cinque)
Nigel Hawthorne (Martin Van Buren)
David Paymer (U.S. Secretary of State Forsyth)
Pete Postlethwaite (Holabird)
Stellan Skarsgard (Lewis Tappan)
Razaaq Adoti (Yamba)
Abu Bakaar Fofanah (Fala)
Anna Paquin (Queen Isabella)
Tomas Milian (Calderon)
Ralph Brown (Lt. Gedney)
Allan Rich (Judge Juttson)
Peter Firth (Captain Fitzgerald)
Jeremy Northam (Judge Coglin)
Arliss Howard (John C. Calhoun)

Before the Civil War settled the issue once and for all, attempts to end slavery in America ended in tragedy and carnage. Slave rebellions were quickly and brutally suppressed. Political and military efforts by whites on behalf of the enslaved met the same fate. The white zealot John Brown and the rebel slave Nat Turner both ended their lives at the end of a rope. Northern congressmen were unable to defeat legislation introduced by Southerners that forbade even the discussion of slavery in the House.

Only one slave revolt was an unqualified success, the only one with a happy ending. The uprising took place aboard the Cuban ship *Amistad*, in 1839, when captured Africans rose up and slew their captors. But instead of instant retaliation by the white establishment, as in the case of Turner and Brown, the rebels found themselves defended by pillars of the white power structure, freed by order of the Supreme Court, and allowed to return home to Africa. Whites even paid for their tickets.

It's no surprise that the story of the *Amistad* victory intrigued director Steven Spielberg enough to turn the real life incident into a fictional film. Of the literally six million stories about the Holocaust, the feel-good director chose to dramatize perhaps the only one with a relatively happy ending, in *Schindler's List*.

Spielberg's *Amistad* cast Anthony Hopkins as John Quincy Adams, who at age 72 defended the Africans before the Supreme Court in a successful bid to gain their freedom, and Morgan Freeman as a composite character based on several black abolitionists of the time who enlists the help of a rich white liberal, Roger Baldwin (Matthew McConaughey), a penniless, bumbling real estate attorney in the film who defends the Africans in court.

McConaughey's Baldwin may have been more fictionalized than Freeman's composite, since the real defense attorney was the well-connected son of the governor of Connecticut and a Yale graduate whose grandfather put his John Hancock on the Declaration of Independence. The film's Baldwin is a Yankee Don Quixote, tilting alone in court at the pro-slavery establishment. In reality, two high-priced lawyers, Theodore Sedgwick and Seth Staples, who later founded Yale's law school, assisted in the defense of the Africans until Adams took over the appeal.

There is some evidence that Cinque, the leader of the shipboard slave revolt, played by Calvin Klein model Djimon Hounsou, may have been a slave trader himself before being captured by Portuguese slavers and sold into slavery. That possibility is not mentioned in the film, since it would detract from the heroic treatment of Cinque, from whose point of view the story is told.

The *Times of London* didn't object to presenting Cinque as an unblemished hero, but complained about the camera's erotic treatment of the buff male model. "Cinque *will* keep taking his clothes off," the *Times* noted and wondered if *Amistad* "was a serious dramatic reconstruction of slavery or a black gay porno flick. There is something vaguely obscene about the way in which Spielberg's camera exoticises the black male form." Howard Jones, author of the nonfiction work *Amistad*, praised the film for its accurate depiction of the horrific Middle Passage of the captives from Africa to America, but the *Times* expressed amazement that after surviving the trip in the crowded hold of the slaveship, Cinque "emerged looking like an Olympic decathlete."

While lauding *Amistad*'s accurate costumes and sets, the *Times* found the dialogue peppered with 20th century anachronisms. It also objected to the marginalization of Morgan Freeman's character when black abolitionists of the time participated fully in the liberation movement.

Historians and religious leaders felt that unlike the black hero, Cinque, the white folks in the film got short shrift. Lewis Tappan, the wealthy New York abolitionist who coordinated the Africans' legal defense, and his brother Arthur "are portrayed more out of political motivation and sensibility. They aren't given the full depth and range of their character," the Rev. Davida F. Crabtree, a minister of the United Church of Christ, said. In the film, Lewis Tappan suggests that the abolition movement might benefit if the Africans were executed and became martyrs for the cause, which contradicts Tappan's real life devotion to freeing the captives. The Rev. Tomas F. Dipko regretted that the film made no mention of the Job-like plagues both Tappans suffered because of their abolitionist activities. Mobs attacked Lewis Tappan's dry-goods store, the largest in New York, and his brother Arthur's mansion. Arthur once found a slave's ear in a box in his mailbox. Insurance carriers canceled their policies after pro-slavery vigilantes put a price on the brothers' heads. None of these camera-ready incidents are depicted in the film.

Not surprisingly, the villains are depicted worse than they actually were. The president at the time, Martin Van Buren, opposed freeing the Africans because he feared losing the upcoming presidential election. (The U.S. was in the middle of its first recession, and Van Buren lost despite his pro-slavery efforts.) But political historians felt Van Buren's portrait had been drawn too harshly. Joyce Appleby, president of the American Historical Association, wondered "why Van Buren had to be turned into an intellectually challenged political hack electioneering in a fashion unthinkable before the Civil War."

Simon Schama, professor of history at Columbia University, complained that John Quincy Adams' closing speech before the Supreme Court lasted two days but was shortened in the film for dramatic purposes. Schama also objected that Adams' speech was rewritten and didn't mention the less than noble argument he made in real life, which was based not on the captives' inalienable right to freedom but on the legality of the slave trade "on the high seas," since Spain claimed ownership of the captives despite several Anglo-British-Spanish treaties outlawing the trade in human flesh. In a *New Yorker* piece, Schama described a dramatic incident that would have improved but didn't make it into the film. A few days before the trial, Adams' horse bolted and killed his coachman, but Adams was not injured. "For the devoutly religious statesman, there could have been no more shocking witness that Providence was watching over the unfolding drama," Schama wrote. The accident occurred in front of the Capitol building, which Schama huffed did not have a dome at the time, as though Spielberg could have shaved off the top of the building for verisimilitude, although who knows what could have been done digitally to the structure in light of *Gladiator*'s magnificent mint-condition, digitized Colosseum.

The film's most unfortunate omission may be its failure to show the ultimate fate of the captives once they returned to Africa. For the sake of a stunning visual ending with their ship sailing into an *ur*-Spielberg sunset, *Amistad* neglects to mention that in order to pay for their passage home, the freed captives were "put on display" by their patrons, who had refused to accept donations for the return trip from the American Missionary Society because the Society accepted contributions from slave holders happy to get troublemaking black freedmen out of the country. The Africans appeared in a series of sold-out "lectures" that were more dog-and-pony show than Bible-reading and lecture.

When the captives' ship docked in the port of Freetown, Sierra Leone, they tore off their "white" American winter clothing and danced naked with relatives who had come to welcome them home, much to the horror of the white missionaries in charge of the voyage. While many of the former captives returned to tribal life, Cinque used the knowledge he had acquired in America to become a successful businessman and entrepreneur.

The mission to Africa had an enduring legacy, which may be the most significant element in the story of *Amistad*, although the epilogue never made it into the film's sun-drenched climax. Missionary-run schools in Sierra Leone sent African students to college in America, where they founded black colleges and universities, among them Fisk and Howard, whose graduates became leaders of the civil rights movement. The ultimate and ironic effect of the *Amistad* nightmare, perhaps too sophisticated a message for the film's "black and white" mind-set, is that the enslavement of blacks in Africa led to their political enfranchisement a century later.

Glory
(1989)

Directed by Edward Zwick
Written by Kevin Jarre, Peter Burchard (book)

CAST

Matthew Broderick (Col. Robert Gould Shaw)
Denzel Washington (Trip)
Cary Elwes (Maj. Cabot Forbes)
Morgan Freeman (Sgt. Major John Rawlins)
Jihmi Kennedy (Jupiter Sharts)
Donovan Leitch (Charles Fessenden Morse)

Pulitzer Prize-winning historian James M. McPherson said that *Glory*, the story of a black infantry unit that stormed a Southern fort during the Civil War, was "not only the first feature film to treat the role of black soldiers in the American Civil War; it is also the most powerful and historically accurate movie about that war ever made." A handful of spoilsports complained that the film lacked historical context, and that the lead was miscast as a wimp. A few mentioned the ironic fact that all the black characters were fictional, while their white leader, the aforementioned wimp, was based on a Harvard-educated Boston Brahmin whose real name was used. Most curiously for a popular entertainment, *Glory* was a feel-good movie about a pyrrhic defeat in which half the Union soldiers died and the Confederacy prevailed!

On July 18, 1863, the largely black 54th Massachusetts Volunteer Infantry assaulted Fort Wagner, an impregnable earthwork that guarded the approach to Charleston, South Carolina. Their leader, Col. Robert Gould Shaw, 25, led the charge and was instantly killed on a parapet by a bullet through his heart. The attack was easily repulsed and the fort remained in Confederate hands. Despite the defeat, the valiant effort disproved once and for all the prevalent opinion among white men that the black man could not fight. Annihilation represented progress of sorts in the even bloodier battle for civil rights.

The film ends with this bloody denouement, and some historians and critics felt that the aftermath of the battle might have provided historical context and an ironic coda to the glory of *Glory*. President Lincoln, who was more Dr. Spin than Honest Abe, snatched victory from the jaws of this Union defeat. Lincoln turned the tragedy into a propaganda bonanza. New Yorkers had recently rioted in protest of the new draft, and Lincoln threw the death of these black soldiers in the face of draft dodgers. "You say you will not fight to free Negroes," Lincoln wrote in an open letter to the New York City rioters. "Some seem willing to fight for you."

While lavishly praising the film, McPherson pointed out some minor errors. In the film, black troops attack Fort Wagner from the south with the Atlantic Ocean on the left when in reality the assault came from the north. (Stop the presses!) Although *Glory* was filmed on the actual site of the battle, problems with building the set that represented Fort Wagner required the geographical change. The great black abolitionist Frederick Douglass looks about 70 in *Glory*, his age when a famous photograph immortalized his lion's head a quarter century after the time period depicted in the film. The real Douglass was only 45 in 1863. Robert Gould Shaw received his commission to lead the 54th while bivouacked in a desolate winter camp in Virginia. The real Shaw declined the offer at first. The film relocates the incident to a more cinematic and elegant drawing room party in Boston, and in the movie Shaw accepts without hesitation—perhaps to buff up the actor who played him, Matthew Broderick, whom *Vogue* magazine unfairly called "a wimp" and whom film critic Stanley Kauffmann said was "the only one on whom a uniform looks like a costume." (Critics

In *Glory*, Matthew Broderick (opposite page) plays the real-life Boston aristocrat Col. Robert Gould Shaw (above), who led an all-black regiment during the Civil War. Unlike Shaw, all the black characters in the film were fictionalized.

love their carp. *The Wall Street Journal* had the bad taste to protest that the Confederacy was demonized in *Glory*.)

More problematic is the fact that while the white guy is real, all the black soldiers are based on fictional composites, which didn't stop Denzel Washington from winning the best supporting actor Oscar for his in-yo-face Private Trip, whose close-up flogging for insubordination is one of the dramatic highlights of the film—if seeing

Trip's scarred back from previous whippings can be called a highlight. And to increase Trip's heroism and avoid the common complaint that movies about blacks are usually filtered through the eyes of whites (see Kevin Kline get double Denzel Washington's screen time in 1987's *Cry Freedom*), Trip leads the boycott that demands the black soldiers receive the same pay as whites, although in real life Shaw instigated the demand for equal pay for equal decimation. McPherson also felt the fictionalization of everyone but Shaw missed some of the compelling real life figures in the 54th, including two of Frederick Douglass' sons and novelist Henry James' younger brother, Garth Wilkinson James. "A dramatic and important story about the relationship of Northern blacks to slavery and the war, and about the wartime ideals of New England culture, could have been constructed from a cast of real, historical figures," McPherson said in one of his few criticisms of the film. He also noted that for obvious dramatic tension, the blacks in the 54th are portrayed in *Glory* as runaway slaves literally fighting for their freedom, while most of the black soldiers of the 54th had been born free men.

With the movie's Wagnerian score and slow-mo slaughter, some critics felt that white director Ed Zwick, a creator of the touchy-feely TV series *thirtysomething*, had created a soft-focus, audience-friendly film about a massacre that occurs in sanguine Technicolor. They might agree with Walt Whitman's prediction that the heroic stories of black soldiers in the Civil War needed to be told by a member of the same race: "The Negro will get his due from the Negro—from no one else," Whitman predicted.

Paging Spike Lee . . .

Dances with Wolves
(1990)

Directed by Kevin Costner
Written by Michael Blake

CAST

Kevin Costner (Lt. Dunbar)
Mary McDonnell (Stands with a Fist)
Graham Greene (Kicking Bird)

Rodney A. Grant (Wind in His Hair)
Floyd "Red Crow" Westerman (Ten Bears)
Tantoo Cardinal (Black Shawl)
Robert Pastorelli (Timmons)
Charles Rocket (Lt. Elgin)
Maury Chaykin (Maj. Fambrough)
Jimmy Herman (Stone Calf)
Michael Spears (Otter)
Doris Leader Charge (Pretty Shield)

For most of the history of American cinema, Native Americans have been portrayed as bloodthirsty and anything but noble savages. While most critics consider John Ford one of the greatest American directors for his epic Westerns, they overlook his treatment of Native Americans, who are so one-dimensional they recall Mark Twain's comment that a cigar store Indian had more life than the endangered Mohicans of James Fenimore Cooper's novels. Their treatment on film was so shabby that Marlon Brando, through a spokeswoman, felt compelled to condemn it in lieu of an acceptance speech at the Oscars in 1973.

So it's no surprise that almost two decades later Kevin Costner's *Dances with Wolves* was welcomed as a much needed antidote to the poisonous portrayal of Native Americans on film, winning best picture and best director Oscars, among others, in 1991.

But Costner replaced the previous Manichean view of Ford and others where the good guys wore white hats and the bad guys wore feathered headdresses with an equally Manichean view that demonized the white man and beatified one Indian tribe while trashing another.

The only good paleface in *Dances with Wolves* is Costner's Lt. John Dunbar. After sustaining a serious leg wound during a Civil War battle circa 1864, Dunbar is sent to recuperate in a deserted outpost in Sioux country in the Dakotas. A burnt-out case *á la* Graham Greene, he re-ignites his spiritual pilot light through contact with noble, peace-loving Sioux right out of some Rousseau romance, falls in love with a white woman captured as a child and raised by the Sioux, and helps them fight bloodthirsty Pawnees, who *Time* magazine felt should hire a "p.r. consultant" for their depiction as the "scourge of the prairies." Finally, Dunbar helps his

As director and star of *Dances with Wolves*, Kevin Costner has one eye on the camera and the other on his girlfriend in the film, Stands with a Fist (Mary McDonnell), a white woman captured as a child and raised by Sioux with a sense of humor about naming children.

adopted tribe escape from the genocidal U.S. Cavalry to temporary safety in a new region for a bittersweet, elegiac ending that serves as a microcosmic example of the macrocosm of the extermination of indigenous peoples.

As director, Costner makes it clear he believes the Sioux were superior to the white men who almost wiped them out. To that end, *Commentary* magazine said, "He simply omits everything from period Indian life that modern film audiences would find repugnant" and leaves the dirty work to the Sioux's archrivals, the Pawnees. At the time the

film takes place, white settlers were encroaching on the ancestral lands of the Plains tribes, including the Sioux, and in response, the Sioux went on a rampage of "killing, raping, pillaging and burning in one of the most savage and bloody Indian uprisings in history," according to Robert Utley in *The Indian Frontier*. The Sioux and other tribes of the Plains scalped, murdered, and tortured captives for entertainment, Utley wrote.

In *Dances with Wolves*, scalping is briefly and discreetly mentioned, but it was far more prevalent in the Old West than in Costner's New West. Besides serving as ornamentation on tent poles and horse bridles, scalps were turned into hair extensions and woven into the victors' hair and decorated with ribbons. In the Costner version, the Sioux always kill quickly, cleanly, and in self-defense, while the victims of the Pawnee die in agony, film critic Richard Alleva noted. And although the U.S. Cavalry committed genocide against Native Americans, the Sioux killed so many Pawnee that during the 19th century their numbers declined from 12,000 to 2,000. The common practice of polygamy is also omitted to make Costner's Sioux more 20th century-friendly.

The production went to archaeological depths to re-create the Native American dress in the film. Leather was "brain-tanned," which meant boiling the brains of buffalo to make a paste for curing hides. Buffalo stomachs served as cooking pots, and buffalo bladders became canteens. Deer sinew instead of synthetic threads was used to sew the leather pieces together. The costumes were dyed with organic colors: yellow from the bloodroot plant, blue and purple from wild grapes, and red from an insect that feeds on prickly pear cactus. One exception to this hyperrealism: turkey feathers had to substitute for eagle feathers, which are illegal. Despite the attention to detail and origins, film critic Richard Grenier felt the costumes were more *haute couture* than High Plains and said Costner's Sioux looked nothing like early photographs of them and "exactly the way Indians dress in the imagination of, perhaps, the couturier Yves Saint-Laurent."

Costner received high praise for taking the commercial risk of having his Native Americans speak in the almost lost dialect of the Lakota Sioux, which meant using subtitles, common in foreign films but dreaded by the multiplex crowd who move their lips while they read. The director hired a college teacher and linguist, Doris Leader Charge, to translate the script into Lakota and serve as an on-set adviser, coaching the star and Mary McDonnell, who plays the white woman raised by the Sioux. Despite her academic credentials, Ms. Leader Charge's command of the language was a bit limited and as skewed as the filmmakers' view in general. *The Nation* pointed out that the males spoke Lakota "in the feminine form . . . Imagine if Costner and his baseball buddies in *Bull Durham* had spoken as if they'd stepped out of *Little Women*!" Was this some subversive feminist subtext or just bad Berlitz?

Costner and screenwriter Michael Blake, on whose novel the film was based, ignore the Sioux's penchant for ritualized, self-inflicted pain. To mourn the loss of a husband, Sioux widows gashed their legs in ritual grief. In the film, Costner stumbles upon McDonnell, a grieving widow who appears to have injured her leg in an accident rather than by her own hand.

Despite their rosy depiction, one of the Sioux actors, Rodney Grant, felt that the Indians got a raw deal when the film showed a child who feared corporal punishment after trying to steal Lt. Dunbar's horse. Grant said the Sioux never punished their children with physical abuse.

Time magazine called *Dances with Wolves'* "ahistoricism risible," and even Roger Ebert, who gave the film four stars and an enthusiastic thumbs up, conceded it was a "sentimental fantasy." Modern day Sioux loved Costner's revisionist re-creation of their past so much they made him and costar McDonnell honorary members of the tribe in a ceremony, coinciding as it did with the film's premiere, that seemed more publicity stunt than tribal induction. And the site they chose, far from the Great Plains, seemed tragically ironic—the nation's capital, the same place from which the original genocidal orders to wipe them out in the 19th century originated.

Critic Richard Alleva suggested a more cynical reason for the director's idealization of the Sioux—which had nothing to do with the apparent desire to right decades of wrong on screen. Not only the whites but the Pawnees were demonized "not from liberal guilt-tripping but from leading-actor egomania. Love me, love my sidekicks," Alleva said.

The Birth of a Nation (1915)

Directed by D. W. Griffith
Written by D. W. Griffith, Thomas F. Dixon, Jr. (novels)

CAST

Lillian Gish (Elsie Stoneman)

Mae Marsh (Flora Cameron)

Henry B. Walthall (Col. Ben Cameron)

Miriam Cooper (Margaret Cameron)

Mary Alden (Lydia Brown)

Ralph Lewis (Austin Stoneman)

George Siegmann (Silas Lynch)

Walter Long (Gus)

Joseph Henabery (Abraham Lincoln)

In *The Poetics*, Aristotle wrote that art must be all three of these: good, beautiful and true. Oscar Wilde maintained that art need only be beautiful. If ever a movie

The Birth of a Nation, set in the post-Civil War South, remains an aesthetic embarrassment: stylistically one of the greatest and most innovative films ever made and also one of the most racist.

sided with Wilde against Aristotle, *The Birth of a Nation* did so in spades, for it remains truly beautiful, but contains little truth and an embarrassing amount of evil.

For better or worse, most critics agree that *The Birth of a Nation* is the *Citizen Kane* of the silent era—the greatest film ever made. Director D. W. Griffith introduced many new film techniques, and visually *The Birth of a Nation* is indeed beautiful. But its story line is morally bankrupt, racist, and saddest of all, led to a revival of the Ku Klux Klan in the 1920s.

President Woodrow Wilson was one of the film's biggest fans. While saving the world for democracy abroad, in the U.S. Wilson was a firm believer in separation of the races and summed up the heady experience of watching the film. "It is like writing history in lightning," he famously said. Forgotten is his *mea culpa* a few years later, when he said, after screenings of the film led to attacks on blacks, that it was an "unfortunate production. My only regret is that it is all so terribly true."

For a man who was a respected academic and historian before assuming the presidency, Wilson's rueful comment on the accuracy on the film is mind-blowing.

It sounds oxymoronic, but *The Birth of a Nation* is a racist classic, which Berkeley history professor Leon F. Litwack denounced as "perverted history." That assessment didn't dissuade its continuing legion of admirers, including the Library of Congress, which in 1992 placed *The Birth of a Nation* on the National Film Registry, certifying it a classic.

The Birth of a Nation's title is also a misnomer. It would have been more accurately titled the *Birth of Reconstruction*, as it focused on the post-Civil War years in the South, when for a brief period of time, newly enfranchised ex-slaves held high political office in the Deep South while whites who fought for the Confederacy lost the right to vote.

The alleged excesses of these newcomers to politics are grotesquely dramatized in the film. Black lawmakers are shown passing bills in state legislatures, wearing no shoes, drinking whisky, and eating the stereotyped staple of African-American cuisine, fried chicken. One of the bills the blacks allegedly enact is one promoting interracial marriage, when in reality the legislators only removed all references to color in the marriage laws.

Miscegenation was the great bogeyman of Southern racists, and Griffith used the fear of interracial sex as a major plot element. A black named Gus in the film tries to rape a white virgin, who keeps her purity intact by leaping to her death. Silas Lynch, a mulatto elected Lieutenant Governor of South Carolina, tries to force another virgin to marry him. She's tied up when he makes the proposal. A title card quotes Lynch proclaiming the hidden agenda of miscegenation: "I will build a Black Empire," he tells his reluctant and gagged fiancée, "and you as my queen shall rule by my side." In an obvious case of projection, blacks are depicted shoving whites off sidewalks and blocking their entrance to polling places. Some torment their former owners and put them in chains.

The Birth of a Nation was a product of its time and reflected white hysteria over the new assertiveness of blacks who between 1890 and 1915, the year of the film's release, founded organizations like the NAACP, which sought to improve the lot of blacks both south and north of the Mason-Dixon line.

The paranoid response to the new "black peril" included among other things the 1905 novel *The Clansman*, by a Southern evangelist, the Rev. Thomas Dixon Jr., who wrote the book as a counterargument against the novel *Uncle Tom's Cabin*, whose stage adaptation revolted Dixon in 1901. A character in *The Clansman* underlines the prevailing obsession with miscegenation when he warns, "There is enough Negro blood here to make mulatto the whole Republic." Both the book and the later film seemed designed to make sure that never happened.

The Birth of a Nation ends on a triumphant note—if you're a white racist—with the end of Reconstruction and the disenfranchisement of blacks, who were thrown out of office.

Griffith justified his celebratory ending by quoting no less an authority than Woodrow Wilson, who wrote in *A History of the American People*, "Negro rule under unscrupulous adventurers was finally ended, and the natural, inevitable ascendancy of the whites, the responsible class, established." Wilson apparently wanted to make the *white* world safe for democracy.

As the sympathies of an apologist like Wilson suggest, the film not only affected the South by reviving the Klan, but it may have had an even more pernicious effect on the North. With its stereotypes of politically corrupt, lazy, dangerous, sexually omnivorous blacks, *The Birth of a Nation* showed Northern lawmakers the reason blacks had to be suppressed and explains why for so many years the Northern establishment ignored the segregationist policies of its Southern neighbors, not to mention the horrors of lynchings and church burnings, which the depredations of the film's dangerous Negroes seemed to justify.

Technically, *The Birth of a Nation* is art, but it is art of the most dangerous kind, whose effects still reverberate amid beatings and lynchings in America today. A Wilde beauty, yes, but a terrible, ugly beauty.

Titanic
(1997)

Directed by James Cameron
Written by James Cameron

CAST

Leonardo DiCaprio (Jack Dawson)
Kate Winslet (Rose DeWitt Bukater)
Billy Zane (Cal Hockley)
Kathy Bates (Molly Brown)
Frances Fisher (Ruth DeWitt Bukater)
Gloria Stuart (Rose Dawson Calvert)
Bill Paxton (Brock Lovett)
Bernard Hill (Capt. Edward John Smith)
David Warner (Spicer Lovejoy)
Victor Garber (Thomas Andrews)
Suzy Amis (Lizzy Calvert)

When it comes to authenticity, it's safe to say that director James Cameron got the details right in *Titanic*, but got his characters all wrong. The film's $200 million

Leonardo DiCaprio does a variation of rearranging deck chairs on the *Titanic* with Kate Winslet in the film of the same name.

budget made it the most expensive movie ever made, and even its detractors, who were legion despite the huge number of fans who turned it into the biggest money-maker of all time with a worldwide gross of over $1 billion, agreed that the money, as they say, was all up there on the screen. If only Cameron, who also wrote the script, had put as much effort into the plot and character development, critics complained, the film wouldn't have degenerated into a "Victorian melodrama" (the *Los Angeles Times*) with a rehashed *Romeo and Juliet* subplot and glaring anachronisms in the dialogue and the protagonists' behavior.

Columbia University's Simon Schama might have been describing *Titanic*, although he wasn't, when he wrote, "A true feeling for period, then, should never be confused with pedantically correct costume-and-decor detail. It's possible to get all the minutiae right and still get the dramatic core of a history wrong."

The details here afforded a heavenly recreation of 1912, the year the *Titanic* disappeared into the freezing waters of the North Atlantic, killing 1,500 passengers. But the director had a devilish time with the fictional love story that occupies centerstage until a pesky iceberg engulfs it.

Cameron's battalion of researchers somehow managed to find the original silverware and china patterns used on the fatal voyage, as well as the wallpaper, all of which were faithfully re-created in the film. When someone suggested building the ship's three-story Grand Staircase with plywood, the director insisted on using the original oak. Some times there were practical reasons for Cameron's anal-retentive obsession with detail. The Grand Staircase had to be made of the original solid wood, because it breaks apart in the film, and plywood doesn't float—or sink—the way oak does. "[Cameron] wanted it to break apart naturally; he wanted it float naturally," the film's resident historian, Ken Marschall, said.

In other matters, Cameron's lust for accuracy seemed like overweening willfulness. The deck chairs on the ship could have been made of cheaper material and painted to look like wood with no floating problems, but the director insisted on the real thing. "The chairs are made of real wood, hundreds and hundreds of them. They could easily have been resin castings, and they could have been stuck together and spray-painted brown, and you would never have known the difference on film. They could have been weighted just right so they would have floated like real chairs. But he said, 'No. I want them to be real wood,'" Marschall recalled.

While clinging to the main outline of his sappy plot, Cameron agreed to change small things in the action. In one scene he wanted furniture in the dining room to careen from side to side as the ship sank, but the on-site expert, Marschall, told the director that the real furniture had been bolted down. "OK. Well, that table's not moving, then. I'll just have to have the actors go in the other direction," the director said. Marschall marveled at Cameron's flexibility. "No other director would do this," the historian said. Once in a while, however, the director ignored blueprints to service the script. Marschall said Cameron wasn't always obsessed with details. "A person couldn't really walk through that wall, because there wasn't a door there, but I'm going to put a door there because I just have to," Cameron told his adviser.

Cameron had a lot of box-office clout from immense hits like *Terminator 2* and *True Lies*, and he demanded and got the bucks to build a replica of *Titanic* that was 90 percent the size of the original—three football fields long. The near-scale model didn't reflect the director's grandiosity but rather his obsession with accuracy. Production designer Peter Lamont explained, "If you have a 50-foot model, the water never looks like the real thing; the bigger the model, the better the water scale becomes."

The main story is framed by a modern subplot that revolves around the sunken wreck. To make sure the production designer faithfully re-created the immersed vessel, Cameron made two trips, two and a half miles down, to the *Titanic* in a Russian mini-sub. With the help of his engineer brother, Michael, he designed a special 35 mm camera and lighting system that could be used on the sub to shoot the wreckage, which provided information for the underwater scenes shot on a set in Nova Scotia.

As careful as the director was about hardware, he was careless about character, which he subordinated to the melodramatic demands of his screenplay. The most glaring historical inaccuracy was the villainous depiction of the ship's first officer, William Murdoch, which resulted in the film's bankroller, 20th-Century Fox (Paramount co-financed), sending an emissary to Murdoch's English hometown to make a formal apology.

The film's Murdoch accepts bribes from first-class passengers and shoots third-class passengers to make room for the rich in the few lifeboats. As the ship slips into the Atlantic, Murdoch uses the gun on himself. The real Murdoch gave a passenger his lifejacket and helped passengers regardless of class into lifeboats before being swept overboard. He did not commit suicide.

Fox made amends by sending a top executive to the town of Dalbeattie, with an engraved plaque in Murdoch's memory and a £5000 donation to the Murdoch Memorial Fund. Scott Neeson, executive vice-president of 20th-Century Fox, in a speech to Dalbeattie's citizens, said, "It was never intended to portray him as a coward." The executive added a sour note to his apology when he admitted that the film wouldn't be changed to correct the erroneous portrayal and no apology would be added to the credits in the video release.

Neeson apparently hadn't seen the movie when he told a startled audience in Dalbeattie, "[Murdoch] did as much as he could to save lives, and I think that was portrayed in the film." *Rich* lives, that is.

Titanic also got the *Titanic*'s final shipboard tune wrong, even though the film's music advisor was on the set with the title and score of the actual song, which the director 86-ed in favor of a sappier musical finale. Ian Whitcomb, who produced the novelty album *Titanic—Music as Heard on the Fateful Voyage*, learned from an eyewitness account given to the *New York Times* at the time by Harold Bride, the ship's radio operator, that the last song heard by the doomed passengers was an upbeat waltz, "Songe d'Automme," a contemporary pop hit by British bandleader Archibald Joyce. Contemporary tabloids, however, erroneously reported that the lachrymose hymn "Nearer My God to Thee" played while the ship sank, and Cameron chose to go with the tabloids of 1912. A few months before the sinking, the ship's bandleader, Wallace Hartley, was asked by a reporter what song he'd select if the *Titanic* went down. Wallace said he'd pick "cheerful stuff" like the pop favorite of the era, ragtime. Wallace added presciently, "I'd never play 'Nearer My God to Thee,'" which he said he planned to save for his own funeral.

The critics ignored minor characters like First Officer Murdoch and the *Titanic*'s fake playlist to save their venom for the main event (not counting the iceberg)—the star-crossed romance of a poor artist in steerage, Jack Dawson (Leonardo DiCaprio), and first class' Rose DeWitt Bukater (Kate Winslet), the reluctant fiancée of a murderous Pittsburgh steel tycoon, Cal Hockley (Billy Zane). After Jack rescues Rose from a suicide attempt, she falls in love with him.

Although *Newsweek* described the film as "quasi-Marxist" and the *New York Times* noted its "rich-bashing populism" for championing *declassé* Jack over aristocratic Cal, other critics, including the *Los Angeles Times*' Kenneth Turan, who wrote five vitriolic pieces on the film, which resulted in Cameron calling for the critic's "impeachment" in a letter to the *Times*, slammed the script for being a "hackneyed, completely derivative copy of old Hollywood romances." Similarly, *Commonweal* dismissed the love story as "Harlequin romance drivel" that owed more to Barbara Cartland than Henry James.

While it served his dramatic purposes, Cameron's championing of steerage over the carriage trade got the *Zeitgeist* of 1912 America wrong. Contemporary reports of the *Titanic's* sinking highlighted the virtues of the rich, while condescending to the humble passengers, who died in disproportionate numbers. 1912 wire service reporters filed dispatches with fictional accounts of John Jacob Astor and other wealthy passengers "stepping aside, bravely, gallantly remaining to die so that the place they otherwise might have filled could perhaps be taken by some sabot-shod, shawl-enshrouded, illiterate and penniless peasant woman of Europe." Hardly the behavior of the film's first officer gunning down the unwashed unworthy to make room for the well-heeled.

Contemporary reports that male passengers already in the lifeboats gave up their seats so women could be saved reinforced the unliberated notions of the post-Victorian world of 1912. A letter in the *Baltimore Sun* gloated, "Let the suffragists remember this. When the Lord created woman and placed her under the protection of man, he had her well provided for. The Titanic disaster proves it very plainly." So much for the film's portrayal of Rose as a proto-feminist.

The dialogue is also filled with anachronisms that screenwriter Cameron must have missed while he obsessed over matching tableware and wall coverings. DiCaprio's Jack seems to paraphrase Bob Dylan when he says, "You can call me a tumbleweed blowin' in the wind." Rose tells penis jokes, which a woman of her class, no matter how liberated, would have never done, and she gives people who annoy her the very late 20th century "finger." Her bright red lipstick would only have been worn by a prostitute of the time. A historian in the Midwest who insisted on anonymity because he didn't want to harm his career in academe by appearing in a pop history book, pointed out to me via email the unlikelihood of an unmarried couple (Rose and Cal) sharing the same suite or the debutante having arguments with her fiancé in her boudoir while wearing a negligée. According to this historian, *Titanic* seems to have lost its class consciousness too. "The classes were strictly segregated. Leonardo DiCaprio wouldn't have been allowed anywhere near Kate Winslet.

And who would have employed a former policeman as a personal valet?" he said about Cal's murderous henchmen (David Warner), who takes potshots at Jack. "The heavy fireplay . . . such nonsense!" the historian said in disbelief. Also unheard of in those days was the film's depiction of a woman smoking in a public place, the Cafe de Paris, the historian added.

Despite the critical barbs and slipshod history, *Titanic* swept the Oscars, with James Cameron winning best director and screenplay awards for his much-maligned script. His hubristic acceptance speech, "I'm king of the world!" led some observers to claim it had replaced Sally Fields' "You like me! You really like me!" exclamation as Oscar's most embarrassing moment. But while Cameron gloated, his triumph may have been diminished if he recalled *Commonweal* film critic Richard Allen's review, which said of *Titanic's* overlong running time of two and a half hours plus:

"I never thought I could be so happy at the sight of an iceberg!"

Reds
(1981)

Directed by Warren Beatty
Written by Warren Beatty, Trevor Griffiths

CAST

Warren Beatty (John Reed)
Diane Keaton (Louise Bryant)
Edward Herrmann (Max Eastman)
Jerzy Kosinski (Grigory Zinoviev)
Jack Nicholson (Eugene O'Neill)
Paul Sorvino (Louis Fraina)
Maureen Stapleton (Emma Goldman)

Diane Keaton and Warren Beatty play Communist sympathizers Louise Bryant and John Reed in *Reds*, a romanticized account of the Russian Revolution.

Activist/novelist Upton Sinclair dubbed American Communist John Reed "the playboy of the social revolution," and it's no surprise that Hollywood's legendary ladykiller and leftist Warren Beatty found directing and starring in *Reds*, a film bio of Reed, irresistible.

It's also proof of Beatty's box-office clout that in 1982, during the "greed is good" Reagan era, the Renaissance star was able to coax $33.5 million out of Paramount to make a heroic film about Godless Communism.

Critics complained, however, that Beatty's liberalism was sabotaged by commercialism and that the co-writer-director-star had relegated the Russian Revolution to a backdrop for the main event, an old-fashioned love story about Reed's tempestuous relationship with his wife, Louise Bryant, played by Beatty's then girlfriend, Diane Keaton.

Much of Reed's political life never made it to the screen while his romantic curriculum vitae got the full Hollywood treatment with soaring music and huge close-ups of the stars in each others' arms. Princeton historian Christine Stansell said, "Too often in *Reds* the enthralling politics . . . become a mere foil for the trials and triumphs of the lovers rather than the opposite way around." No mention was made of Reed's attempts to infiltrate American labor unions with Communist activists, and Beatty lost a dramatic windfall when he failed to include Reed's documented meetings with Alexander Kerensky, Leon Trotsky, and Vladimir Lenin, the Big Three of the Russian Revolution. Reed also engaged in famous shouting matches with Theodore Roosevelt, but their verbal sparring didn't make it into *Reds*, despite the fact that with a running time of three hours-plus there should have been plenty of room for all these lost dramatic opportunities, which might have included a comment from Walter Lippmann, the most influential political columnist of the 20th Century and Reed's Harvard roommate. Lippmann dismissed Reed for "what many people believe to be the central passion of [Reed's] life, an inordinate desire to get arrested."

Downplaying radical rhetoric, Beatty not only heightened the romance, but invented scenes from the Reed-Bryant affair that gave *Reds* a David Lean–*Lawrence of Arabia*–*Doctor Zhivago* cinematic sweep even though those scenes popped out of Beatty's typewriter and not the historical record. The film's climactic sequence, which provided a handsome image for movie posters and newspaper ads, shows Beatty and Keaton embracing at a Moscow train station after being separated. To get to this reunion, Keaton's Bryant is shown preposterously walking across the Russian Steppes from Finland in the dead of an Arctic winter. When her trek is rewarded with the embrace of Hollywood's most handsome matinee idol, the arduous journey seems worthwhile—except for the fact that Bryant never schlepped through the Steppes to get her man. Bryant, a feminist and less talented writer than her husband, never covered World War II from the French trenches as the film shows her doing— an unheard of job for a woman of that time. For obvious reasons, Bryant's less than heroic life after Reed's death from typhus at the age of 33 in 1920 wasn't mentioned since it entailed her sad descent into drugs and alcohol. After marrying a wealthy American diplomat, Bryant became a socialite, abandoning her politics and career. Divorced, she died in poverty in Paris in 1936. An ironic coda to the Reed-Bryant romance wasn't depicted in the film, perhaps because it would have suggested Bryant was more careerist than romantic. Although she faithfully nursed her dying husband in the hospital, shortly after his death, the grieving widow stuffed her sorrow and kept an appointment to interview Lenin for an American newspaper.

To add a documentary flavor to a film that was more melodrama than docudrama, *Reds* used an innovative device (later parodied by Woody Allen to hysterical effect), interviewing "witnesses." These real but unidentified people—old reds and pinkish fellow-travelers—allegedly knew Reed and Bryant in their heyday. Beatty may have failed to identify them on screen for a good reason. Of the 30-odd "witnesses" whose reminiscences are sprinkled throughout the film, only two or three actually knew the couple, according to Princeton's Christine Stansell, who took the trouble to find out who they were. Some of the ancient witnesses were actually children during the time they "recalled" 1910's bohemian Greenwich Village milieu in which Reed and Bryant participated. Among the name-droppers, journalist Rebecca West lived in England while Reed and Bryant were in Greenwich Village and Russia. Novelist Henry Miller, the thinking man's pornographer, authoritatively analyzes Reed with psycho-babble, although Stansell says he barely knew him. And painter Andrew Dasburg, who *did* know Bryant—in the biblical sense—makes no mention on screen of his affair with her, perhaps because it would have undercut *Reds'* primary preoccupation with the lush romance between Reed and Bryant.

Film critic Kenneth Turan believed that the savvy director had held a moistened finger to the wind and realized that an adulatory account of an American red would not go down well in a white-bread America tilting to the right and Ronald Reagan. Beatty was charged with subconsciously desaturating Reed until he was something less than a pinko, and much less a Technicolor red. "Beatty had the intuition to see beyond the politics, to realize, first of all, how a patina of distance and romance would safely neutralize Reed's beliefs until he seems no more threatening than a Rotarian," Turan wrote in the defunct *California* magazine.

The violence of the Bolshevik hijacking of the Russian Revolution with its bloody purges, artificial famines and forced collectivizations doesn't appear in Beatty's re-creation of a bloodless coup. The uprising seems to consist of nonviolent political debates climaxing with Reed, Bryant, and a proletariat cast of hundreds launching the revolution simply by singing the Communist anthem, "The Internationale," as they bloodlessly march down the streets of Petrograd.

For Beatty, the revolution is a lovefest, symbolized by lovemaking with Bryant in a freezing apartment while the *leitmotiv* of "The Internationale" plays on the Victrola in a reprise of the street scene. Film critic Steve Chagollan felt Reed's outspoken eloquence got lost in the whitewash, while Beatty's trademark screen personality of the stammering, inarticulate but charming hunk burst to the surface of a film that was *all* surface with little depth. "Beatty is noticeably repetitive as Reed, relying on that same boyish charm and stammering innocence that have marked his previous roles," Chagollan wrote.

Director Paul Morrissey, who managed to make nearly X-rated films for Andy Warhol while holding on to right-wing views that seemed incongruous with his cinematic *ouevre*, was enraged by *Reds'* Communist sympathies and nicknamed it "Commie Dearest." But Beatty is a limousine radical and a mainstream moviemaker who never let politics get in the way of a terrific (however fictionalized) tale. Film critics Kenneth Turan and Peter Rainer encapsulated Beatty's *Weltanschauung* best. "Beatty has chosen Hollywood over history." (Turan) "Warren Beatty is less social historian than showman." (Rainer)

The Untouchables (1987)

Directed by Brian De Palma
Written by David Mamet

CAST

Kevin Costner (Eliot Ness)
Sean Connery (Jim Malone)
Charles Martin Smith (Oscar Wallace)
Andy Garcia (George Stone)
Robert De Niro (Al Capone)
Billy Drago (Frank Nitti)
Patricia Clarkson (Ness's Wife)

About the only thing that is the same in Eliot Ness's 1950s autobiography and the 1987 Kevin Costner film allegedly about the Prohibition-era crime buster is the title, *The Untouchables*.

Director Brian De Palma, whose borrowings from classic films verge on plagiarism rather than *homages*, threw out the real story of how clever accounting practices, resulting in a tax evasion conviction, brought down Chicago gangster Al Capone and substituted mythic elements from *The Seven Samurai*, *The Magnificent Seven* (the latter an American remake of the former Japanese classic), and even *Robin Hood*. The archetypal story of the *The Untouchables* but not the Untouchables offers a band of outnumbered men who join forces to battle a more powerful world of evil, winning against overwhelming odds, led by an innocent novice who grows into his role with the advice of his elders. That sells more popcorn than trying to squeeze drama out of accounting fraud like double-bookkeeping.

The screenplay by Pulitzer Prize-winning playwright David Mamet even changes Ness' professional affiliation. Ness was a special agent in the U.S. Prohibition Bureau sent to clean up Chicago's bootlegging and other forms of organized crime because the local police department and politicians were hopelessly corrupt. In the film, Costner's Ness works for the Treasury Department, which puts him closer to the government or-

Kevin Costner gives an arresting performance as Prohibition-era crime buster Eliot Ness in *The Untouchables*.

ganization that actually sent Capone to prison for 11 years for grossly underestimating his taxes on a vast criminal enterprise that personally earned him $100 million a year.

The real Ness assembled nine men to bust organized crime in Chicago. To make the odds more uneven, Costner's Ness only employs three: an accountant named Oscar Wallace (Charles Martin Smith), who does resemble the owlish Frank Wilson, who nailed Capone by examining both sets of his books; an entirely fictional Italian-American (Andy Garcia) who has anglicized his name to George Stone; and a crusty old Chicago cop (Sean Connery) named Malone. The real Ness had no Italians on his team, and one critic speculated that Garcia's Italian-American character was added so the film wouldn't seem like unrelenting dago-bashing. The real Chicago police department was so rife with corruption, Ness never would have found one of its members to recruit. The real Malone worked for the Treasury Department and had no affiliation with Ness. Connery was injected into the story to set up scenes where a wise old cop mentors a wet-behind-the-ears youngster, Costner's archetypal reworking of Ness. While offering plenty of advice and Irish-brogue-sweetened homilies, Connery does not engage in the real life Malone's more dramatic accomplishment of infiltrating Capone's organization and uncovering the tax evasion evidence that sent Capone to the slammer for eight years in 1931.

The real Ness was not married during the Capone era, but the film gives him a wife and baby who can be placed in harm's way and rushed from their home to a safe place. The climax of the film has Ness, finally corrupted by the corruption all around him, violate the civil rights of Capone's No. 2 man, Frank Nitti, by hurling him off the roof of a tall building. Nitti crashes through the roof of a car to his death, which allowed Costner to allegedly ad lib the film's best line. When a colleague asks about Nitti's whereabouts, Costner deadpans, "He's in the car." The real Nitti and Ness never went *mano a mano*, and Nitti died in 1943 of that rarest of gangster deaths, suicide. To justify Ness' murderous vengeance on Nitti, the crime buster only acts after learning Malone has been killed by Capone's henchmen. The nerdy accountant is also felled by gangsters. However, not one of Ness' real life associates was ever killed. Crime historian Martin Short said that if Ness "had ever perpetrated such a crime" against Nitti, "he would have deserved a 10-year jail sentence himself."

Ness was never shot at, as he is in the film when bootleggers defend their operations with guns. In real life, when Ness' team showed up at illegal breweries, the booze-makers sneaked out the back door and set up shop elsewhere.

Other fictionalized scenes go heavy on the gore, especially one in which a little girl is blown to pieces by a bomb intended for a bar whose owner refused to sell Capone's beer. De Palma's *homage* to the famous baby carriage careening down the Odessa Steps in Eisenstein's classic, *Potemkin*, is relocated to the dizzying staircase of a railway station. A heart-stopping scene, but also one that never happened in real life. De Palma, who belongs to the auteurist school of dice 'em and slice 'em with films like *Dressed to Kill* and *Carrie*, actually decreased the body count in *The Untouchables'* most memorable moment. Robert De Niro plays Capone as a genial psychopath, as charming as he is lethal. During a lavish banquet scene, De Niro complains about the job performance of one of his henchmen, then bludgeons the underachiever to death with a baseball bat. The deadly banquet took place, but Capone, who didn't believe in golden parachutes, killed three unproductive cronies at the feast—two more than De Palma gives him. Of all the fictional screen mayhem, the hoakiest has to be the portrayal of the Royal Canadian Mounted Police, who join Ness on a joint venture to bust rum runners on the U.S.-Canadian border. The real Mounties never participated in the collar for the simple reason that alcohol was not illegal in Canada. A real Mountie felt the portrayal of his colleagues owed more to *Rocky & Bullwinkle* and *Rosemarie* than Canadian history. De Palma took their official name literally and put the Canadians on horses, even though the Mounties hadn't battled crime on horseback since the 1870s, according to Corporal Pierre Belanger, a spokesman for the organization at the time of the film's release.

The fate of the real Eliot Ness was as anticlimactic as Al Capone doing time for stiffing the IRS. Although widely reported to have been a suicide, Ness died in 1957 of a heart attack after a business venture to waterproof checks to prevent forgery went bust and devastated him emotionally and financially. He died a broken and broke man, $9,000 in debt . . . in his own bed.

Pearl Harbor
(2001)

Directed by Michael Bay
Written by Randall Wallace

CAST

Ben Affleck (1st Lt./Capt. Rafe McCawley)
Josh Hartnett (1st Lt. Danny Walker)
Kate Beckinsale (Nurse Lt. Evelyn Johnson)
William Lee Scott (Billy Thompson)
Greg Zola (Anthony Fusco)
Ewen Bremner (1st Lt. Red Winkle)
Alec Baldwin (Maj./Col. Jimmy Doolittle)
Catherine Kellner (Nurse Lt. Barbara)

Jon Voight (President Franklin D. Roosevelt)
Cuba Gooding Jr. (Doris "Dorie" Miller)
Mako (Admiral Isoroku Yamamoto)

Director Michael Bay boasted that he would show Pearl Harbor as it had never been shown before, to which naval historian David Suid replied, "In that, he has succeeded." But Suid didn't mean that as a compliment because he then proceeded to describe a film that "fails to provide even a reasonable facsimile of history." Suid, the author of *Sailing on the Silver Screen*, claimed that about the only thing Bay and screenwriter Randall Wallace (who similarly warped the historic William Wallace in *Braveheart*) got right was the date of the attack, "which will live in infamy." You get

Pearl Harbor's T&A treatment of naval nurses was so sexist even the U.S. military complained, but Kate Beckinsale's nurse Evelyn Johnson shows she's more than a pretty face as she tends to a casualty of the Japanese air strike.

the feeling that Suid feels *Pearl Harbor's* release date, May 25, 2001, will be remembered with only slightly less ignominy.

Perhaps more than any film in recent memory, *Pearl Harbor* epitomizes the debate about the duty of filmmakers when creating a film based on fact. Is their first obligation to give the audience a history lesson or an ahistorical roller-coaster ride? Historians and film critics alike agreed that *Pearl Harbor* was almost all—one hates to use the term "pure"—entertainment with virtually no instruction or information about one of the most critical events in the history of the Republic.

In his defense, Bay noted that he interviewed more than 100 survivors of the attack plus several military advisers vetted the script, including Jack Green, a U.S. naval officer and an expert on the subject; Lt. Melissa Schuerman at the Defense Department and the film's liaison to the military; the family of Jimmy Doolittle, the bomber pilot who led the first raid on Tokyo in April 1942 and who figures prominently in the film; and Col. C. V. Glines, Doolittle's biographer and also an expert on Pearl Harbor's infamous day.

Then, it seems, Bay and Wallace ignored all his expert advice in order to make an entertaining film, or as Suid said, "given the alternatives of dramatization or reality, the filmmakers too often chose to create a cinematic vision that lacked plausibility or any resemblance to history. . . . In fact, Randall Wallace's original script showed virtually no awareness of actual history."

Bay made the standard defense in response to critics that the film wasn't intended as a history lesson. But Suid feels filmmakers have a duty that takes precedence over entertaining, and he perfectly capsulizes the argument that fiction doesn't excuse grotesque distortion of the facts in order to sell more popcorn. "If films fabricate and distort the truth, viewers have no basis for knowing what actually happened and why it happened and so may well conclude that historical accuracy remains unimportant."

In descending order of most egregious inaccuracies and omissions in *Pearl Harbor*: there's the scene *Time* magazine called a "howler," in which FDR (Jon Voight), a paraplegic, rises, unaided, from his wheelchair, and gives a rousing speech to his defeatist Cabinet members, implying that if he can stand up, anything is possible. *Rolling Stone's* Peter Travers found this temporary cure worthy of Lourdes "exciting," while anyone familiar with paraplegia would call it preposterous.

Both Bay and Wallace have said that if this scene didn't happen in real life (it didn't), it should have. The *Wall Street Journal* complained that the film made the emaciated president look "fattish and sweaty," with no hint of FDR's charisma or his "enormous flair and magnetism" that rallied a nation demoralized by the surprise attack on Pearl Harbor and its carnage.

To its credit, the film ignores the bogus conspiracy theories that Roosevelt knew beforehand of the Japanese attack and did nothing so that an isolationist America would go to war (especially against Nazi Germany, which FDR found a greater menace than Japan). Doris Kearns Goodwin, who won the Pulitzer Prize in 1995 for *No Ordinary Time: Franklin and Eleanor Roosevelt: The American Homefront During World War II*, wrote, "It is inconceivable that Roosevelt, who loved the Navy with a passion, would have intentionally sacrificed the heart of his fleet, much less the lives of 3,400 American sailors and soldiers, without lifting a finger to reduce the risk."

Moving down the list of inaccuracies and omissions, next up has to be the film's treatment of the Japanese. The filmmakers give the attackers kid-glove treatment at best, a "whitewash" at worst—to use one critic's term for the film's depiction of Japan's culpability. The whitewash wasn't dictated by political correctness or even a desire to rectify decades of "Jap-bashing" in American films about World War II. Financial considerations were paramount. Neither the Japanese nor the Germans in the film are depicted as villains because Japan and Germany are huge film markets, and Disney, which bankrolled *Pearl Harbor*, didn't want to offend Japanese and German ticket buyers. Indeed, *Pearl Harbor* seems to justify the attack when a Japanese commander says with regret, "We have no choice but war," because the United States has cut off oil to Japan.

"From this Disney version of events," the *Wall Street Journal* said, "moviegoers who know little or nothing of the history of the world may well conclude that a peace-loving Japan had been forced into an act of war by the American embargo of its oil supply." And so the sorrowful Japanese commander doesn't explain why the U.S. pulled an OPEC-like freeze on oil exports to his country. The *Sunday Times of London* didn't share the filmmakers' P.C. and box office delicacy and explained that Japan's invasion of China and the atrocities it committed there prompted the America's oil embargo. "The same cruel and imperialistic Japanese forces that were engaged in the brutal massacre of 300,000 Chinese soldiers and civilians in Nanking in

1937 are portrayed as honourable men doing what they had to do to survive . . . [*Pearl Harbor*] is a drama that declares everyone innocent."

In another nod to Japanese sensibilities, a line in the film that accurately described Japan's execution of captured American pilots as war criminals was cut. And Admiral Isoroku Yamamoto (Mako), who against his better judgment followed orders and orchestrated the attack on Pearl Harbor, is depicted in the film as a pacifist and sage, despite the fact that Robert Love, an expert on Pearl Harbor and a professor at the U.S. Naval Academy, has called Yamamoto a "lunkhead." In the film, Yamamoto's sagacity and prescience are underlined when he utters the famous line "I fear all we have done is to awaken a sleeping giant," which *Time* called an "accurate, prophetic warning." But David Suid pointed out that the line was lifted from the 1970 film *Tora! Tora! Tora!*, and was never uttered by the real Yamamoto.

Director Bay was correct when he said *Pearl Harbor* wasn't a history lecture. It's an old-fashioned romance with a classic (the critics used the term "stale") love triangle involving two dashing American pilots, Rafe (Ben Affleck) and Danny (Josh Hartnett), who fall in love with the same beautiful nurse, Evelyn (Kate Beckinsale). Rafe goes off to fight in the RAF (the British air force), promising to return. When Rafe is reported lost in action, Evelyn falls in love with his best friend, Danny. Then Rafe returns and a hoary drama that dates back to the silent film era ensues. Evelyn tries to comfort Rafe with a speech about her love for both men, then ends with a line that had one preview audience howling. "And then all *this* happened"—"this" being the attack on Pearl Harbor.

Ironically, at a time when Washington and Hollywood itself were engaged in self-flagellation about movies being too violent, *Pearl Harbor* was criticized for going soft on the gore because Disney demanded a PG-13 version so the all-important teen audience wouldn't be locked out of theaters. "The scenes of the dead floating in the water look for all the world as though they had been choreographed by Busby Berkeley." *Time* said. "Photographs from the day show the true hell of Pearl Harbor—blown-apart boats and bodies, oil fires everywhere, the sea aflame. Bay's bay is, by contrast, vivid, colorful, almost clean . . . The grimness is missing." Pundits called this Pearl Harbor another Disneyland, "the happiest place on earth."

In retribution for the attack, FDR calls for a bombing raid on Tokyo, which had little strategic value but was designed to give Americans a feeling of "gotcha" and revenge. Leading the raid was Capt. Jimmy Doolittle (Alec Baldwin). Despite consultation with the Doolittle family, *Pear Harbor* gets the naval hero all wrong. Baldwin's Doolittle portrays an obscenity-spouting (within PG-13 constraints) technological bimbo who doesn't know what a slide rule is, despite the fact that the real Doolittle held a doctorate in aeronautical engineering from MIT. To heighten the danger, the film's Doolittle claims no plane has ever taken off from an aircraft carrier when in fact pilots had been practicing carrier takeoffs and landings in Virginia to prepare for the raid on Tokyo.

During the raid, the American planes are hit by Japanese antiaircraft guns, but historian David Suid insists that "Japanese gunners and airplanes inflicted virtually no damage on any of the bombers."

Also during the raid, Evelyn, the nurse, listens to the attack on a short-wave radio transmission from Doolittle's planes. In reality, only FDR and top military leaders knew about the raid. The American public, including presumably the fictional Evelyn, only learned of the raid afterward when news of the attack was broadcast on Japanese radio. The short-wave radio transmission from Doolittle's planes also never happened because Doolittle had the radios removed from his planes to save weight. The scene serves a dramatic purpose, allowing Evelyn to fret over the fate of her two lovers, but absent the radios on Doolittle's bombers, the scene was also a technological impossibility.

The *Village Voice* pointed out the grimly amusing fact that no native Hawaiians seem to live in Disney's Hawaii, and in the film's epilogue, which explains the aftermath of Pearl Harbor, no mention is made of the United States' imprisonment of 120,000 Japanese American citizens, which the magazine said "has engendered comparisons with Europe's concentrations camps." In this sunny E-ticket ride, there is no room for any kind of holocaust.

Just as Japanese atrocities were omitted, American racism also doesn't exist in the film despite the fact that Jonathan Okamura, a professor of ethnic studies at the University of Hawaii, notes that "anti-Japanese sentiment and violence were widespread by 1941 and the film hardly hints at such hatred." There are no "Japs" in Pearl Harbor, only Japanese.

More than one critic blasted the T&A treatment of the nurses in the film, and even the American military, not exactly known for its feminist activism, complained after reading the final draft of the script about the *Playboy* pictorial flavor of the film. Phil Strub, special assistant for audiovisuals in the Defense Department's public affairs office, sent the film's producer, Jerry Bruckheimer, a note that the naval nurses' portrayal was "anachronistic and also a bit crude, fixated on how their breasts will appear." The *Wall Street Journal* said the nurses' debate about which flier had the cutest butt sounded as though the dialogue was lifted from an episode of *Sex and the City*.

In a happy world where crippled presidents walk and ER nurses talk trash, where war crimes don't exist and there's no "Yellow Peril," anything seems possible, including a sanitized depiction of an attack that claimed 3,500 American lives.

Or as *Time* wrote, "To make money on one of the costliest films ever made [$145 million], Disney wanted to preserve its PG-13 rating to draw the widest possible audience. The movie burnishes the golden glow around World War II, a vicious slaughter that now seems distant and Olympian."

It's a small, small, *sanitized* world after all.

Bonnie and Clyde (1967)

Directed by Arthur Penn
Written by Robert Benton, David Newman

CAST

Warren Beatty (Clyde Barrow)
Faye Dunaway (Bonnie Parker)
Michael J. Pollard (C. W. Moss)
Gene Hackman (Buck Barrow)
Estelle Parsons (Blanche)
Denver Pyle (Frank Hamer)
Velma Davis (Gene Wilder)

Bonnie and Clyde (Warren Beatty, Faye Dunaway) glamorized the life of two incompetent petty theives and major murderers who in their two-year crime spree during the Depression netted a grand total of $2,000 by robbing banks, gas stations, and dry cleaners.

The most memorable moment in *Bonnie and Clyde* occurs when Faye Dunaway, as Bonnie Parker, pistol in hand, announces the couple's occupation:

"We rob banks."

Bonnie robs banks with her lover, Clyde Barrow (Warren Beatty). Bonnie's claim is only one of the many elements in the controversial film that were glamorized and hid ugly truths about the real pair of robbers who terrorized the Midwest and the Southwest from 1932 to 1934.

Dunaway would have been more historically accurate, but not so cool, if she had listed the pair's more typical targets—filling stations, dry cleaners, and grocery stores.

Although Bonnie Parker and Clyde Barrow now occupy the same pantheon as such big-time gangsters as Al Capone, John Dillinger, and Machine Gun Kelly, they were in reality petty, incompetent crooks who during their crime spree netted a total of $2,000. At one point during their two-year binge, their total cash assets amounted to $8.

The glamorization of the couple, who were described by the *New York Times* as "human rats," began with the casting of the lead roles. Hunky Warren Beatty portrays Clyde Barrow as a likable, charismatic figure who just happens to rob banks. The real Barrow was no stud, burdened with a weak chin and out-sized ears. A biographer described him as "altogether unheroic in physical appearance. In other words, he was no Warren Beatty." Clyde's cruelty, which included killing civilians and not just lawmen, began in childhood, when he frequently tortured animals. His specialty was breaking birds' necks and wings. His blasé attitude about killing innocent bystanders revolted even his criminal colleagues, with John Dillinger describing Barrow as "kill crazy" and claiming the pair gave bank robbers a bad name!

At the time the film was made, Faye Dunaway was a starlet and former fashion model, beautiful and statuesque. The real Bonnie Parker was four feet ten, weighed 90 pounds, and was flat-chested and hard-faced. She had unsightly burns all over her body after their car crashed during a getaway. Suave operators in the film, the real couple were incompetent crooks. Their car had crashed because it ran out of gas, dim bulb Clyde having forgotten to fill up the tank before the robbery.

Nervous screenwriters deviated even more from the historical figures when it came to portraying their love life. In the late 1960s, depictions of homosexuality in any media were still taboo, and writers David Newman and Robert Benton completely excised that fact that Clyde was a bisexual pedophile who often joined Bonnie in *ménage à trois* with a 17-year-old mechanic and gang member, played by 28-year-old Michael J. Pollard. Director Arthur Penn dismissed the omission by calling it a "dreary story" when embarrassing would have been a more accurate explanation for the excision of Clyde's homosexuality.

Instead, the fictional Clyde is beset with impotence. He abruptly interrupts his lovemaking with Bonnie by conceding that he's "no lover boy." Bonnie challenges him to resume his life of crime (he had spent two years in the state pen before they met) as a powerful substitute for his weakness in bed. Stroking his gun, Bonnie challenges him with, "You wouldn't have the gumption to use it." Sexual dysfunction leads to crime, according to the film's psycho-sociology.

Bonnie's criminal influence on Clyde was actually based on the career of another couple of sociopaths: Kathryn Thorne goaded her husband, George Kelly Barnes, a small-time bootlegger, into becoming the famous gangster Machine Gun Kelly.

Bonnie and Clyde's benevolent treatment of the little people was borrowed from John Toland's biography of John Dillinger, which the screenwriters credited as a source. Dillinger committed heists with big payoffs, not Bonnie and Clyde's petty dry-cleaner robberies, and it was Dillinger who avoided killing innocent bystanders, unlike the film's hero and heroine.

Omitted from the story line because it diminished their heroic image was their cold-blooded killing of two men who took second jobs as part-time cops to support their families during the Depression. One victim left behind five motherless orphans, the other a widow and three children with no life insurance.

The genuinely heroic lawman who brought down the couple is portrayed as a villain in the film. Frank Hammer, a retired policeman, had a well-paying job with a Houston oil company when the Texas Rangers asked him to help capture the gang. Hammer gave up his $500-a-month job (a handsome salary during the Depression) out of a sense of public service. In the film, Bonnie and Clyde capture Hammer, who wears the traditional villain's black hat and tie him up. When Bonnie kisses him, Hammer spits in her face. The film's Hammer escapes and vows revenge for his humiliation. The real figure was never captured and never met the pair before their final, fatal run-in with the authorities.

The heroic treatment of two petty hoods galled many critics of the film, who resented their depiction as modern-day Robin Hoods. The film emphasized that the couple robbed banks (as opposed to the corner grocery store) because banks were widely reviled during the Depression, when thousands of financial institutions foreclosed on mortgages or went out of business, losing their customers' life savings.

The Robin Hood theme is emphasized after their first holdup, when the couple are hiding out in an abandoned farm, shooting at a bank foreclosure sign for target practice. The former owner of the farm drives by and explains he no longer lives there because the bank has foreclosed on his home. Clyde gives the farmer his gun and invites him to take potshots at the symbol of his dispossession, the foreclosure notice. "We rob banks," Clyde tells the man, as though their crime spree is an act of revenge against heartless bankers. No such episode happened in real life. In another scene, while holding up a bank, Clyde refuses to take money from an obviously poor depositor in line, suggesting his gang only robbed institutions, not individuals. That suggestion and the scene itself are pure fiction.

The film's Bonnie and Clyde are lionized by the public for their Robin Hood style, and they achieve folk hero status. In reality, the public was more fascinated by their ability to evade the law for such a long time, their use of fast cars to outrun the police, and their relentless self-promotion in the press, which seemed to anticipate today's birthright of 15 minutes of fame for all. Bonnie sent photographs of the gang to local newspapers, including one famous picture showing her holding a gun and smoking a cigar. Her literary aspirations and longing for fame no matter how dubious its source also prompted her to send her poems to newspapers, which dutifully printed them while vilifying the pair as "ugly and evil desperadoes." In the film, Dunaway reads Beatty a poem the real Bonnie sent to a newspaper: "Someday they'll go down together/They'll bury them side by side/To a few it'll be grief/To the Law a relief/But it's death to Bonnie and Clyde."

The real Bonnie's aunt sided with "the Law" and said of their brutal demise, "I'm glad she's dead. She is surely in hell."

The violent depiction of their death epitomized what some critics found most loathsome about the film, while others praised it as perfectly reflecting the equally violent 1960s. Cornered in their car by the police, the two are riddled by bullets in a slow-motion sequence that has an almost beautiful, balletic quality.

Released a few years after the assassination of President Kennedy, while America's inner cities were going up in flames and American boys were dying in a faraway place called Vietnam, *Bonnie and Clyde* was a symbolic representation of the violent present, according to admirers and the film's creators. Director Arthur Penn said his film was a "commentary on the mindless violence of the American Sixties and an esthetic evocation of the past." The film embodied Santayana's caution about repeating past mistakes, and Penn pointed out that the violence of the Depression era continued in the 1960s, citing "the ridiculous war" in Vietnam as an example of an ignorant society condemned to repeat the mistakes of its past. "We have a violent society. America is a country of people who act out their views in violent ways [and who lack] a strong tradition of persuasion, of ideation, of law," Penn said.

Screenwriters Newman and Benton were even less apologetic about the violence they had created and considered their hero and heroine perfect avatars of the present decade—blithely acknowledging the grim statistic that their "heroes" killed 15 people during their two years on the lam. "If Bonnie and Clyde were here today," Newman and Benton wrote in a book about the making of the film, "they would be hip. Their values have been assimilated in much of our culture—not robbing banks and killing people, of course, but their style, their sexuality [pedophilia?!], their bravado, their delicacy, their cultivated arrogance, their narcissistic insecurity, their curious ambition have relevance to the way we live now." Who needs Charles Manson when you have Barrow and Parker as role models?

Like many movies that grossly distort the historical record, *Bonnie and Clyde* made amends of sort by getting the details right. The screenwriters went to Dallas to study the region and the culture, although both must have changed a great deal in the 30-odd years separating the subject matter and the film. They also brought along a tape recorder to capture the regional accents.

The opening of the film displays photos of the real Bonnie and Clyde, along with their birthdates, birthplaces, and the "back story" before they met. In the film, Clyde recounts a true incident from his stay in prison, where he cut off two toes to get out of work detail. The couple's first meeting near Dallas is also accurately portrayed. They eventually team up with Clyde's brother and sister-in-law, Buck (Gene Hackman) and Blanche (Estelle Parsons). In 1933, the police almost caught the foursome in a cabin motel, and the movie identifies the actual place where this occurred, Platte

City, Missouri. When her husband is mortally wounded by the authorities, Blanche becomes hysterical, especially after she's blinded in one eye by flying glass. (A photograph of the incident shows Blanche screaming, and one of her eyes is clearly injured.)

In the end, on film and in real life, a member of their gang betrays them to the authorities. (Michael C. Pollard in the film; in real life, a member of their gang named Henry Methin turned them in in return for immunity.)

Bits and pieces of historical trivia also help re-create the 1930s. Rudy Vallee sings on the radio. After robbing a bank, Bonnie and Clyde hide out in a movie theater, where the feature is the ironically titled *Goldiggers of 1933*, and for further irony, the scene they watch is a lavish chorus number with dancers waving giant coins over their heads, singing, "We're in the money." Leftover posters for Franklin Roosevelt's 1932 run for the presidency, Burma Shave signs on the highway, and Ford V-8s, the car model Clyde favored, enrich the period film visually and aurally.

Just as the casting got the "Hollywood treatment," wardrobe also provided more glamorous togs for the fashion model turned actress Faye Dunaway. Despite her lower class roots as a waitress, Bonnie sports chic 1930s gowns by Oscar-nominated costume designer Theadora van Runkle, which spawned a fashion trend after the movie's release. Despite the careful attention to period details, Dunaway's makeup and hairdo remain resolutely circa 1967. The plucked eyebrows and helmet-like bobs of the era would have detracted from the photogenic actress' appearance.

Although he claimed Bonnie and Clyde were genuine symbols of 1960s violence, director Penn insisted he was dealing in mythology, which justified all the historical distortions and omissions.

"This is not a case study of Bonnie and Clyde," Penn said. "We did not go into them in any depth. We weren't making a documentary." The film, he added, was only interested in the "mythic aspects of their lives."

BIOGRAPHY AND SOCIAL HISTORY

Quills
(2000)

Directed by Philip Kaufman
Written by Doug Wright, based on his play

CAST

Geoffrey Rush (The Marquis de Sade)
Kate Winslet (Madeleine LeClerc)
Joaquin Phoenix (The Abbé du Coulmier)
Michael Caine (Dr. Royer-Collard)
Jane Menelaus (Renee Pelagie)
Billie Whitelaw (Madame LeClerc)

In the fall of 2000, liberal U.S. senator and vice presidential contender Joseph Lieberman launched an unlikely, conservative-style jihad against Hollywood's alleged smut peddlers, and in a masochistic orgy of *mea culpas*, the entertainment industry promised to try to do better and feted Lieberman at several gala Hollywood fund-raisers for the man who had excoriated their artistic output.

Not all of Hollywood, however, welcomed Lieberman's crypto-conservative criticism, and one filmmaker in particular responded with what *Los Angeles* magazine called a "really grand 'fuck you' to those who would control the content of movies." Director Philip Kaufman's biopic about the Marquis de Sade, *Quills*, was the cinematic equivalent of a slap in the face to Lieberman and his fellow travelers on the other side of the aisle, Republicans like Senator Jesse Helms and Monicagate's Grand Inquisitor, Kenneth Starr.

Quills presents the notorious Marquis de Sade (Geoffrey Rush) as a First Amendment/free speech martyr, and not as the real-life sadist who mutilated prostitutes and molested little boys.

Instead of portraying the real-life sexual sadist and child molester, Kaufman's Marquis comes across as a First Amendment advocate and victim, an *ancien régime* Larry Flynt (as interpreted by Mike Nichols in 1996's *The People vs. Larry Flynt*), an early crusader in the fight against censorship, and a genius whom lesser minds envy and try to destroy. This literary conceit amounted to deceit, according to *The New Republic's* Stanley Kauffmann, who was appalled by the filmmakers' hero worship of a man who was a monster first and a minor literary figure a distant second. "The screenplay's worst offense," Stanley Kauffmann complained, "is that it very nearly converts a deliberately dangerous soul into a card-carrying member of the ACLU."

The director and screenwriter, Doug Wright, who adapted his 1991 play for the film, chose a prickly character to turn into what one reviewer called a "cuddly hero." The historic aristocrat was what the British call a nasty customer. He loved to torture prostitutes and sodomize little boys, whom he abducted with the help of his wife, who eventually repented and entered a convent in 1791.

Donatien Alphonse François de Sade was born into one of France's most noble and ancient families in 1740. His ancestors included kings of France. Under the tutelage of his corrupt uncle, a priest, the adolescent Marquis was introduced to perversion and eventually surpassed his mentor. What separates the Marquis from your garden-variety pervert seems to be his ability to describe his perversions in a literary style that was shocking in its day for its candor and later influenced generations of self-consciously decadent writers who adopted the Marquis as their spiritual founder, especially France's poets *maudits*.

If you were a woman, especially a prostitute, or a young boy, you would not want to have known the Marquis de Sade. At a time in France when the common people had no rights under an oppressive monarchy and aristocracy, de Sade's sexual torture of low-born prostitutes was so severe that the aristocratic establishment sided with the common folk. De Sade was imprisoned for the first of several times in 1768 after Rose Keller, a streetwalker he had imprisoned and mutilated, escaped and made her story public.

In *Quills*, the Marquis is not imprisoned for his real life crimes of eponymously sadistic passion, but because the graphic depiction of sexuality in his novels has offended public morality and sensibilities. *Quills'* aristo is a martyr for free speech, not the perpetrator of deeds so triple-X and horrific they had to be sanitized for the film to receive an R rating.

Quills begins in 1794, three years after the nobleman, played by Geoffrey Rush, has been incarcerated in an insane asylum at Charenton. There, as better dramatized in the 1964 play *Marat/Sade (The Persecution and Assassination of Jean-Paul Marat as Performed by the Inmates of the Asylum of Charenton Under the Direction of the Marquis de Sade)* by Peter Weiss, he stages his obscene productions using the other inmates as actors. (The lunatics may not be running the asylum, but one of them is directing its theater.) Nothing can suppress the creative vitality of this literary genius, including incarceration. In *Quills*, the psycho-sexual show must go on.

The film mounts inaccurate productions of de Sade's plays at Charenton. *Quills'* plays within a screenplay are foul-mouthed odes to everything from necrophilia to coprophilia (the sexualization of feces). The real Charenton productions, according to de

Sade biographer Francine du Plessix Gray, were more like drawing room comedies and so G-rated that local notables visited the asylum to take in a good, not grotesque, show.

Screenwriter Doug Wright insisted, "There's a lot of truth in the film," then did an about face and admitted, "As for the facts, we made free with them."

Indeed, de Sade's real plays (before they were sanitized for Charenton's tony audience) contain such shocking prose, Wright was forced not to bowdlerize the original text, but create new dialogue for the crazed inmates to perform in *Quills'* madhouse plays. In fact, all the alleged quotations from de Sade's novels and plays in the film were actually written by the screenwriter, not de Sade. It's beyond ironic that a film that purports to support free speech and damn censorship doesn't censor but deletes its First Amendment hero's X-rated rants and domesticates his literal bestiality. Joe Lieberman and Tipper Gore couldn't have been more pleased.

Some liberals were not. *W* magazine's Aaron Gell resented making the sadistic de Sade a martyr of the Enlightenment: "In turning de Sade into a champion of free expression, the film portrays him as a harmless, if horny, old codger. So what if he brutalized a few prostitutes and children? Kaufman deserves a spanking." The man who gave his name to sadism probably would have come up with a much crueler punishment for the adapter of his life and life's works.

Other "facts" the filmmakers "made free with"—or, more accurately, fabricated—are both minor and major. While the caretaker of the asylum, the kindly Abbé Simonet de Coulmier, was in real life a bulbous, four-foot-tall hunchbacked dwarf, he is played in the film by *Gladiator*'s mad emperor, Joaquin Phoenix, an actor of average height and no spinal misalignment.

In *Quills*, de Sade's wife (played by Rush's real-life wife, Jane Menelaus) visits him in his cell, whereas the real Marquise had voluntarily committed herself to a convent years before. Omitted from the film is the fascinating factoid that before Mme. de Sade got religion, she helped her husband get boys and participated in his rape and mutilation of the young victims. In the film, de Sade's alleged masterpiece, the novel *Justine*, is smuggled out of prison by a fictional creation, a laundress played by Kate Winslet. In fact, the novel had been published before de Sade's incarceration. The laundress's risky business of smuggling the Marquis' prose is attributed to her appreciation of its literary merit, a dubious judgment, and an unlikely one, *The New Republic* pointed out, for a woman of her station, who probably would have been illiterate.

Some of *Quills'* most dramatic episodes were entirely fictional, including his use of blood and his own excrement to continue writing when the title's writing implements are taken away from him. Also invented was the climactic scene in which he is literally silenced by having his tongue cut out. Never happened.

But as in many historical biopics, the "hero"—if that's the right term for a man who derived sexual gratification from feces and mutilation—is hijacked for modern purposes, not dramatized for historical accuracy. "Kaufman and Wright are less interested in the historical Marquis de Sade than in giving him contemporary resonance. For them, Sade's voice is a cry against the whitewashing of our culture," *Los Angeles* magazine's James Greenberg wrote.

But the filmmakers' bad boy is so bad, they had to whitewash his work, and over that fresh coat of paint impose their own viewer-friendly version of the corrupt antihero—an irony that de Sade himself, a master ironist, would have enjoyed. If such a place exists, somewhere in hell the aristocratic pornographer is laughing. And maybe mounting an accurate production of his plays with his fellow hellmates.

Nicholas and Alexandra (1971)

Directed by Franklin J. Schaffner
Written by James Goldman, Robert K. Massie (book)

CAST

Michael Jayston (Nicholas)
Janet Suzman (Alexandra)
Roderic Noble (Alexis)
Ania Marson (Olga)
Lynne Frederick (Tatiana)

Candace Glendenning (Marie)

Fiona Fullerton (Anastasia)

Harry Andrews (Grand Duke Nicholas)

Irene Worth (Marie Feodorovna)

Tom Baker (Rasputin)

Jack Hawkins (Count Fredericks)

Timothy West (Dr. Botkin)

The creators of *Nicholas and Alexandra*, the story of the doomed last emperor and empress of Russia, had an impossible task: turn two clueless twits into figures of grand tragedy. Their source material was not promising even though James

In *Nicholas and Alexandra*, Michael Jayston and Janet Suzman play the last emperor and empress of Russia as heroic, tragic figures, while the real life Nicholas was a clueless, reactionary twit and his wife a paranoid religious fanatic.

Goldman's screenplay was based on the bestseller of the same name by Pulitzer-Prize-winning historian Robert K. Massie.

If *Nicholas and Alexandra* were a piece of pure fiction, a critic might capsulize the problem as "great plot, thin characters." Indeed, the *New Republic* called the film's protagonists, the tsar and tsarina, "two silly people" and the *New York Times* dismissed the supporting cast, the leaders of the Russian Revolution, as "cartoon characters."

The story is the stuff of epic drama, but the little people in this big picture keep getting in the way. Except for them, *Nicholas and Alexandra* has all the right stuff: the birth of the imperial couple's hemophiliac son, Alexis, who is saved from death by the intervention of the mad monk Rasputin. The tsarina's infatuation with the lecherous holy man, whose meddling in politics had fatal consequences for her and her family. Rasputin's comic-grotesque death, where it takes more bullets and poison to kill him than a werewolf. The portentous Russo-Japanese War of 1905, in which Russia's humiliating defeat by a seemingly backward Asiatic power led to constitutional reforms that were too little and too late to avoid the bloodbath of the 1917 Revolution. The second humiliating defeat of Russia by Germany in World War I, which sealed the tsar's fate. His grudging abdication followed by the rifle and bayonet murder of the entire imperial family, including those achingly photogenic kids.

Biographer Massie was hoodwinked by the imperial couple, with whom he seemed to have fallen blindly in love when the worst epithet he could summon to describe Nicholas was "irresponsible." The best the screenwriter and director could do was present Nicholas as a weak ruler, but a great dad. Even that's too kind a depiction when compared to the historical record. During the depths of the Russo-Japanese war, a huge crowd demanding political reforms and an end to the war in Asia, marched on St. Petersburg. With the tsar's approval, the city's garrison fired on the unarmed demonstrators, killing 100 and giving the massacre its famous name, "Bloody Sunday." Leon Trotsky, not the most objective of sources, wrote in *The Russian Revolution* that "at the very dawn of [Nicholas'] reign, Nicholas praised the Phangoritsy regiment as 'fine fellows' for shooting down workers. He always 'read with satisfaction' how they flogged with whips the bob-haired girl-students, or cracked the heads of defenseless people during Jewish pogroms," which the tsar promoted, hoping to use the Jews as scapegoats to distract attention from his attempt to seize Korea, which led to the disastrous Russo-Japanese war.

The film fails to portray Nicholas as the reactionary bozo he was, a man whose political myopia was only topped by that of another ditzy autocrat, Louis XVI, who on July 14, 1789, the day the Bastille fell, wrote in his diary, "Nothing [happened today]." The historical—but not the movie's—Nicholas was a not-so-benevolent despot who embodied the divine wrong of kings, a concept of all-powerful sovereignty that was already under attack 300 years before and had already separated two kings and a queen from their heads.

The *New York Times* described the film's Alexandra as "gently neurotic," but historians and forensic psychiatrists have diagnosed her as a "paranoiac" whose Rasputin-backed interference in politics reinforced her husband's autocratic rejection of Russia's fledgling attempts at democracy and parliamentary government. The *New Republic's* Stanley Kauffmann was too harsh when he called the title figures in this flabby tragedy "two silly people who got what they deserved" (no one deserves to be bayoneted to death), but it is true that their intransigence *led* to what they got.

Produced during one of the peaks in the Cold War, the film's portrayal of the leaders of the Bolshevik Revolution reflected "viewpoints having more to do with American orthodoxies rather than Russian history," *Newsweek* said, complaining that it presented Lenin as a "Russian Hitler." Actually, the revolutionaries are more cartoonish than totalitarian here. Poor Lenin gets howlers from Goldman, who served another pair of royals, Henry II and Eleanor of Acquitaine, much better in *The Lion in Winter:* "Trotsky, you've been avoiding me," and "Well, Stalin has been exiled to Siberia . . . *again.*" *Newsweek* felt the film's Stalin resembled Jimmy Durante and was reduced to introducing himself by saying, "Hello, my name is Josef Stalin . . ." Cliff Notes have more eloquence.

Rasputin also comes across as a refugee from an X-rated Tom and Jerry cartoon, a boozy Lothario shown literally rolling in the hay with three milkmaids while failing to display any of the well-documented charisma that bewitched an empress, "healed" her hemophiliac son in what must be history's first recorded instance of the placebo effect, and dictated Russia's domestic and foreign policy until his murder in 1916. Perhaps fearing unintentional farce, the script neglects to mention that the ringleader of Rasputin's assassins, Prince Yussoupov, was a transvestite. The film got some of the details of Rasputin's end right and some wrong. He was poisoned and shot by disgruntled aristocrats while "Yankee Doodle Dandy played on a Victrola," which the film accurately portrays. But it fails to show his place of burial, the Neva River, into which his half-dead-half-alive body was unceremoniously dumped. "Still, the little poisoned cakes look scrumptious," the scholarly journal *Films & Filming* said of the toxic dessert that failed to kill Rasputin and necessitated the use of bullets.

At least the production's pastry chef did his job.

Lawrence of Arabia (1962)

Directed by David Lean
Written by Robert Bolt

CAST

Peter O'Toole (T. E. Lawrence)
Omar Sharif (Ali ibn el Kharish)
Alec Guinness (Prince Faisal)
Anthony Quinn (Auda abu Tayi)
Jack Hawkins (General Allenby)
Jose Ferrer (Bey of Deraa)
Anthony Quayle (Col. Harry Brighton)
Claude Rains (Mr. Dryden)
Arthur Kennedy (Jackson Bentley)

Lawrence of Arabia won seven Oscars and influenced a generation of future *auteurs*—among them a teenage Steven Spielberg, who abandoned plans to become a surgeon after seeing the film in 1962—but critics complained that the epic air-brushed a flawed hero, glossed over his homosexuality and sadomasochism, and hid a racist British imperialist under the burnoose of a champion of Arab self-determination. Defenders of

In the title role of *Lawrence of Arabia*, Peter O'Toole champions Arab rights and nationalism, although the historical Lawrence has been called a racist and a tool of British imperialism.

Lawrence felt the film portrayed too flawed an anti-hero and fabricated war atrocities he never committed while focusing on too narrow a period in a variegated life.

Even the actor who played him and talked to friends and colleagues of Lawrence found the man unknowable. "It was impossible to find any two men who could agree on Lawrence," Peter O'Toole said when the film was released in 1962.

The disagreements continue to this day.

T. E. Lawrence was the illegitimate son of an Irish aristocrat who changed his name and ran away with his children's governess, Lawrence's mother. Many historians and psychologists speculate that the stigma of illegitimacy created an overachiever whose heroic exploits in battle became the stuff of legend and a cinematic classic.

A Cambridge-educated archaeologist fluent in Arabic, Lawrence went to work for British intelligence in Cairo during World War I, when he was tapped to lead an Arab revolt against the Turks, Germany's ally. The British hoped the rebellion would distract Turkey and Germany from the European theater of operations, which had turned into the muddy, bloody stalemate of trench warfare.

Lawrence united the squabbling Bedouin tribes of the Arabian peninsula and ousted the Ottoman Turks from the Middle East in a climactic battle for Damascus, in the process butchering Turks and putting two Arab allies on the thrones of Jordan and Iraq. But Lawrence's dream of Arab independence was destroyed when Britain and France turned the new Arab nations into colonies. The film's Lawrence is a tragic hero whose idealism was betrayed by European imperialism and colonialism.

Arabs have never bought the Western view of Lawrence as a failed liberator and would-be midwife of their infant nationalism. Some dispute that Lawrence even led the campaign that freed them from Turkish rule. "He did not lead the revolt. It was an Arab revolt. He was one among many," according to Suleiman Mousa, a Jordanian historian and revisionist biographer of *T. E. Lawrence: An Arab View*, which documented errors in Lawrence's autobiography, *The Seven Pillars of Wisdom*, a main source for the film. Sari Nasir, a University of Jordan sociologist, considers Lawrence a racist who felt that only superior Western Europeans could free the primitive Bedouin tribes, and Lawrence's own writings revealed his condescending attitude toward his desert allies when he described them as a "limited, narrow-minded people whose inert intellects lay fallow in curious resignation."

Lawrence himself might have felt uncomfortable with his hagiographic treatment by director David Lean and screenwriter Robert Bolt. According to his brother and literary executor, Prof. A. W. Lawrence, a retired Cambridge archaeologist, Lawrence felt his desert campaign deserved the Disney treatment—as an animated cartoon! "T. E. thought Disney could do it justice—you know, cartoon trains dynamited into kaleidoscope patterns in the air. Grotesque and funny. T. E. thought his role in the Arab revolt could best be understood through humor," his brother said in 1962. But Lawrence's sibling wasn't laughing when he saw his brother's life depicted on the big screen. "I didn't recognize my brother in the film," he said, and he wasn't referring to the fact that the handsome six-feet-tall O'Toole didn't look anything like his brother, a runty five-feet-four inches, whom one acquaintance said resembled Stan Laurel.

Professor Lawrence objected most to a scene where O'Toole shouts, "No prisoners!" then supervises an Arab massacre of the Turks. His brother called that scene and another where T. E. confesses he enjoyed killing an Arab "pure fiction." The scholar blamed Robert Bolt's political bias for portraying his brother as a bloodthirsty maniac and turning the film into anti-war propaganda, citing Bolt's earlier arrest for a civil disobedience campaign that demanded unilateral nuclear disarmament. Bolt denied the charge and could point to Lawrence's own words to justify the portrayal. Indeed, Bolt took the words right out of Lawrence's mouth—actually, his memoirs, where he wrote, "By my orders we took no prisoners" during the Arab massacre of Turks at Deraa on the Syrian-Jordanian border.

One critic called the film's portrayal of Lawrence's personality "pre-psychological," and Professor Lawrence felt that rather than psychoanalyze his complex brother, the film psychosimplified him. "They have used a psychological recipe: take an ounce of narcissism, a pound of exhibitionism, a pint of sadism, a gallon of bloodlust, and a sprinkle of other aberrations and stir well. This completely misrepresents my brother," Lawrence said. Missing from the professor's stew and barely hinted at in the film was Lawrence's homosexuality and documented masochism.

In 1962, homosexuality was still taboo, the love, in Oscar Wilde's phrase, that dare not speak its name, and it remained mute due to the Victorian censorship of Hollywood's Motion Picture Production Code. In a powerful scene, Lawrence is captured by the Turkish governor of Deraa (Jose Ferrer), who subjects his prisoner to a beating, which Lawrence seems to enjoy. The real life incident was expurgated into near meaninglessness by the screen depiction, and its lifelong aftereffects omitted altogether. (When *Lawrence of Arabia* was re-released in 1970, it was rumored that a deleted scene showing Lawrence's homosexual activities would be restored, but no such scene existed.) The bowdlerized film version of "Lawrence's homosexual humiliation," in the words of *The New Republic*, was "badly skimped—symbolized by a lascivious pinch [Ferrer's], a flogging and his being thrown out into the mud."

Lawrence himself hinted that he got more than a beating in Deraa when he later wrote in *The Seven Pillars of Wisdom*, "That night the citadel of my integrity had been irrevocably lost." He was even more forthcoming in a letter to the wife of his friend and champion George Bernard Shaw, when he confessed that "he had broken under the torture and agreed to please the Turk," according to *Life* magazine.

T. E. Lawrence (Lawrence of Arabia) (1888–1935). *Courtesy of the Library of Congress.*

The flogging left more than stripes on his back. Not surprisingly, unmentioned in the film is the claim by one of his biographers, psychiatrist John E. Mack, that the otherwise asexual Lawrence suffered a "flagellation disorder," a compulsion that led him to re-create the beating for the rest of his life.

The Arabs in the film come off only slightly better than the bestial Turk. Edward W. Said, a professor of English literature at Columbia University and a member of the Palestine National Council, felt the depiction of Arabs was flat-out racist. As Prince Faisal, the future king of Iraq, Alec Guinness seemed to be reprising his film role as Fagin, the schlocky Shylock of Lean's *Oliver Twist*, with "an annoying admixture of oiliness thrown in for good measure," according to Professor Said. Anthony Quinn's warrior, Auda, whom Lawrence praised in "Homeric terms," is a "semi-moronic thug out of *West Side Story*," Said added.

Disillusioned by the British betrayal of Arab nationalism, Lawrence sought refuge in obscurity after the war, going so far as to enlist in the RAF as a private under a pseudonym—psychologists theorized as revenge against his father's assumed name and shame over his own illegitimacy. But for someone trying to avoid the limelight, Lawrence cooperated with his biographer, Lowell Thomas, who turned his subject into a household name. Then wrote his own wildly successful attempt at self-promotion, his derring-do account of the Arabian campaign, *The Seven Pillars of Wisdom*.

That account, while inspiring Bolt's screenplay, was filled with more tall tales than truth, according to a revisionist 1955 biography by Richard Aldington, who called his subject the most preposterous liar since Baron Munchausen, noting Lawrence's Paul Bunyanesque claim that he had read "the best part" of the 50,000 volumes in the Oxford Union Library. His hagiographer, Lowell Thomas, also admitted that he had "not hitherto been entirely frank" in his biography, *With Lawrence in Arabia*, having spent only a few days with his hero there and omitting information that would have diminished his heroic portrait.

Lawrence himself, when questioned about inconsistencies in his memoirs, gleefully retorted, "History isn't made up of the truth anyhow, so why worry?"

Although it opened to now forgotten mixed reviews, including Bosley Crowther's dismissal as a "camel opera" in his *New York Times* review, *Lawrence of Arabia* achieved instant classic status with its Oscar sweep, including best picture and director. With time, nostalgia and the adulation of Spielberg and Scorsese, the critical consensus has only improved. But *Lawrence of Arabia* remains a co-opted classic and bad history. Professor Said of Columbia best described its dual location at the summit of art and the pits of Arab ethnography: "On its merits as a cinematic experience, *Lawrence of Arabia* is an engrossing, enjoyable film. As an attempt either to narrate history or to provide insight into the Arab world, however, it has the retrospective nostalgia of an imperial daydream, stubborn and still influential."

Just ask Steven.

Sergeant York
(1941)

Directed by Howard Hawks

Written by Harry Chandlee, Sam Cowan, Abem Finkel, John Huston, Howard Koch

CAST

Gary Cooper (Alvin C. York)

Walter Brennan (Pastor Rosier Pile)

Joan Leslie (Gracie Williams)

George Tobias (Michael T. Ross)

Stanley Ridges (Maj. Buxton)

Margaret Wycherly (Ma York)

Ward Bond (Ike Botkin)

Noah Beery, Jr. (Buck Lipscomb)

June Lockhart (Rosie York)

Dickie Moore (George York)

Howard Da Silva (Lem)

Charles Trowbridge (Cordell Hull)

When writers and directors fiddle with the truth, it's usually to heighten the dramatic content of the story with the happy side effect of increasing a film's box-office performance. In the case of *Sergeant York*, box-office considerations forced the creators of the film to stick closer to the truth than usual.

When *Sergeant York* went into pre-production in 1940, America was overwhelmingly isolationist and did not want to participate in the war going on in Europe. The isolationism was due in part to disillusionment with World War I, which by the 1930s had come to be viewed with the same cynicism and disenchantment the Vietnam War engenders today. In 1937, a Gallup poll showed that 37 percent of Americans felt that their nation's participation in World War I had been a mistake, motivated by munitions manufacturers more interested in profits than making the world safe for democracy. A Congressional investigation in the late 1930s revealed that American industry had made huge profits off the war and that American banks had promoted U.S. involvement because they feared losing loans made to France and Britain. These revelations fueled the national cynicism.

In the face of the prevailing pacifism of the time, making a movie about the most famous hero of World War I, Alvin York, seemed like madness. The studio did not want to be seen to be creating a propaganda piece that glorified war or carried the message that America should throw itself into the conflict raging in Europe. To that end, the production bent over backward to present a balanced and accurate portrait of Alvin York's exploits in the First World War.

They had another reason to pursue accuracy. *Sergeant York* would be the first major Hollywood film to portray a living character. (Hollywood had had great success with biopics of dead Europeans like Emile Zola and Benjamin Disraeli.) Besides fearing lawsuits from York and other people portrayed in the film, the biggest nightmare was the possibility of its subject publicly denouncing the film for inaccuracy.

From the moment World War I ended, York was besieged with offers to turn his life into a movie, all of which he rejected. It's easy to see why Hollywood wanted to tell York's story. It was filled with character conflict, big battles, and even bigger acts of courage under fire. Before the start of the war, Alvin York was a hard-drinking, loose-living native of the hills of Tennessee. When his fiancée demanded he change his ways in return for her hand in marriage, York became a sober, church-going fundamentalist and a pacifist, which oddly contrasted with his almost superhuman ability as a crackshot with a rifle. (Once, blind drunk on his horse, he shot at six turkeys in the dark and didn't miss a single one.)

But after his conversion to an offshoot of Methodism whose tenets included pacifism, this crack shot and future war hero applied for conscientious objector status. After losing four appeals, he was shipped to France and dropped in the middle of the Meuse River–Argonne Forest in France in the front lines of the war. In the action that would make him world famous, York found himself advancing against the Germans, who had positioned machine-gunners on a hill and were cutting the American troops below to pieces. Crossing enemy lines, York stumbled upon 15 German soldiers and took them prisoner. Then the machine-gunners spotted York and opened fire. Like in his turkey shoots in Tennessee, York wiped out his attackers one by one. By the end of the day, the former conscientious objector had conscientiously killed 25 Germans and captured 132.

York returned to a hero's welcome, a ticker-tape parade in New York, movie deals and the offer of huge sums to lend his name to product endorsements. York turned down all offers, explaining, "Uncle Sam's uniform—it ain't for sale." Instead, unlike Charles Lindbergh, he returned to a simple life in Tennessee, where he received the gift of a heavily-mortgaged farm that caused him major financial problems for years. Despite these difficulties, during the next two decades, York resisted all efforts (and lots of money) to turn his story into a film. As revelations about the financial basis for the war were revealed, York felt disgust for the conflict that had made him a national hero. In the mid-1930s, York's isolationism made Lindbergh seem like a hawk. York said he didn't feel America "did any good" by entering the war, and his disillusionment spilled over onto the next war he felt was about to erupt. If the nations of Europe started another conflagration, he believed we "should let those fellows fight their own battles and we'll fight ours when the time comes." By the late 1930s, as Hitler gobbled up large chunks of Europe, York was beginning to feel that the time had come. He promoted military preparedness and financial aid to Britain. An early interventionist despite public opinion favoring isolationism, Alvin York was adored by FDR, another early opponent of Hitler.

In 1940, most Americans hadn't come around to York's way of thinking, and the film's producer, Jesse L. Lasky, went to great lengths to distance the production from present-day politics, insisting "this is in no sense a war picture."

But it was money, not politics, that prompted York to accept Lasky's film offer after having rejected so many others. By this time, York had already cleared personal debts associated with his farm, but he wanted funds to open an international Bible school in Tennessee. York proved to be as tough at the bargaining table as he been in battle and extracted a much larger cut of the film's profits than Lasky had originally offered. He also got a contractual guarantee that he would be portrayed accurately and had a great deal of input into the film, making it one of the most accurate filmed re-creations up to that time. One clause in his contract guaranteed that the film would "redound to his credit."

The film's authenticity was further enhanced by the producer's fear of lawsuits from real life people portrayed in the film. Supposedly unsophisticated Tennessee "hillbillies" turned out like York to be tough negotiators, and some refused to sign a release until they were assured of the film's accuracy. Some also held out for more money, with a lucky few getting the then princely sum of $1,500 apiece. Pastor Rosier Pile, who counseled York when he applied for conscientious objector status, felt the script inaccurately portrayed his attitude toward war, and rather than risk a defamation suit, the writers reworked his part per the minister's specifications, lending further authenticity to the project.

York objected to an early draft of the script that portrayed him before marriage as a womanizing drunk and to a completely fictionalized scene in which his future wife scratches his face after he kisses her. York insisted he had had only a few flings before marriage and demanded the script be changed to reflect his early years more accurately.

With financing from Warner Bros., which specialized in socially conscious films, Lasky sent a camera crew and a writer to Tennessee's hill country to photograph the locals and their homes to help the set designers provide an authentic backdrop for the film. The writer, Harry Chandlee, interviewed members of York's family and other principals in the story.

The result of all this research ended up on a backlot in Hollywood in the form of an expensive 40-foot Appalachian mountainside constructed of wood, cloth, plaster, rock, soil and 121 real trees. The most money, however, went for re-creating the battlefield where York performed his heroic exploits. Three hundred workers converted a verdant California farm into a blackened terrain of trenches and barbed wire. The transformation required five tons of dynamite. Four hundred trees were stripped of their leaves, and 5,200 gallons of paint were used to spray the foliage black.

York did allow the addition of one fictionalized character to help the film appeal to a broader audience. Fearing urbanites might not be interested in a movie about a backwoodsman, the filmmakers decided to give their hero a buddy from Brooklyn.

In the most egregious case of mythmaking, the writers dramatically changed York's conversion from dissolute living to Bible thumping pacifist. Like Saint Paul's experience on the way to Damascus, the film's York is struck by a bolt of lightning and knocked off his horse, which leads to his spiritual transformation. York complained but did not stop the filming of this hokey fabrication, even though he insisted his conversion had been the product of much thought and introspection rather than a bolt from the blue.

York allowed other bits of fiction to creep into the script. In the film, as a reward for his exploits, he receives a lavish farmhouse with rich fields and a lot of farm animals—not the heavily mortgaged property with no dwelling that he got in real life.

Another scene of pure fiction shows York trying to win money to buy a farm before the war by taking part in a turkey shoot. York never impressed his superiors by hitting a series of bull's-eyes on the shooting range as he does in the film, nor did he quote the Bible to his commanding officers. The writers omitted York's belief that God would protect him from harm in battle because it lessened the dramatic tension and made his success seem inevitable.

More accurately, in its casting, the film portrayed the rather large disparity in the ages of York and his wife. Gary Cooper, who played York, was 39, and his on-screen bride (Joan Leslie) was 15, the same age as the real Mrs. York when she met her future husband, then 28.

By the time *Sergeant York* was ready for release in the summer of 1941, it turned out that the studio need not have worried about turning off isolationist movie-goers. By then, Hitler had conquered France, Belgium, Poland, and the Netherlands. Just a few weeks before the film opened, Germany invaded the Soviet Union.

The winds of war had stirred up American public opinion, and *Sergeant York* became one of Warner Bros.'s biggest moneymakers up to that time. Instead of being condemned (and worse, boycotted) for war-mongering, *Sergeant York*, *Time* magazine said, was "Hollywood's first solid contribution to the national defense."

The Last Emperor
(1987)

Directed by Bernardo Bertolucci
Written by Bernardo Bertolucci, Mark Peploe, Enzo Ungari

CAST

John Lone (Pu Yi)
Joan Chen (Wan Jung)
Peter O'Toole (Reginald Johnston)
Ruocheng Ying (The Governor)
Victor Wong (Chen Pao Shen)
Maggie Han (Eastern Jewel)
Ric Young (The Interrogator)

As an entertainment reporter for the *New York Times Syndicate* in 1988, I had the curious experience of being backstage at the Oscars when Bernardo Bertolucci won the best director award for *The Last Emperor*. Bertolucci, like all the other winners, came backstage after winning his award to talk to the press. His film told the story of China's last imperial ruler, Pu Yi (1905-1967). The production had been highly praised for its authenticity, sweeping the Oscars with awards for cinematography and costume design, which re-created the world of the last emperor down to the last detail. Backstage, I posed this question to the director: After all the effort he had put into making the film so accurate, why did he omit one important fact—that Pu Yi was homosexual? The film portrayed him as a raging heterosexual who has sex with two women at a time.

The director flew into a rage after all the softball questions the other journalists backstage had lobbed at him during his moment of triumph. "It would have opened up a whole new can of worms," Bertolucci told me in a huff, to examine the Emperor's homosexuality.

That didn't stop the director from filming in detail the last *empress'* lesbian dalliance with a Japanese spy in a scene that had the spy sucking on the toes of the empress. There is no historical evidence that Pu Yi's consort was a lesbian. There are at least two biographies, Arnold C. Brackman's *The Prisoner of Peking* (1980) and Edward Behr's *The Last Emperor* (1987), that describe the emperor's homosexual orientation.

Cynics might say Bertolucci displayed typical male heterosexual bias by avoiding any depiction of male homosexuality while indulging in a favorite fantasy of heterosexual males, lesbian sex.

One excuse for the omission of the Emperor's homosexuality is that the film was based on his autobiography, and Pu Yi didn't care to out himself in his memoirs, which were written in China, where homosexuality is deeply taboo. One critic suggested that because of the taboo the Chinese government never would have given Bertolucci the privilege of filming in Beijing's Forbidden City, which housed the former emperor's palace. That doesn't explain why the Chinese greenlighted the explicit lesbian scene. Even stranger was the government's insistence on cutting a scene in the Chinese release in which the Emperor has sex with two women.

Pu Yi was crowned emperor of China at the age of three and ruled briefly before being deposed by the forces of Sun Yat-sen. When the Japanese invaded Manchuria, they reinstalled Pu Yi as their puppet to gain legitimacy for Japanese rule. At the end of the war, the Russians captured the emperor and turned him over to the Communist Chinese in the early 1950s. Accused of collaboration with the Japanese, Pu Yi spent 10 years in a brutal reeducation camp, where he became a model Maoist. He gained his freedom in the early 1960s and spent the rest of his life as a humble gardener in Beijing.

The Last Emperor generated a lot of controversy over Bertolucci's depiction of Pu Yi's reeducation. Through gentle prodding by a humane prison warden, he comes to see the error of his fascist, imperialist ways and embraces Communism in a strict but not harsh prison environment.

A French journalist, Lucien Bodard, who interviewed Pu Yi in prison in the 1950s, described a far different reeducation. Bodard wrote that the emperor, "his brain well and truly washed, wallowing in humiliation, quaking with fear, pale-faced and sweating," sat for the interview while his prison warders looked on. As Pu Yi recited his "catalogue of misdeeds," he appeared to be a "crushed convert" play-acting a "grim, repulsive charade."

Bertolucci's version, according to the *New York Times*, treats the Emperor's reeducation as benevolent "psychotherapy . . . There are no rituals of submission, verbal or physical. There is only the aging [emperor] emerging as an illustration of the Maoist technique of creating a better, more self-reliant individual."

Historians also pointed out that Pu Yi's prison uniform in the film is of better quality than the clothing most unimprisoned Chinese wore at the time, and none of the prisoners suffers from malnutrition, despite the fact that thousands died of starvation in Chinese reeducation and labor camps.

Apologists for the director responded that he was only following Pu Yi's own account in his autobiography, and Bertolucci also had to please the Chinese government or lose access to the Forbidden City. Bertolucci's defenders neglected two more compelling reasons for the film's pro-Communist leanings: Pu Yi's autobiography was actually ghostwritten by a committee of party hacks, and the director is more than a Communist sympathizer. Every time his name appears in the co-production agreement he signed with the Chinese, it says: "Bernardo Bertolucci, member of the Italian Communist Party." One critic went so far as to call Bertolucci a "Maoist filmmaker."

The director's leftist leanings may also explain his depiction of the Japanese, whom historian Paul Pickowicz said appear as "crude, one-dimensional caricatures of Japan that have appeared time and again in Chinese films since 1937." Indeed, 30 seconds of the film, showing newsreel footage of Japanese atrocities during the Rape of Nanking, offended the Japanese film distributor Shochiku Fuji, which removed the footage before the film hit theaters in Japan. (After an international uproar, the distributor restored the snippet.)

Other scenes never happened, according to the emperor's brother Gioro Pu Jie, a Communist party official. The film opens with Pu Yi slashing his wrists while in prison. His brother insisted the emperor never tried to commit suicide. A concluding scene gave the story a nice rosy glow when Pu Yi toward the end of his life returns as a tourist to his old home, the Forbidden City, and finds tucked under his throne a pet from childhood, a cricket in a cage, still alive after all these years. Anyone familiar with the ephemeral life span of insects finds this preposterous scene amusing rather than touching. Also fictionalized, per Gioro Pu Jie, is a scene where Pu Yi stops young Red Guard members from abusing his former warden, now a prisoner of the Cultural Revolution. (The Chinese release cut this episode too, despite the fact that the government has denounced the Cultural Revolution of the 1960s and 70s, which imprisoned and executed top government officials and intellectuals.)

Pu Jie also took issue with the film's central conceit, that his brother became a dedicated Communist during his reeducation in prison. According to his sibling, the emperor never gave up his dream of restoring the imperial Manchu dynasty and insisted that Pu Jie call him "Your Majesty" while they were in prison together. The emperor's brother-in-law Guoburo Runqui, a consultant on the film, disagreed with the French journalist's recollection of a terrified, brainwashed emperor and even felt Bertolucci's humane treatment of his conversion to Communism was too harsh.

Finally, one justification for Bertolucci's Mao-friendly take on Pu Yi's life—that it gave him access to the Forbidden City—was undercut by his own Oscar-winning production designer, Ferdinando Scarfiotti, who claimed, "I created everything" on soundstages in Italy. "The only place the Chinese let us shoot, *very quickly*, was the Room of the Supreme Harmony," the last emperor's last throne room.

Despite the Oscar sweep, the *New Republic* dismissed *The Last Emperor* as "slightly sophisticated DeMille" for replacing substance with spectacle. The *New York Times* agreed, calling the film "an elegant travel brochure."

Michael Collins
(1996)

Directed by Neil Jordan
Written by Neil Jordan

CAST

Liam Neeson (Michael Collins)
Aidan Quinn (Harry Boland)
Julia Roberts (Kitty Kiernan)
Alan Rickman (Eamon De Valera)

Michael Collins was one of the founding fathers of modern Ireland and a prime mover in the nation's 700-year-old fight for independence from Britain. Collins was also a man who ordered assassinations of British officials sent to Ireland to put down the rebellion there. Collins participated in the 1916 Easter Uprising in which the forerunner of the IRA took over the Dublin post office and declared Ireland's independence. The revolt failed and 16 of the rebels were executed. The leader of the movement and future first president of Ireland, Eamon De Valera, was spared because he was half American and Britain desperately wanted the U.S. to enter the war against Germany on its side. Collins was also spared and sent to a prison camp in Wales. After escaping, the two men returned to Ireland and launched a guerilla campaign against the occupying British that led to negotiations to grant Ireland limited independence while keeping Northern Ireland a part of Britain. The results of that compromise are still with us in the form of the 30-year clash between the IRA and Britain.

De Valera and Collins were approximately the George Washington and Thomas Jefferson of Ireland respectively, except that the 1996 film about Collins strongly implies that Ireland's George ordered Tom's assassination. An Irish Protestant from Belfast, Liam Neeson, plays Collins with the same melancholy Danish reluctance Neeson brought to another equivocal hero, the compiler of Schindler's List.

The typecasting of Alan Rickman, the villainous Everyman of cinema, telegraphs the film's estimation of De Valera. *Michael Collins* claims that De Valera sent a reluctant Collins to England in 1921 to negotiate Ireland's independence knowing full well that Collins would come back with a deal unacceptable to a vocal—and violent—minority of Irish. The film intelligently condenses the complex compromise Collins agreed to in which southern Ireland would have its own parliament, or Dial, while still swearing allegiance to the hated British crown. Ireland was granted Dominion status, which Canada found acceptable, but which De

Valera and his cronies found intolerable. Britain's refusal to let Northern Ireland join the new Irish Free State in the south was equally repellent to De Valera's large faction.

When Collins signed the Anglo-Irish Treaty in 1922, he said to his British counterpart, "I may well be signing my own death warrant." According to *Michael Collins*, that's exactly what he did.

When Collins returned to Ireland with the treaty, the Dial ratified it by a close vote. De Valera denounced the treaty, and Ireland erupted into civil war. As the new commander-in-chief of military forces in the Irish Free State, Collins found himself in the agonizing position of killing fellow Irishmen to quash the internecine struggle.

On August 22, 1922, while Collins was leading a military convoy in Beal na mBlath in Cork, Ireland, a sniper shot and killed him. Although he seemed to have lived a lifetime, Collins was only 31. The film shows his rival, De Valera, agonizing over the decision to kill Collins. De Valera became Ireland's first president. With what one historian called Stalinesque ruthlessness, De Valera excised his rival from Irish history books and refused to let the slain leader's relatives erect a monument to him. Collins became an Orwellian nonperson, forgotten in Ireland and unknown to the rest of the world until Warner Bros. gave Irish director Neil Jordan $35 million to resurrect the Collins legend on film.

Because of his Irish citizenship, the British condemned Jordan's partisan depiction of the British in Ireland as biased and unrelentingly villainous. Both Irish and British historians insisted there was no proof De Valera ordered Collins' assassination. And British critics complained that the director lost a terrific opportunity to mend Anglo-Irish relations by failing to dramatize Collins' affair with a British aristocrat.

Even American critics took the director to task for justifying the assassinations of British agents in Ireland by Collins' henchmen. "Assassinations, yes, but of villains, not innocents. The movie shows most of the targets executing some nasty deed before being bumped off," the *Village Voice* said.

Most historians say there is no evidence De Valera signed off on Collins' murder, and the accepted fact that De Valera had been in Beal na mBlath earlier in the day was merely a coincidence just like the little known fact that Nixon had been in Dallas earlier in the day Kennedy was shot. Critics couldn't resist comparisons between

JFK director Oliver Stone's paranoid conspiracy theories about Kennedy's assassination, and Jordan's portrayal of De Valera as Collins' killer.

Jordan apparently hadn't seen his own film when he insisted in an interview with the *Boston Globe* that it didn't finger De Valera as the mastermind behind the assassination. "De Valera was earlier that day only 300 yards from where Collins was shot, but I don't mean to imply that he had him assassinated. He had a nervous breakdown after Collins was killed," Jordan said. Others reported that De Valera wept when he heard the "news."

The *Times of London* compared *Michael Collins* to Leni Riefenstahl's Nazi monsterpiece *Triumph of the Will*, and other British critics eviscerated the film for its depiction of the infamous Bloody Sunday massacre in Dublin when British troops fired on innocent spectators at a soccer match. In the film, a primitive British tank rolls onto the playing field, indiscriminately shooting at the soccer players and the people in the stands. Nitpickers objected because the actual British gunmen fired from a nearby bridge, not from a tank. Splitting grotesque hairs, the *Times of London* said, "British soldiers [did not] fire on crowds from armed vehicles, *only on foot*." As if mass murder is okay if committed by pedestrians. Saves gas. Jordan conceded that he changed the position of the British, but only to lessen the film's brutality. "It would have been incredibly brutal because you would actually see the faces of those soldiers [on the bridge] that were shooting up this innocent crowd. You would actually come to hate them because they did go in and shoot 13 people," Jordan said, undercutting critics who felt *Michael Collins* would enflame the present standoff in Northern Ireland.

Before leaving to negotiate the treaty in London, Collins became engaged to his best friend's girlfriend, Kitty Kiernan. According to some historians, Collins began an affair with Lady Hazel Lavery, wife of society painter Sir John Lavery, when the couple opened their London home to Collins while he negotiated the 1922 treaty. By omitting this symbolic proof that the Irish and English could get along, the *Times of London* said Jordan missed an opportunity "to fight sectarian nationalism if it had made Irish people confront the reality that one of their first leaders loved Lady Lavery." Jordan, however, believed Lady Lavery was a groupie and an erotomaniac who fantasized her affair with the handsome rebel. "I didn't get into a romance Collins was supposed to have had with Lady Lavery in London. I'm convinced that the romance was mostly her admiring him, and that it was unconsummated," Jordan said. The *Times of London*, however, insisted that the romance was mutual, as evidenced by the fact that Lady Lavery's and not poor Kitty Kiernan's love letters were found on Collins' body after his assassination.

In an electrifying montage that comprises the high point of the film, the Irish use car bombs to eliminate British officials in Ireland. Historians with no political ax to grind pointed out that car bombs weren't used by the IRA until 70 years later. Jordan justified the anachronism because it allowed him to create literally explosive scenes. Another fictional scene Jordan conceded adding was the British torture and murder of a turncoat agent, Ned Boyd, who died in his sleep in 1972, but defended the episode by saying it symbolized other documented cases of British torture-executions of prisoners. Pressed for a better justification than symbolism, Jordan said of his critics, "Well, fuck them!"

The *Village Voice* felt that the writer-director left the zing out of Collins' romance with Kitty Kiernan (an expensive cameo by the $20 million-per-pic Julia Roberts), saying, "Kitty is a poor excuse for a subplot . . . with little chemistry between her and Collins." *Newsweek* said, "It fizzles on screen." Jordan referred all complaints to a primary source, the couple's love letters, which he described as "chaste . . . Collins would exchange letters with Kitty about going to Mass!" No wonder he died carrying Lady Lavery's turgid mash notes.

American film historian Joseph Roquemore objected to Jordan's black-and-white whitewash of the complex history of "The Troubles" in Ireland, which continue to this day. The trouble with Michael Collins, per Roquemore, is "all of Jordan's English and pro-union Irish are genocidal totalitarians [the prevailing fashion in today's Hollywood—see *The Patriot*]. Director Neil Jordan's hagiographic bio pic belongs in Fantasyland's cartoon vaults, not in history lovers' video libraries."

Roquemore's criticism misses the fact—or perhaps fiction—that *Michael Collins* suggests that Ireland's first president colluded in the film hero's death, which makes it something less than an apologia for the Irish Republican side.

The message of *Michael Collins* is less pro-Irish/anti-British and more reflective of the historical truism that revolutions devour their children. Just ask Robespierre, Garibaldi, and Trotsky. Or Michael Collins.

Chaplin
(1992)

Directed by Richard Attenborough
Written by William Boyd, Bryan Forbes, William Goldman, Diana Hawkins

CAST

Robert Downey Jr. (Charlie Chaplin)

Geraldine Chaplin (Hannah Chaplin)

Paul Rhys (Sydney Chaplin)

John Thaw (Fred Karno)

Moira Kelly (Hetty Kelly/Oona O'Neill)

Anthony Hopkins (George Hayden)

Dan Aykroyd (Mack Sennett)

Marisa Tomei (Mabel Normand)

Penelope Ann Miller (Edna Purviance)

Kevin Kline (Douglas Fairbanks)

Maria Pitillo (Mary Pickford)

Milla Jovovich (Mildred Harris)

Kevin Dunn (J. Edgar Hoover)

Deborah Moore (Lita Grey)

Diane Lane (Paulette Goddard)

Nancy Travis (Joan Barry)

James Woods (Lawyer Scott)

Sometimes a filmmaker's access to primary sources diminishes rather than heightens the authenticity of a biographical film. A good example of too much access leading to excess is *Chaplin*, director Richard Attenborough's film portrait of the greatest actor of the silent era.

In telling the story of Charlie Chaplin, Attenborough and a quartet of credited screenwriters relied on the subject's autobiography, plus sources the late star may have not been happy to supply, but his widow, Oona O'Neill Chaplin, happily turned over to the director. "I met her about 20 times," Attenborough said of the woman

Actor Charles Chaplin (1889–1977) dressed as the "tramp" in a scene from *The Circus*, 1928. *Courtesy of the Library of Congress.*

Chaplin married when she was an underage teen, his favorite type of love interest. "It was not an intimate relationship, but she was sweet enough to say I could see everything: letters, diaries, and ask questions, even if they seemed somewhat indelicate."

The participation of Chaplin's last wife seems to have co-opted if not hijacked a more balanced picture of the subject, or as the *Sunday Telegraph* in London said, "The overall finished portrait is thin on warts."

Not quite. With the exception of Oona and his third wife, actress Paulette Goddard, the women in Chaplin's life are all presented as bimbo harpies, and indeed, *some* of them were. The misogyny is all the more pronounced because it contrasts with the hagiographic presentation of the title character. (Attenborough was so smitten with his subject, he shed a tear on the set when he told a reporter about Chaplin buying a house for his chauffeur-gofer.)

Some of the star's misogyny seems justified and may have dated back to his childhood. At the age of 16, living on the streets of London, Chaplin was forced to institutionalize his mentally ill mother, a sometime vaudeville performer who had introduced her two sons, Charles and Sid, to the theater. The film takes a vaguely psychoanalytical approach that suggests Chaplin's lifelong yen for jailbait arose from parenting an older woman, his mother, who he felt had abandoned him. And if Chaplin did resent some women (including most of his wives), he had reason to. In the 1940s, he had to endure a headline-making trial based on a paternity suit, which was a set-up, filed by an underage actress, Joan Barry. Although a blood test proved he wasn't the father of Barry's child, the trial revealed he had been intimate with the teenager, and a scandalized jury forced him to pay child support.

Despite its access to all the minutiae of Chaplin's life, the film gets both small and large things wrong. Chaplin was on a vaudeville tour of America when Keystone Kops director Mack Sennett caught his act and sent him a telegram offering Chaplin his first movie contract. Chaplin's autobiography says the epochal telegram arrived when he was performing in Philadelphia, but the movie for inexplicable reasons relocated the incident to dusty Butte, Montana.

While only Trivial Pursuit purists might object to minor errors like that, historians felt an important period in the U.S. was misrepresented in *Chaplin*. Because of alleged Communist ties, despite the historical record that shows Chaplin was an apolitical humanist, when he tried to return from his native Britain to America in 1952, the State Department let him know he would not be granted a visa because of his left-wing political associations, although the real reason was the government's disgust over his yen for young girls, despite the fact that after marrying Oona when he was 53 and she was 17 over the virulent objections of her father, playwright Eugene O'Neill, he remained faithful to her until his death more than 30 years later. But the simplifying demands of moviemaking call for evil to be personified, so instead of a faceless State Department bureaucracy hounding Chaplin out of the country, the film creates out of whole cloth a conspiracy engineered by the favorite whipping boy of paranoid leftists, the late FBI director and cross-dresser J. Edgar Hoover, who pursues Chaplin throughout the film with Lt. Gerard-like persistence, even though Chaplin's autobiography mentions Hoover only once, in a nonpolitical context, and the star's definitive biography by David Robinson omits all mention of the G-man.

Chaplin also relies on a hoary gimmick which has the additional misfortune of being entirely fabricated. The film begins with a fictional editor (Anthony Hopkins), who is less than satisfied with Chaplin's autobiography, trying to coax out of the dying star more compelling tidbits, which seem to be mostly about sex. As Chaplin's memory is jogged, the film implies that he (and it) are telling the real story you won't find anywhere, including Chaplin's own memoirs.

With or without the sensationalistic fictional elements, Chaplin was such a juicy role major stars like Robin Williams, Dustin Hoffman, and Billy Crystal sought the part, but in the interest of accuracy, they were rejected by Attenborough despite their marquee value because, without his tramp costume and cookie-duster, Chaplin looked like a matinee idol. The director felt the character actor stars who wanted to play him were not handsome enough. Attenborough picked a slightly more photogenic actor, Robert Downey Jr., and his choice received the blessing of the movie industry when Downey earned a best actor Oscar nomination.

Surprisingly, for all the over-dramatization of other parts of Chaplin's life, the director truncated perhaps the most touching moment in his career, when he returned, finally forgiven, to the U.S. in 1972 to accept an honorary Oscar. Video clips show Chaplin going on stage while the audience rose to its feet, applauding and cheering. That and Chaplin's acceptance speech are not dramatized. The film ends instead with the 83-year-old standing in the wings, waiting for his entrance cue.

Ironically, *Chaplin* offers the best advice for excavating Chaplin when the star tells his editor, "If you want to understand me, watch my movies."

Citizen Kane (1941)

Directed by Orson Welles
Written by Herman J. Mankiewicz, Orson Welles

CAST

Orson Welles (Charles Foster Kane)
Joseph Cotten (Jedediah Leland)
Dorothy Comingore (Susan Alexander)
Agnes Moorehead (Mrs. Mary Kane)
Ruth Warrick (Emily Norton)
Ray Collins (Boss James W. Gettys)

Perhaps it's not fair to criticize the accuracy of a film that does not claim to be a fact-based biography, but *Citizen Kane* is such cinema *à clef* that it's inevitable to compare its portrayal of the title character, Charles Foster Kane, with the real life figure, newspaper magnate William Randolph Hearst, on whom the film was so transparently based.

"For most of us Charles Foster Kane and William Randolph Hearst are indistinguishable; they morphed into the archetype of the demagogic press baron who menaces democracy by cynical manipulation and enriches himself in the process," historian and editor Harold Evans wrote.

The historical consensus is that the real life newspaper mogul was a much, much nicer guy than the cynical, megalomaniac warmonger and reactionary created by

Citizen Kane (with Orson Welles as Charles Foster Kane and Dorothy Comingore as his second wife) is a thickly veiled account of demagogic press baron William Randolph Hearst.

writer Herman Mankiewicz and director Orson Welles, who rewrote much of Mankiewicz's script to fit his vision of the film's anti-hero.

What personal animus against Hearst caused Welles to distort Hearst's character? In the director's case, it was more than the need to fictionalize reality "so the facts wouldn't get in the way of a good story." Hearst's real life contained more than enough drama, tragedy, sex, ups and downs, and glamour to make a viable film. Indeed, in 1985, a highly rated TV movie, *The Hearst and Davies Affair*, proved that.

Welles' vendetta against Hearst derived from a profound disappointment based on what Hearst had once been and had become. The director felt Hearst had betrayed his original socialist ideals and become a reactionary. And he was right.

Hearst had been a radical Democrat who fought the corruption of New York's Tammany Hall, which got its revenge on the publisher by rigging the city's 1905 mayoral election, robbing Hearst of a sure victory. His newspaper empire was based in the West, and his clout in that region of the country helped FDR win the 1932 presidential election. But Hearst soon became disillusioned with the New Deal and the expanding power of the federal government. The radical Democrat became a registered Republican in 1936.

Hearst's reactionary politics got worse. Welles has been criticized for replacing positive elements of Hearst's life with made-up negative ones. (A critic said *Citizen Kane* amounted to "slander.") But Welles could have painted an even more damning portrait with facts that are little known today but still have the power to shock.

Historian David Nasaw in *The Chief* speculated that Hearst became such a diehard anti-Communist because he felt Fascism and Nazism had been created in reaction to it. That would mean his hatred of the left was based on a revulsion for the right. But Hearst's actions in the 1930s suggest that rather than revulsion, the publisher embraced—or at least propagated—the radical right's message in his newspapers.

This astounding factoid would have made a great scene or series of scenes in *Citizen Kane*. In the 1930s, Hearst hired both Mussolini and Hitler to write columns that ran in his newspapers in 17 cities with a combined daily circulation of five million. The employment histories of these columnists from hell would be funny if their message hadn't been so hellish. Mussolini, it turned out, was greedy and demanded more than the $1,500 per column (multiply by 10 for an equivalent sum in today's money) Hearst offered the Italian dictator. His columns also had to be completely rewritten because the Fascist leader, a former schoolteacher, was nearly illiterate. Hitler was a more typical writer—always missing the newspapers' deadlines.

But Hearst did more than propagate the views of these dictators. He shaped his reportage to downplay the horrors of Nazism. In a cable to his New York editors, he ordered them to tell the chain's Berlin correspondent to stop filing critical dispatches on the Nazi regime. "Von Weigand [the Berlin reporter] articles and cables seem too incendiary. Think he should be instructed to send generally interesting news with partisanship," Hearst said in one cable.

To his credit, the Hearst papers did a better job reporting the Nazi's escalating violence against Jews than the *Times of London* did. And when the publisher met his "foreign correspondent," Hitler, he begged him to halt his persecution of the Jews. Even so, Hearst remained an appeaser and an isolationist who used his papers to blast FDR's campaign to enter the war on Britain's side.

Welles tampered with details of Hearst's personal life to add melodrama while ignoring facts that would have legitimately heightened the drama.

In the film, Kane is an independently rich heir to a silver mine fortune when he decides as a lark to buy his first of many newspapers. The man on whom Kane is based was rich, but not independently so. After his father's death in 1891, the entire Hearst fortune went to his schoolmarm mother, Phoebe, not her son. A Medean figure, Phoebe extracted a terrible price to bankroll Hearst's journalistic dreams. In 1895, when he wanted to buy the bankrupt *New York Journal* for the fire sale price of $150,000, Mrs. Hearst gave him the money but only on the condition that he dump his longtime mistress, Tessie Powers, a waitress he had lived with for almost 10 years. Hearst's ambition was bigger than his heart, and he agreed to his mother's terms, thus launching one of the most spectacular publishing careers in history.

Perhaps *Citizen Kane's* biggest departure from fact involves the love of Hearst's life, silent screen star Marion Davies, and chatelaine of his fabled central Californian mansion, San Simeon. Despite a paralyzing stutter, Davies, a beautiful Ziegfeld girl, had a successful film career during the silent era. (It helped that audiences couldn't hear her speech impediment.) To promote his mistress' career, he bought Cosmopolitan Productions in 1919 and had its staff writers create star vehicles for Davies.

Publishing magnate William Randolph Hearst (1863–1951), the inspiration for the title character in *Citizen Kane*, circa 1906. *Copyright © J. E. Purdy, courtesy of the Library of Congress.*

In the film, the Davies character is called Susan Alexander (Dorothy Comingore), and she's a no-talent saloon singer whom Kane tries to turn into an opera star. When no opera house will have her, he builds his own, but her lack of talent makes her career unsalvageable and his insistence on her continuing to pursue it leads to a suicide attempt. Also, the revelation in the rival press that the married Kane has a mistress destroys all his political ambitions on the eve of what would have been an election victory for the Senate. Kane marries his mistress and together they lead a lonely, isolated existence in a mausoleum called Xanadu (a much tackier pile than the sprightly San Simeon) until their divorce.

Hearst's love life couldn't have been further from Welles' portrayal of it. Unlike Comingore's sullen and bored mistress, Davies joyfully presided over famous weekend house parties at San Simeon, which were attended by major movie stars and leaders in other areas of American life. Hearst never married Davies because his Catholic wife refused to give him a divorce, but the couple stayed together happily for three decades, and unlike Kane, who dies alone among the gloomy splendor of Xanadu, Hearst had Davies at his bedside when he died in August 1951. Both Davies and her film counterpart, however, suffered from alcoholism, which Kane ignores but which broke Hearst's heart.

Hearst has been credited with inventing yellow journalism, and he certainly didn't shy away from "inventing" the news to raise circulation. *Citizen Kane* is at its most accurate when it depicts the publisher virtually creating a conflict that didn't exist, the Spanish-American War of 1898.

An unnerving scene in *Citizen Kane* shows the magnate dancing with chorus girls in the newsroom while joyfully dictating a telegram to painter Frederic Remington, hired to illustrate the Cuban conflict for Kane's newspaper chain: "You provide the pictures, and I'll provide the war."

Hearst came close to doing the same with front-page stories that were often pure fabrications about the Spanish mistreatment of Cuban colonials, which sparked America's involvement in the Cuban revolt. One article was headlined "DOES OUR FLAG PROTECT WOMEN?" and described brutish Spanish police aboard an American ship, ordering three young Cuban women to submit to a strip search in the hope of finding rebel letters. A competing paper later reported that the girls had been properly searched by a matron, not policemen.

Hearst famously tried to suppress *Citizen Kane* and had his henchwoman Louella Parsons badmouth both the film and its director in her influential gossip columns, syndicated by the Hearst chain. Perhaps for that reason, Welles always denied that his movie was anything more than a portrait of a fictional character, a claim belied by the fact that many of Kane's lines are verbatim quotes attributed to Hearst.

Welles was ultimately forgiven for playing fast and loose with the facts of William Randolph Hearst's life because as a piece of fiction rather than a docudrama, *Citizen Kane* is universally considered the finest American film ever made, regularly topping critics' "best" lists, including the American Film Institute's recent Top 100.

Gandhi (1982)

Directed by Richard Attenborough
Written by John Briley

CAST

Ben Kingsley (Mahatma Gandhi)
Candice Bergen (Margaret Bourke-White)
Edward Fox (Gen. Dyer)
John Gielgud (Lord Irwin)
Trevor Howard (Judge Broomfield)
John Mills (Lord Chelmsford)
Martin Sheen (Walker)
Ian Charleson (Charlie Andrews)
Athol Fugard (Gen. Smuts)
Geraldine James (Mirabehn)
Alyque Padamsee (Mohammed Ali Jinnah)
Roshan Seth (Pandit Nehru)

When director Richard Attenborough told Indian Prime Minister Jawaharlal Nehru of his plans to make a film about his mentor, Mahatma Gandhi, Nehru begged the director, "Whatever you do, do not deify him—that is what we have done in India—and he was too great a man to be deified."

But Attenborough couldn't resist the temptation to canonize the Indian leader, and *Gandhi*'s adoring picture of the founder of modern India is achieved by ignoring

To protest the British monopoly on wool in India, Ben Kingsley in the title role of *Gandhi* spins his own in an act of civil disobedience recorded by photographer Margaret Bourke-White (Candice Bergen).

many unflattering aspects of the subject's life and character. (The fact that the $22 million film was largely financed with funds provided by the Indian government may have something to do with the worshipful treatment, but that possibility remains equivocal, given Nehru's orders to the contrary.)

Gandhi created and used the concept of *satyagraha*—civil disobedience and passive resistance to the British who ruled India until 1947. The film begins with a dramatic example of this—except that it never happened. At the turn of the century, South Africa, where Gandhi at the time practiced law, ordered all Indians to carry special identity passes. In the film, Gandhi burns his pass and the police respond by savagely beating him. In reality, although the South African police once kicked him out of a whites-only compartment on a train, they never resorted to physical abuse the entire 20 years Gandhi lived there.

To demonstrate Gandhi's impact on Indian independence, other important activists who participated in the struggle—Vallabhai Patel, Maulan Kalam Azad, J. R. Kripalani and Abdul Gaffar Khan—are given cameo roles. Only Nehru receives a well-rounded treatment. Mohammed Ali Jinnah, the brilliant leader of the Muslim League, whose energy and political skills led India's Muslim population to form Pakistan, is reduced in the film to a lazy and ill-tempered dandy. Jinnah's success in founding Pakistan seems inexplicable based on the film's lackadaisical portrayal of him.

The British violently opposed Indian independence for decades, and they become the villains of the piece, portrayed as bigoted dim bulbs whose ability to rule a vast colonial empire on which the sun never set seems impossible. One critic said the British act more like the S.S. than members of a colonial government that tolerated Gandhi's activism for decades. The British policy of pitting the Hindu population against the Muslim minority in order to maintain colonial rule is in the film blamed for the bloody battles between the two sects, which doesn't explain why the enmity between the two countries continues to this day long after the British pulled out.

Like the rest of its one-dimensional portrayals, the assassin of Gandhi isn't even named in the film, nor are his motives explained. (The murderer was a member of a fundamentalist Hindu sect that felt Gandhi had sold out to the Muslims.)

Gandhi achieves sainthood in *Gandhi* with the help of huge omissions of facts and incidents. Although his concepts of civil disobedience and passive resistance inspired Martin Luther King Jr. and Nelson Mandela, sometimes the Indian leader promoted his philosophy in ways that seemed suicidal. The film fails to mention an open letter he sent the British in 1940, urging them to surrender to the Germans who were bombing London into rubble, then use passive resistance in the form of massive demonstrations to drive the Nazis out. Gandhi seemed to have no idea of the threat posed by totalitarian regimes compared to the relatively benign (if paternalistic) rule of Britain. While Japanese troops approached India's eastern border, Gandhi redoubled his efforts to expel the British and lose the protection their army provided against the encroaching Japanese.

The pathological elements of Gandhi's private life are completely absent from the film. Although he used his wife's dowry to pay for his own education as a barrister, he insisted that his wife remain illiterate. When the long-suffering woman contracted

Mahatma Gandhi (1869–1948), circa 1943. *Photo by Kamu Gandhi, courtesy of the Library of Congress.*

pneumonia, Gandhi adopted a Christian Science-like attitude toward modern medicine and refused to allow her to be treated with penicillin, explaining, "If God wills it, He will pull her through." His wife died within days. But Gandhi didn't rely on divine intervention when he became ill with malaria and took quinine to treat the disease. He wasn't a much better father, refusing to educate his sons despite his own law degree.

Although the film gives no hint of it, Gandhi was a Puritan with strong authoritarian impulses. During a 1936 meeting with birth-control proponent Margaret Sanger, he announced his "ruthless determination to destroy pleasure wherever he saw it." Even sex between married couples should be forbidden—by law if need be—after they have had three or four children. "If the social reformers cannot impress this idea on people," he told a shocked Sanger, "why not a law?" In later life, his Puritanism seemed to mask the desires of a dirty old man. Purportedly to prove that he had forsworn all pleasures of the flesh, at the age of 80 he began sleeping naked with groupie-like teenage girls who never left his side.

Gandhi's famous pacifism wasn't all it was cracked up to be. He once announced he "would not flinch from sacrificing a million lives for India's liberty" and one acquaintance described his "fierce joy of annihilation."

Plagued by bouts of paralyzing depression, the leader of India's struggle for independence often abandoned the cause for long periods of time, which only worsened the squabbling among his fractious political disciples and rivals. The film omits its hero's disastrous detachment.

Nehru felt his mentor was too great to be deified. Director Attenborough and screenwriter John Briley apparently felt Gandhi was so great he *had* to be deified. Or as historian Geoffrey C. Ward described the writer and director's anti-aesthetic, "*Gandhi* is a work of worship, not art."

Frances
(1982)

Directed by Graeme Clifford
Written by Eric Bergren, Christopher De Vore, Nicholas Kazan

CAST

Jessica Lange (Frances Farmer)
Jordan Charney (Harold Clurman)
Jeffrey DeMunn (Clifford Odets)
Sam Shepard (Harry York)
Kim Stanley (Lillian Farmer)

The life of 1930s movie star Frances Farmer had enough drama in it to fuel a very long, two-and-a-half-hour feature, *Frances*, that starred Jessica Lange in the title

In *Frances*, Jessica Lange plays 1930s movie star Frances Farmer, whose descent into madness and mental institutions was fueled by alcohol and speed.

role. There were terrific sources for the screenwriters, including a primary one, the actress' posthumous autobiography, *Will There Really Be a Morning?* and a definitive biography, *Shadowlands*, by *Seattle Post-Intelligencer* film critic William Arnold.

Farmer was the original rebel *with* a cause. As a precocious teenager, she won a *National Scholastic* magazine contest for her essay that proclaimed the death of God. In college, she won another contest for selling the most subscriptions to a Communist newspaper, and her prize was a free trip the Soviet Union, where as Stalin's guest she visited the birthplace of the Method, Stanislavsky's Moscow Art Theater. Failing to make it as a stage actress, she moved to Hollywood and became a contract player at Paramount, where her performance in 1937's *Come and Get It* prompted gossip columnist Louella Parsons to predict a bigger career than Garbo's. Farmer rejected the studio system (with its iron-clad seven-year acting contracts) by leaving Hollywood to appear on Broadway in Clifford Odets' *Golden Boy*. She then created a scandal by having an affair with the married playwright, who dumped Farmer to return to his wife and colluded in stopping her from reprising her role in the film version. In her spare time, she raised money for both the leftist Loyalists during the Spanish Civil War and migrant farm workers in the San Joaquin Valley.

Many of Farmer's wounds were self-inflicted. Her alcoholism and Benzedrine addiction led to a series of misfortunes. She assaulted a studio hairdresser in her trailer for rubbing—actually combing—her the wrong way. In 1942, she was arrested for driving with her headlights on during a World War II blackout. Very unpatriotic and typical of a Communist sympathizer, columnists tut-tutted, although Farmer always denied any affiliation with the party, despite her politically unfortunate sojourn in Moscow as Stalin's guest. After her arrest, she screamed obscenities at the cops in the Santa Monica, California, police station and at the judge she appeared before. Her domineering mother, a right-wing paranoid, helped commit Farmer to a mental institution in Washington State that was straight out of Hogarth. There, she was subjected to repeated electroshock therapy, drugged, gang-raped by orderlies and soldiers from a nearby base, and according to her autobiography forced to have a transorbital lobotomy that finally took the fight out of her.

All this dramatic fare wasn't enough for first-time director Graeme Clifford and a trio of screenwriters, whom one film critic accused of turning Farmer's tragic life into a "screeching cross between *The Snake Pit* and *Mommie Dearest*." Christina Crawford had an easier life.

Farmer was a proto-feminist who shocked Hollywood by driving a beat-up car and refusing to pluck her bushy eyebrows. And yet in *Frances*, the writers and director made her dependent on a man, a fictional character named Harry York (Sam Shepard), based on a questionable real life figure, Stewart Jacobson, a Seattle elevator operator who claimed to have had a decades-long affair with the star. In fact, the producers maintained that the film did not rely on film critic Arnold's definitive biography but on Jacobson's account. Harry York flits in and out of the film, reappearing at crucial times to save the feckless victim, even smuggling her out of an insane asylum. "No such man ever came to save her from anything," feminist author Joyce Sunila said.

The trouble with Harry is that he's based on laughable claims made by Jacobson, a convicted pimp with a rap sheet dating back to 1939 that included arrests for murder, vagrancy, tampering with a witness, and assault, although he beat all charges. Jacobson's chronology alone should have raised the eyebrows if not the suspicions of the film's creators. He claimed he first met Farmer in 1931 when he was a police detective. He would have been 17 at the time! He also claimed to have acted as go-between for an affair Farmer had with Supreme Court Justice William O. Douglas, to have convinced Senator Joseph McCarthy not to denounce Farmer for her Communist sympathies, and to have arranged Farmer's last job as hostess of a movie show on a local Indianapolis TV station. Jacobson also said publisher William Randolph Hearst put out a contract on Farmer after she witnessed him murder his mistress' boyfriend aboard a yacht in 1924, although Farmer would have been a precocious 10 at the time. Jacobson explained the absence of any photos of himself and Farmer together by saying they had been destroyed, and Farmer's failure to mention him in her autobiography resulted from his "direct orders."

Louis Kibbee, who ghostwrote the actress' memoirs and interviewed her over a period of several months, said, "I'm sure that Jacobson was not her lover." Biographer Arnold was harsher. "I think he's a complete fraud. He has no credibility at all. If you listen to [Jacobson's taped interviews], he implicates everyone from JFK to William Randolph Hearst," Arnold said. None of this deterred *Frances* co-producer Marie Yates from claiming the film was based on "extensive interviews" with Jacobson, who also supplied the film's narrative voice. "Jacobson provided the love story and viewpoint that we wanted to present," Yates said.

Although one film critic derided Kim Stanley's over-the-top performance as Farmer's mother, Lillian, as "an overheated exercise in villainy—a merger of Joan Crawford and Bette Davis in *What Ever Happened to Baby Jane?*" the real Mrs. Farmer was worse and the screenwriters felt the need to cosmetize her. No mention is made in *Frances* that Lillian threw a pair of scissors at her daughter when she was a child. Or that Communism wasn't the only thing she was paranoid about. She once led a crusade to close every bakery in Seattle because she claimed they used "dark and evil food substitutes" in their bread recipes. Mrs. Farmer's husband, a leftist intellectual and attorney, tried unsuccessfully to have his wife committed to a mental institution twice. A great real-life scene the director passed on would have shown Lillian denouncing her daughter at a press conference, where she said, "If I must sacrifice my daughter to Communism, I hope other mothers save their daughters before they are turned into radicals in our schools." Joan Crawford could only aspire to such bad parenting.

And as Dickensian as the film depiction was of her six-year stay in the mental institution, *Frances* doesn't show Farmer's hydrotherapy treatment, where she spent eight hours in ice cold water and almost chewed off her bottom lip from the pain.

Despite feminist Sunila's reductive argument that Farmer was "destroyed by misogyny," the foul-mouthed alcoholic-addict may have been her own worst enemy. Still, it's profoundly sad that so many other people in her life could have laid claim to that title.

Patton
(1970)

Directed by Franklin J. Schaffner
Written by Francis Ford Coppola, Edmund H. North, Ladislas Farago (book), Omar N. Bradley (book)

CAST

George C. Scott (Gen. George S. Patton Jr.)
Karl Malden (Gen. Omar N. Bradley)
Michael Bates (Field Marshall Sir Bernard Law Montgomery)
Ed Binns (Maj. Gen. Walter Bedell Smith)
Richard Munch (Col. Gen. Alfred Jodl)
Karl Michael Vogler (Field Marshal Erwin Rommel)

Patton was described by its creators as a warts-and-all biography of the famous World War II general. Unlike previous sentimentalized portrayals of military heroes, *Patton* depicted a lot of the choleric leader's warts, but not all of them.

The movie presented an equal if not greater dose of heroism with the curious result that Patton seemed to be all things to all people, or as the *New Yorker* described the contradictory elements of George C. Scott's Oscar-winning portrayal, the script

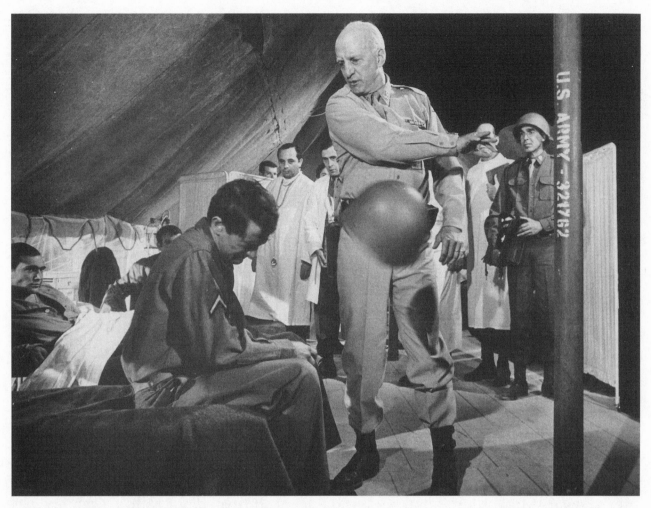

As the flinty World War II general in *Patton*, George C. Scott slaps a soldier whom he accuses of faking illness to avoid combat. (It turned out the GI had malaria.)

"appears to be deliberately planned as a Rorschach test," with viewers on all points of the political spectrum identifying with the most controversial general of the Second World War.

If ever a historical film reflected the time in which it was made, *Patton* embodied the violent public debate in 1970 over the Vietnam War. To hawks, the film's Patton was an honorable military genius. To doves, he appeared to be "the worst kind of red-blooded American mystical maniac who *believes* in fighting, symbolic proof of the madness of the whole military complex," the *New Yorker* said, but added approvingly that the film makes Patton seem both crazy and heroic at the same time. Hollywood usually has trouble depicting duality in characters, preferring black-and-white heroes and villains, with no shades of gray. Movie stars don't like to play anti-heroes. *Patton*'s palette is a vivid gray.

The general's halo is supported by horns, and it's arguable which head ornament the film favors. The halo effect is enhanced when German generals are depicted praising their opponent's brilliant knowledge of military strategy. The Nazis also hold back troops because they fear Patton's military genius will annihilate them. The movie's Patton is gruff (actually, the real Patton had a high-pitched, squeaky voice, which was simply out of the vocal range of George C. Scott's whiskey-soaked baritone), but he's also a classy, kind man—most of the time. He writes poetry, speaks French, loves fine wine and gourmet food, and his bedside manner is terrific—again, *most* of the time. One scene shows him on the verge of tears as he bends down to comfort a soldier covered with bandages in a hospital ward.

Because they were so famous, the movie was unable to omit two less than tearful experiences Patton had while visiting the wounded, although the two events are condensed into one. The film dramatized the real life incident involving Charles Kuhl, who was suffering what was called "shell shock" during World War I, battle fatigue during World War II, and post-traumatic stress syndrome during the Vietnam War. When Patton noticed that Kuhl seemed uninjured in a hospital tent, Kuhl self-deprecatingly replied, "I guess I can't take it." Patton flew into a rage. He not only slapped the apparent malingerer, he also kicked him in the pants, called him a coward, and ordered him back to the front. It turned out Kuhl's disability was not purely psychological. A medical examination uncovered the fact that he also had a 102-degree temperature on the day Patton smacked him, chronic diarrhea, and an undiagnosed case of malaria. When the true story was leaked to the press, General Eisenhower sacked the slap-happy commander.

The director valiantly tried to preserve the subject's heroic image with an exculpatory scene that precedes the slap heard around the world. Patton is shown driving down a road filled with badly injured soldiers. Then, in the hospital tent, he is overcome with sympathy when he sees more soldiers who are visibly wounded before coming upon the apparently intact Kuhl. But the final image that emerges remains "warty." George C. Scott has a demonic look in his eyes as he strikes out at his malaria-stricken victim.

Patton was a thoroughly researched film. In addition to various books on the general, the screenwriters read autobiographies by men who knew him, including General Omar Bradley, President Eisenhower, and Field Marshal Sir Bernard Law Montgomery (who comes off in the film as superficial, supercilious, and more effeminate than the real British commander). Eisenhower contributed more than his autobiography to the film. He wrote a personal and confidential letter to the director with his assessment of Patton. Although he was Patton's frequent defender during the war and saved him from being sacked on several occasions, Eisenhower revealed in his letter that he thought Omar Bradley was a better soldier but praised Patton for his relentless pursuit of the enemy in battle.

If the dialogue rings true in the film, that's because the screenwriters reproduced verbatim many of Patton's speeches, including one before a women's group in England, which not only repeated the entire speech, but was shot in the town where Patton spoke.

As usual, Hollywood poked fun at the British. Not only Montgomery, but Scottish troops wearing kilts are depicted as effeminate compared to their burly American counterparts. A comment actually made by another field marshal is put in the mouth of the luckless Montgomery, who says, "Don't wince, Patton. I shan't kiss you." The director even put Montgomery in short pants! The film gives Patton most of the credit for driving Rommel out of North Africa, ignoring the important contribution of the British there, as well as in campaigns in the Mediterranean, France, and Germany.

The film may be most interesting for what it omitted about Patton's life, mostly personal elements that were just too warty. Patton's flagrant infidelity is completely ignored. Despite his wife's protests, the general carried on a long-term affair with his niece Jean, who volunteered as a Red Cross donut girl. Also unexamined is Patton's ill-conceived and unethical raid on a German POW camp to rescue his son-in-law, a tragedy that resulted in many American casualties and failed to free a single prisoner.

While Patton is shown arriving at Buchenwald, the director curiously omitted a famous incident that occurred while he was there, the sight of the tough general vomiting as he came upon mountains of corpses and the near dead. Despite his sympathy for victims of the Holocaust, Patton was an anti-Semite whose hatred of the Jews (and Russians) is on the record but not in the film. He also objected to the Allies' de-Nazification program and admired German military expertise—both issues

General George S. Patton (1885–1945). *Courtesy of the Library of Congress.*

ignored in the film. The general's very public criticism of the Allied attempts to bring former Nazis to justice was the last straw, and the infinitely patient General Eisenhower sacked him, but this never happens in the film. Patton considered Eisenhower's cautious, life-saving military tactics more cowardly than humane, and he thought Britain's King George VI was a drunk with subnormal intelligence. Those embarrassing opinions also never made it into the script.

Historian Paul Fussell regrets the omission of one incident that the screenwriters, Francis Coppola and Edmund North, almost certainly never learned of. After one of Patton's particularly long-winded speeches, a junior officer muttered to another, "What an asshole!" Fussell speaks with authority on this comment because he was the officer who made it.

Besides winning seven Oscars, including best picture, director, screenplay, and actor (which Scott, in keeping with the nihilism of the times, rejected as a symbol of the establishment), *Patton* earned critical raves for appealing to Everyman, dove and hawk, left and right. The *Wall Street Journal's* review had the headline "Viewing Patton: Pick Your Angle." *Variety's* headline said, "Left, Right Hail War Picture," while the *Los Angeles Herald-Examiner* summed up the effect with "Patton: Reaction Divided."

Patton had something for everyone, no matter how contradictory, according to the *Los Angeles Herald-Examiner's* Richard Cuskelly, who imagined liberals saying, "See that's the sort of freak America produces and idolizes during wartime." Conservative fans would feel "what we need are more leaders and Americans like Patton."

Patton's mixed messages influenced more than the generation of filmgoers who saw it in 1970. According to historian Robert Brent Toplin, the general's macho posturings increased Richard Nixon's courage in much the same way viewers of the Super Bowl reportedly experience a burst of testosterone during the big game. Emboldened by Patton's dismissive attitude toward propriety and ethics, Nixon, a big fan of the film, increased domestic surveillance of perceived enemies, which led directly to Watergate, according to Toplin.

Indeed, George C. Scott's *basso profundo* performance surpassed Patton's influence. During Desert Storm, General Norman Schwarzkopf confessed that Scott's portrayal was more influential in his battle strategy than his own military training!

Ever since the end of the Second World War and Patton's untimely death in 1946, his family had tried to keep any depiction of their famous relative off the screen. But Robert H. Patton, the general's grandson, became a booster of the film and summed up its combination of fact, fantasy, and omissions. "Despite the obscuring, myth-making inflation that *Patton* brings to the subject, it led me to consider for the first time in my life that my grandfather was somebody real."

Real enough to inspire warriors five decades later in the middle of a desert in the Middle East.

Bugsy
(1991)

Directed by Barry Levinson
Written by James Toback, Dean Jennings (book)

CAST

Warren Beatty (Benjamin "Bugsy" Siegel)
Annette Bening (Virginia Hill)
Harvey Keitel (Micky Cohen)
Ben Kingsley (Meyer Lansky)
Elliott Gould (Harry Greenberg)
Joe Mantegna (George Raft)
Bill Graham (Charlie Luciano)

Hollywood loves to glamorize gangsters. They represent our unfettered ids, acting out the murderous fantasies we civil folk would never engage in, bigger than life in real life, and even bigger on the big screen.

It seems inevitable that the life of gangster and alleged visionary Bugsy Siegel would get the Hollywood glamour boy treatment. Siegel was glamorous and so photogenic he once made a Hollywood screen test in the hope of becoming a movie star. (He failed the test, but made it big in the world of crime for a longer time than most movie stars' careers last.)

The casting of matinee idol Warren Beatty clues us in immediately that Siegel will be portrayed as a hero, however flawed, and not the sociopathic thug he really was. The casting of aristocratic Annette Bening as his gun moll Virginia Hill elevates the social status and graces of the real Hill, a lowlife who never, it seems, met a gangster she didn't sleep with. (She learned so many mob secrets during pillow talk with gangsters she bedded that her alleged suicide in Austria in 1966 was more likely a mob hit that liquidated a potential police informant.)

The film wisely focuses on only two periods of Siegel's life: the Hollywood years, when he hobnobbed with major stars in the glittering nightlife of Sunset Strip clubs, and his manic stay in Las Vegas, a town the movie inaccurately claims Siegel invented.

Bugsy (with Warren Beatty in the title role) romanticizes the life of gangster Ben "Bugsy" Siegel as a visionary who invented Las Vegas rather than the psychopathic contract killer and embezzler he was.

His "formative years" as a contract killer, hijacker, and burglar, far less glamorous than his role as visionary builder of a gambling empire, do not make it into director Barry Levinson's antiseptic portrait of a great-looking multiple murderer.

"He's classically heroic," Annette Bening said of her costar's character, her rose-tinted view clouded perhaps by the fact she had fallen in love with her leading man during filming and was carrying his child. But even a more objective observer, the *New York Times*, bought into the film's myth when the paper declared Siegel was "the archetypal American dreamer."

The movie depicts Siegel dreaming up Las Vegas. He stands in the middle of a barren desert that would one day become the Strip, and declaims, "It came to me like a vision, like a religious epiphany." Siegel then goes on to build the legendary Flamingo Hotel from the sand up.

In reality, the Flamingo was already under construction, the brainchild of Billy Wilkerson, owner of the Sunset Strip's Ciro's nightclub and founder/publisher of the *Hollywood Reporter*. Wilkerson ran out of money during construction, and Siegel bought into the project with $1 million of mob money. Siegel was just the financier, not the Vegas auteur of the film, and allowed Wilkerson to retain creative control of the project.

As for turning the sand dunes into the home of the Dunes *et al.*, Vegas was not the undeveloped backwater the film suggests when Siegel showed up in 1946. Two major hotels had already been built on the Strip by then.

Wilkerson's son, William Jr., was furious his dad had been airbrushed out of the picture. "It was his vision, his idea, and what happened was he just ran out of money. So it's infuriating to see a film like *Bugsy* roll over history. It's just plainly not true," Wilkerson said.

That complaint could be made about most of Bugsy's characterization. The film presents Siegel as an idealist with no eye on the bottom line. Gangster Meyer Lansky says in the film, "He isn't even interested in money. He's interested in the idea."

The real Siegel was very interested in money, and that, not his more serious crimes like murder for hire, led to his downfall. Siegel grossly inflated the cost of building the Flamingo, charging the mob $6 million to build the place, then pocketing $2 million. Skimming, not killing, killed Bugsy Siegel. In 1947, while staying at

Legendary gangster Benny "Bugsy" Siegal (1906–1947). *Photo by the Associated Press, courtesy of the Library of Congress.*

Virginia Hill's rented Beverly Hills mansion, a hit man blew his head to pieces with a .30-30 carbine.

Hill's character is whitewashed as much as Siegel's. As a famous newsreel of Hill testifying before a Congressional committee on organized crime shows, she spoke with a lower-class Brooklyn accent. But either out of ignorance or calculation, Bening uses her own finishing school voice in the film. Beatty and Bening have lovers' quarrels in *Bugsy*, but they remain true to one another. The real Hill spied on her lover for the mob and may have even turned over the information about his skimming from the Flamingo that led to his death. Hill was conveniently in Paris when Siegel was murdered in her home. Like her Brooklyn accent, also omitted from the film is the incident in which Hill had sex with several men while their girlfriends watched.

The most outrageous truth that had to be ignored to portray Siegel heroically was the fact that as segregationist Jim Crow laws were slowly being repealed across the country, Siegel introduced them in Las Vegas. Black entertainers were not allowed to eat or sleep at the casinos where they entertained white folk and had to hole up in shantytowns on the other side of town. When Lena Horne refused to lodge on the wrong side of the tracks, Siegel allowed her to occupy a poolside cabana, but gave orders that her sheets were to be burned every morning! The absence of segregation in *Bugsy*, Las Vegas documentary filmmaker William Drummond said, was "like telling the story of the Civil War without mentioning slavery. It's a grave oversight never to mention that this was a guy who decided he was going to institutionalize segregation in the entertainment industry." (The ban wasn't lifted in Las Vegas until the 1960s, when Frank Sinatra put his foot—and considerable prestige—down and demanded that his buddy Sammy Davis Jr. receive accommodations in the hotel where he worked.)

Bugsy has a lot of fun with its hero's hare-brained scheme to assassinate Mussolini, showing him plotting the hit on the phone while wearing a ludicrous chef's hat as he cooks dinner for his family in the suburbs. He may have been a gangster, the film implies, but he was a patriotic gangster. The real Siegel actually did business with Il Duce, who gave him $40,000 as a down payment on an explosive device Siegel had invented. To finalize the deal, Siegel went to Italy, where he socialized with Mussolini as well as visiting Goebbels and Göring.

Film historian Joseph Roquemore summarized the distasteful effect of transforming a monstrous Frankenstein into an idealistic Dr. Frankenstein: "All of this adds up to shameless glamorization of an ugly, sleazy story."

Mommie Dearest
(1981)

Directed by Frank Perry
Written by Robert Getchell, Tracy Hotchner, Frank Perry, Frank Yablans, Christina Crawford (book)

CAST

Faye Dunaway (Joan Crawford)
Diana Scarwid (Christina Crawford, adult)
Mara Hobel (Christina Crawford, child)
Steve Forrest (Greg Savitt)
Howard Da Silva (Louis B. Mayer)
Rutanya Alda (Carol Ann)
Harry Goz (Alfred Steele)
Jocelyn Brando (Barbara Bennett)
Priscilla Pointer (Mrs. Chadwick)
Michael Edwards (Ted Gelber)

How did a heartbreaking memoir about childhood abuse turn into one of the campiest, funniest movies of all time? In the case of *Mommie Dearest*, which did to the memory of Joan Crawford what Firestone did to vulcanized rubber, not only the director and writers, but the makeup and hair people have to take the blame for a movie that generated more one-liners than an installment of *Comic Relief*.

In between beatings, Faye Dunaway's Joan Crawford celebrates her daughter (Mara Hobel) Christina's birthday in the unintentional camp classic *Mommie Dearest*.

A comparison of just one scene as rendered in the autobiography by Crawford's adopted daughter, Christina, and the movie's re-creation of it reveals the problem. We feel something close to Aristotle's famous recipe for classic tragedy—fear and pity—when we read Christina's account of her violent punishment for hanging her expensive dresses on wire rather than padded hangers. In the film, when Crawford screams, "No . . . wire . . . hangers . . . EVER!" as she beats Christina with the source of her rage, audiences across the country screamed with laughter. Why? A bit of the blame falls on the actress who impersonates Crawford, Faye Dunaway, whose line readings don't begin to be covered by the term "over the top." (Dunaway's performance in *Mommie Dearest* recalls novelist-turned-screenwriter F. Scott Fitzgerald's rueful warning about writing screen vehicles for Crawford. "Never write a stage direction like, 'Pretend to tell a lie,' because she'll do Benedict Arnold handing over West Point to the British.) But Dunaway alone can't take the rap for putting *Mommie Dearest* in the camp classics hall of fame. When she delivers her wire hangers speech, Dunaway is wearing a fright wig, padded shoulders that look as though they should have the name of a football team stenciled across the back, and face cream that seems inspired by classic Japanese theater. With the aid and abetment of hair and makeup and a director who doesn't believe less is more, *Mommie Dearest* becomes *kabuki* mommie. *Playboy* said Dunaway was "made up to resemble Groucho Marx as a female impersonator, or maybe a demon being exorcised by Max Factor." The *New York Times* was arguably kinder when it called her work "serious caricature." Even Dunaway's bushy eyebrows, which anticipate Mariel Hemingway and Cindy Crawford but don't reflect the look of the film's 1940 through 1960 settings, fail to present the historical Crawford easily referenced and enshrined in coffee table books like *The Art of the Great Hollywood Portrait Photographers*.

Similar sins committed by bad hair and makeup, worse acting, and the worst direction and script make Dunaway's rose garden strategy in the "Tina, bring me the ax!" scene another unintentional howler. (The film's producer, Paramount, responded to derision from both critics and moviegoers by retooling its original marketing campaign with new advertisements that had a coat hanger dangling from the title letters with the tag line "The biggest mother of them all." The ads were withdrawn after attorneys for the producer and co-screenwriter, Frank Yablans, filed suit against the studio.)

Mommie Dearest makes wan attempts to give a psychological explanation for Crawford's abusive behavior, but its psychohistory is based on apocrypha. The scene just before the rose garden butchery shows Crawford being fired from MGM by its chief, Louis B. Mayer, who even refuses to walk her to her car. Her humiliation seems to explain if not justify the ensuing midnight madness among the shrubbery. The only problem is MGM didn't fire Crawford; she walked out on the studio after it kept casting her in B-movies.

And if another famous line, "Don't fuck me with me . . . FELLAS!"—Crawford's warning to Pepsi board members who try to retire her as the company's spokeswoman and ask for the repayment of a "loan"—is as unlikely as it is funny, that may be because the real actress never made the threat.

Even Crawford's luxe home wasn't luxe enough for the director, whose aesthetic seems embodied by Oscar Wilde's opinion that "nothing succeeds like excess," so an even more palatial home was created on soundstages.

Fans of Crawford, if any existed after the film's *I Remember Monster* character assassination of the star, might object that the film only mentions two of her films, *Mildred Pierce* and *Ice Follies of 1939*—when the workaholic alcoholic made dozens of them in a career that spanned almost the entire history of the movies. Her marriage to Douglas Fairbanks Jr., which made headlines at the time and earned them the title of Hollywood's royal couple, isn't mentioned. Another husband, Franchot Tone, the actor-socialite who had a profound effect on helping the actress overcome her wrong-side-of-the-tracks pedigree, is only briefly referenced, while two other marriages are composited into one nameless husband.

Dunaway told the *New York Times* that she studied photos of Crawford and worked her jaw muscles to duplicate the shape of the star's mouth, which seems like wasted effort since all we see is a diagonal slash of lipstick where her mouth is supposed to be. Dunaway never intended to give a camp performance. She took her role seriously and felt it "was similar to playing Greek tragedy." Perhaps if Aristophanes had been the rewrite man. Dunaway didn't pull any punches—literally. After a face-slapping scene, Diana Scarwid, who doesn't quite lose her native Georgia accent as the teenage and adult Christina, said, "My ears rang for days."

As she does in the book, Christina had the last word on her mother and the woman who turned her into a Krafft-Ebing cartoon. Forewarned by negative reviews, Christina waited until she had recovered from a stroke so a screening wouldn't prompt another seizure. "Faye Dunaway's portrayal was absolutely ludicrous," Christina carped. "I've read she is saying she has been haunted by the ghost of Joan Crawford—and after seeing her performance, I can see why. I also heard she did a lot of research trying to make it a balanced portrayal—but I didn't see anything resembling it."

Warts-and-all biographies have become a cliché. *Mommie Dearest* introduced a new genre that might be called tumors-and-more.

Hoffa
(1992)

Directed by Danny DeVito
Written by David Mamet

CAST

Jack Nicholson (James R. Hoffa)
Danny DeVito (Bobby Ciaro)
Armand Assante (Carol D'Allesandro)
J. T. Walsh (Frank Fitzsimmons)
Kevin Anderson (Robert Kennedy)

Director Danny DeVito said of his film's title character in *Hoffa*, "Jimmy Hoffa was a man who dedicated every waking hour to benefiting peoples" and added that the late Teamsters leader would have made a great president.

Critics and historians begged to differ—vehemently. The *New Republic* said of the 1992 film starring Jack Nicholson, "Every single frame of this storyline is a lie or a half-truth."

One critic objected that the film, written by Pulitzer Prize-winning playwright David Mamet, amounted to a "deification" of the union leader and presented him as a tireless crusader in the fight for the working man and a martyr of jealous Teamster officials and mob associates who feared he would testify against them.

Nicholson's Hoffa reluctantly gets in bed with gangsters to protect striking workers against company-hired scabs and thugs who beat the strikers. But in the film, he always keeps his mob cronies at arm's length. Robert F. Kennedy, who as attorney general unsuccessfuly pursued Hoffa, is presented as an effete East Coast Harvard-educated brat, or as Nicholson calls him, "You little fag."

In contrast to the film's portrayal of Hoffa as a passive partner of organized crime, he had, in his own words, close ties to the mob, although he denied his associates were in the organization. In a 1975 interview in *Playboy*, which is not referenced in the film although verbatim transcripts of his denial of crime ties at congressional hearings did make it into the script, the magazine's interviewer asked

Jack Nicholson's *Hoffa* is the heroic champion of the working man, whereas the real union leader, Jimmy Hoffa, used the Teamsters' pension fund as his personal piggy bank and disastrously allied the union with organized crime.

Hoffa, "Aren't you and mob boss Meyer Lansky good friends?" Hoffa: "I know him . . . My opinion, he's another victim of harassment. *Playboy*: "The [congressional] Mc-Clellan Committee said that Lansky and Frank Costello were organized-crime members, members of the Mafia." Hoffa: "It's a complete, 100 percent lie." *Playboy*: "What about Johnny Dio?" Hoffa: "Friend of mine. No question about that . . . I don't believe there is any organized crime, period. Don't believe it. Never believed." Johnny Dio, who doesn't make an appearance in the film, was a convicted New York City labor extortionist who was also charged with blinding investigative journalist Victor Riesel by throwing acid in his face because of Riesel's negative reportage on him.

When Hoffa wasn't actively involved with organized crime, he created a "mob-friendly" atmosphere for it to flourish in the Teamsters union. Hoffa created phony local unions to facilitate the relationship. In his hometown of Detroit, Hoffa allowed

Jimmy Quasarano and Peter Vitale to use a fake local as a front for distributing drugs. He conspired with Johnny Dio to take control of the New York Teamsters with votes from other phony locals. He tried to herd New York's 30,000 cab drivers into the union, which Dio was in charge of.

None of Hoffa's coziness with the mob appears in *Hoffa*. The film creates a fictional scene where Hoffa reluctantly calls on mob thugs to prevent striking Teamsters from being beat up by scabs. His only goal is to help the working man survive. Mob help was the only way, however distasteful, to accomplish that. But the real genesis of Hoffa's links to organized crime had nothing to do with fighting corporate bosses. The corrupt alliance began in 1941, when he called on mob muscle to fight a rival union, the Congress of Industrial Organizations (the CIO, which later merged with the American Federation of Labor as the AFL-CIO). As Arthur A. Sloane's biograpy, *Hoffa*, points out—and the film ignores—it was Hoffa who made overtures to Detroit's "East Side crowd," led by "Scarface" Joe Bommarito. The local mob did not seek Hoffa out. Together, the unholy alliance forced the CIO local out of Detroit. According to Sloane, who is considered Hoffa's definitive biographer, the mob from then on worked with Hoffa on a daily basis. During Hoffa's long tenure that spanned decades until his disappearance in 1975, notorious gangsters like William Presser, Louis "Babe" Triscaro, and "Tony Pro" Provenzano, an alleged capo in the Genovese family, held leadership positions in the Teamsters. (Provenzano, a convicted murderer, was president of Teamster Local 560.) DeVito and Mamet's argument that Hoffa had to embrace organized crime to save his union flies in the face of the historical record and the example left by other unions and their leaders, such as Walter Reuther, who led the squeaky clean United Auto Workers.

Also absent from the film is the allegation by a congressional subcommittee that Hoffa may have killed John F. Kennedy! While quoting at length from transcripts of other congressional investigations that portrayed Hoffa as a tireless champion of working stiffs, the director ignored the startling report of the House of Representatives subcommittee that concluded "mobsters Carlos Marcello, Santos Trafficante, and Jimmy Hoffa had the motive, means and opportunity" to kill JFK. Indeed, author Dan Moldea (*The Hoffa Wars*) called *Hoffa* "the worst case of Hollywood retelling history since *JFK*," director Oliver Stone's paranoid fantasy that a cast of thousands conspired to kill the president.

Hoffa never was convicted of mob ties, but he did spend five years in prison for jury tampering, fraud, extortion, wire tapping, and bribery. Hoffa's incarceration is never mentioned in *Hoffa*.

Hoffa also gets small details wrong. His famous mangled syntax, which included neologisms (recorded on film) such as "unsubstantuated," doesn't infect a single line of dialogue in the film. Nicholson is also much taller than he diminutive leader, who stood five feet six inches tall. The opening scene, set in the 1930s when Hoffa was in his 20s, was played by a then 55-year-old Nicholson who looks nowhere near as young as Hoffa at the time.

The film's ending, in which Hoffa's disappearance in 1975 is presented as a mob hit, is a complete invention that adds a tragic dimension to his reluctant use of organized crime to preserve his beloved Teamsters. (A few weeks before he vanished, it was discovered that this "friend" of the working man had looted the Teamsters' pension fund of hundreds of millions of dollars. "Hoffa was a dishonest person," according to Ron Carey, the reformist leader of the Teamsters. "You just have to look at all the pensioners around the country who lost money as a result of his actions.") *Hoffa* ignored biographer Sloane's equally fanciful contention that Richard Nixon ordered Hoffa's murder because he was afraid the Teamsters boss would reveal that Nixon had given Hoffa's successor, Frank Fitzsimmons, $6 million to deposit in a Swiss bank account for safekeeping!

Danny DeVito rejected Sloane's theory, saying, "I don't think any of that's true; for a start Hoffa always voted for Nixon and always boasted of the fact . . . Hoffa had been betrayed [by his prison sentence] and he was mad as hell, and too many people were scared of what he'd say. Particularly the mob."

Hoffa's son James Phillip Hoffa, was brought to tears by the ending because it was "too graphic," he told *People* magazine. Despite the film's heroic treatment of his father, the younger Hoffa also felt Nicholson's snarling portrayal didn't jibe with the real, kinder, gentler Jimmy Hoffa his son knew. "My dad was a very upbeat and happy person. He was a great kidder and always had a ready smile," his son insisted.

According to the FBI, despite the film's conclusion, the case on Jimmy Hoffa remains open.

So why did Hoffa get the kid gloves treatment in *Hoffa* other than for the usual dramatic necessity of presenting a good guy the audience can root for? *Time* magazine

James R. "Jimmy" Hoffa (1913–1975), Teamsters Union leader, 1959. *Photo by the Associated Press, courtesy of the Library of Congress.*

speculated that Hoffa's executive producer Joseph Isgro had something to do with the whitewash because of Isgro's alleged ties to the Gambino crime family. Biographer Dan Moldea offers an even more sinister reason: "You can't make a movie about the mob in Hollywood without the mob's permission." Moldea also pointed out that at the time of the film's release in 1992, executive producer Isgro had been reindicted on 57 counts of racketeering. But mob-related theories that try to explain *Hoffa*'s deified Hoffa fall apart when the film's ending blames the mob for its hero's death.

Hoffa was a critical and commercial flop. Its failure to win any major Oscar nominations, despite Nicholson's critically acclaimed performance (the film was only nominated for cinematography and makeup and didn't win either, perhaps in the latter case because of Nicholson's risible bulbous nose prosthesis), may have reflected the general distaste for turning a thug into the savior of the working class. The first sentence of Dan Moldea's *The Hoffa Wars* describes the toxic effect that was the real legacy of the Teamsters leader: "James R. Hoffa's most valuable contribution to the American labor movement came at the moment he stopped breathing on July 30, 1975."

A Beautiful Mind (2001)

Directed by Ron Howard
Written by Akiva Goldsman
Sylvia Nasar (book)

CAST

Russell Crowe (John Nash)
Ed Harris (Parcher)
Jennifer Connelly (Alicia Nash)
Christopher Plummer (Dr. Rosen)
Paul Bettany (Charles)

Adam Goldberg (Sol)
Jason Gray-Stanford (Ainsley)
Judd Hirsch (Helinger)

A Beautiful Mind is the multiple-Oscar-winning story of John Forbes Nash, a brilliant mathematician who with the help of a loving wife overcame schizophrenia and went on to win the Nobel Prize. *A Beautiful Mind* seems like a *Rocky* for eggheads: troubled geek goes the distance.

The only problem, however, according to the *New York Times*, is that "the story is almost entirely counterfeit."

A Beautiful Mind's "sins" are mostly those of omission rather than commission. And Akiva Goldsman's script, based on Sylvia Nasar's biography, omits so much that when you learn what was left out of the film, the viewer is likely to feel betrayed or at the very least duped for shedding tears over a beautiful mind that did not, unfortunately, belong to a beautiful man.

The real John Nash was a brilliant but arrogant student at Princeton in the late 1940s who went on to teach math at MIT. By the time he was 30, his genius seemingly turned into schizophrenia, for which he was hospitalized. After a three-decade struggle with mental illness, he underwent a miraculous remission and won the 1994 Nobel Prize for his "non-cooperative games" theory described in his doctoral dissertation.

The rest of the "facts" of his life as presented in the film and what it omitted generated so much condemnation that it was feared allegations of falsifying Nash's life would cost *A Beautiful Mind* its Oscar haul, just as similar complaints knocked 1999's *The Hurricane* out of the Oscar race. That didn't happen. *A Beautiful Mind* swept the Oscars, winning most of the major awards except best actor, which was attributed to loutish behavior by Russell Crowe, who played Nash and received an Oscar nomination but lost to Denzel Washington, who starred in a film, *Training Day*, that no one seems to have seen except Academy voters.

What ugly truths did *A Beautiful Mind* omit? The omissions were so egregious, the *New York Times* paid the film the ultimate insult by implying it could have been directed by Oliver Stone and claiming it was a "piece of historical revisionism on the order of [Stone's] *JFK*," the bête noire of those who believe films based on fact should stick to the facts.

Critics felt *A Beautiful Mind* airbrushed its portrait of Nobel Prize-winning mathematician John Nash by omitting his alleged anti-Semitism and his arrest for indecent exposure in a public restroom.

A Beautiful Mind depicts Nash being saved by the love and care of his long-suffering wife, Alicia (Jennifer Connelly in a best supporting actress Oscar win). The film neglects to mention that Alicia divorced her husband, and the couple remarried only six months before the film's release for what the *Sunday Times of London* called "cynical movie-marketing purposes."

Screenwriter Goldsman cherry-picked Nasar's 1998 biography and left out a lot of the embarrassing stuff: Nash's alleged anti-Semitism; his homosexual liaisons; a mistress who bore him a son he abandoned to poverty; his arrest in a public restroom in Santa Monica, California, for indecent exposure, for which he was fired by the Rand Corp. after it yanked his security clearance; and the existence of another son who suffers from the same mental illness as his father.

Ironically, the most persuasive defender of the film's treatment of Nash may have come from the woman whose book was trashed by the filmmakers. In an Op Ed piece in the *Los Angeles Times*, Sylvia Nasar, a professor of journalism at Columbia University and a former economics reporter for the *New York Times*, defended the film and rebutted many of the claims that it had airbrushed Nash's life into unrecognizability.

After the *New York Post* quoted a letter Nash wrote in 1967 that contained anti-Semitic ravings, Sylvia Nasar pointed out that Nash had been an ardent champion of Jewish mathematicians—colleagues who were victims of anti-Semitism at American universities in the 1930s and 1940s. Most tellingly, Nasar puts Nash's alleged anti-Semitism in its proper context—time. "The letter the *New York Post* quotes was written eight years after Nash was diagnosed with paranoid schizophrenia, when he not only felt himself threatened by Jews and the state of Israel, but also believed himself to be Job, a slave in chains, the emperor of Antarctica and a messiah living, not in his mother's home in Virginia, but in hell, refugee camps, bomb shelters and prisons. These were signs of paranoid delusions," Nasar said, not anti-Semitism.

The film also depicts Nash as an intrepid Cold War patriot, but critics pointed out that at one time he tried to renounce his U.S. citizenship in a bid to promote a world government. Nasar said the renunciation attempt also occurred during the 1960s, when Nash was severely delusional.

Nasar claims the bust in the public toilet was police entrapment and notes that the charge of indecent exposure was later dropped. Strangely, she attributes the homophobic arrest to the McCarthy witch hunt. By omitting the arrest, the film lost a dramatic opportunity to depict that despite his innocence on the indecent exposure charge, his employer, the Rand Corp., took away his security clearance and fired him, saying it didn't care that the police had lied.

The allegation of bisexuality seemed to rankle the real John Nash more than the accusations of anti-Semitism or a market-driven motivation for his remarriage only six months before the film's release. Nasar admitted that Nash had "intense emotional relationships with other men in his 20s, but no one I interviewed [out of hundreds] claimed that Nash ever had sex with another man." That wasn't enough vindication for the normally reclusive Nash, who apparently was so upset with the accusations about his sex life he appeared on TV's *60 Minutes* with his wife, who insisted her husband was straight. By way of "proof," Alicia said, "I should know."

Nasar conceded that Nash and Alicia were divorced in 1963, but noted that they stayed together after the separation for 38 years.

The *Hollywood Reporter* called Nash an "adulterer," but Nasar said Nash's affair with the mother of his illegitimate son had ended by the time he married Alicia.

L.A. Weekly only slightly overstated the case against the director of *A Beautiful Mind* when it said, "If Ron Howard had made *Ali*, there'd be no Black Muslims or womanizing, and Ali would've won that first fight against Joe Frazier."

Quiz Show
(1994)

Directed by Robert Redford
Written by Paul Attanasio, Richard N. Goodwin (book)

CAST

Ralph Fiennes (Charles Van Doren)
John Turturro (Herbie Stempel)

Rob Morrow (Dick Goodwin)

Paul Scofield (Mark Van Doren)

David Paymer (Dan Enright)

Hank Azaria (Albert Freedman)

Christopher McDonald (Jack Barry)

Elizabeth Wilson (Dorothy Van Doren)

Mira Sorvino (Sandra Goodwin)

After the Vietnam War, Watergate, Iran-Contra, Monica Lewinsky, and Al Gore's bizarre association with a bunch of Buddhist nuns, the TV quiz show scandals of the 1950s seem like a tempest in a TV set today. In 1994's *Quiz Show*, Professor Mark Van Doren reflects the present estimation of the controversy rather than the hysteria of his own time when he tells his guilty son, Charles, "Cheating on a game show is like plagiarizing a comic strip."

But cheating on prime time quiz shows was no laughing matter in the age of Eisenhower and fathers who knew best. Of course, the 50s were not, despite the period's later nostalgic depiction on TV and in film, a more innocent time, merely an era when the newfangled box in everyone's living room was a national obsession, and the quiz show scandals generated front-page headlines, congressional investigations, the death of careers, and perjury convictions—although all the sentences were suspended, reflecting perhaps the only measured reaction to the hysteria of the time.

Quiz Show is director Robert Redford and screenwriter Paul Attanasio's lyrical meditation on America's loss of innocence when it discovered that its prime time heroes weren't quite as bright as they seemed—not to mention guilty of fraud. It was also perhaps the only time in the nation's history that pointy-headed intellectuals became genuine American heroes on a par with baseball players and movie stars.

Quiz Show focuses on the most famous (or infamous) of these pointed-heads, Charles Van Doren, a lecturer in English literature at Columbia University who made the cover of *Time* magazine and became a national cynosure for the seemingly supernatural wealth of knowledge he displayed as a contestant on NBC's *Twenty-One*, one of the plethora of network gameshows at the time.

A member of America's intellectual aristocracy whose father was a Pulitzer Prize-winning poet and literary critic, Charles Van Doren was literally the fair-haired boy of prime time, an *über*-WASP, a Charles Lindbergh who flew via the airwaves. He was brought down by his opposite number, a lumpen Jewish grad student from Queens, Herb Stempel. Stempel preceded Van Doren on *Twenty-One* and matched his rival's encyclopedic store of arcane trivia, returning week after to week on a show that drew 40 million viewers in pre-cable America. The overarching irony of *Quiz Show*'s story is that network executives and the show's producers, some of whom were Jewish, felt Stempel was too "ethnic," read too Jewish, for gentile viewers—or as one executive in the film says, "Herbie Stempel—now there's a face made for radio." On the night of December 5, 1956, Stempel reluctantly agreed to take a fall, flubbing a maddeningly easy question for a contestant with an IQ of 170—"Which film won the best picture Oscar in 1955? Answer: *Marty*" (Stempel had seen the film three times!)—so the more telegenic Van Doren could become the new champion and boost ratings.

A blizzard of riches and public adulation fell on the new Great WASP Hope, who became the darling of talk shows and earned a $1,000 fee per appearance on *The Dave Garroway Show*, which particularly irritated Stempel, who within a year of his ouster had blown his $50,000 winnings on a bookie. Stempel began to regret his decision and took his story to the *Journal-American*, which ran a front page article on August 28, 1958. (An internal investigation of *Twenty-One* by NBC that same year announced that the network had found "Stempel's charges to be utterly baseless and untrue." It was later revealed that the network based its conclusions solely on assurances from the show's producers that nothing had been rigged.)

Enter, in the film but not in real life, Richard Goodwin, a Harvard Law School graduate and congressional investigator, on whose book, *Remembering America*, *Quiz Show* is based. The movie's Goodwin goads Congress into holding hearings, which ultimately led to Van Doren and a parade of others—including child star Patty Duke and pop psychologist Dr. Joyce Brothers—admitting that they had been fed the answers on *Twenty-One* and other game shows, like *The $64,000 Question*. Van Doren, who had earlier perjured himself in testimony before Congress, saw his promising career as an academic and TV talking head evaporate overnight, and he ended up writing entries for the *Encyclopedia Britannica*. The eccentric Stempel, despite his role in exposing the scandal, fared almost as badly, claiming he was kicked out of his school's doctoral program. Stempel ended up teaching high school.

Observers argued that while condemning dishonesty, the director was guilty of the same thing. They pointed out that events that took place over three years were telescoped into a few months. Dialogue between Van Doren father and son was fabricated, and Goodwin's role in unmasking the scandal was inflated. *Newsday*'s film critic Jack Matthews wrote, "Redford's willingness to alter history for dramatic effect says as much about the corrupting qualities of the media as the events depicted in the film itself."

Retired New York judge Joseph Stone maintained that he had played Goodwin's role as the head of the Manhattan district attorney's crime bureau at the time and had led the investigation and prosecution of the principals involved in *Twenty-One*, etc. Goodwin, Judge Stone insisted, got involved months after the first inquiries began. "As far as I am concerned, the movie is a farce. It's full of baloney from beginning to end," Stone said.

While Charles Van Doren comes across as the tragic anti-hero of the piece who sold his soul for fame and money to supplement his $4,000-a-year teacher's salary, and Stempel as his eccentric foil (*Time* magazine was more critical, calling John Turturro's Stempel the "most offensively stereotyped Jew in modern American cinema"), the real villain of the morality play is the late Dan Enright, co-producer of *Quiz Show*, who is shown coaching Stempel to flub the *Marty* question.

Enright wasn't alive to refute the film's allegations, but *Twenty-One*'s co-producer and Enright's partner, Albert Freedman, was. "All of my conversations [in the movie with Enright] were fiction. Everything that they have me saying is fantasy," Freedman said, taking particular umbrage at a scene where he tries to soothe Stempel by saying, "What did you do wrong? Everybody knows the magician doesn't saw the lady in half."

Another heavy, Judge Mitchell Schweitzer, is shown conspiring with Enright to obstruct justice by quashing the investigation, although there is no evidence of a conspiracy.

Addressing a hostile audience of TV executives after a screening of the film in 1994, Redford defended his film's mix of fact and fiction by pleading the usual case: *Quiz Show* was not a docu-drama. Redford admitted that "dramatic license was taken to make either a moral point or an ethical point [but] not move too far out of what could possibly have happened."

Film historian Joseph Roquemore sided with Redford and felt that Van Doren, Enright, and Stempel had been accurately portrayed in what Roquemore called "one of the finest movies ever made about the fifties."

JFK
(1991)

Directed by Oliver Stone
Written by Oliver Stone, Zachary Sklar, Jim Garrison (book), Jim Marrs (book)

CAST

Kevin Costner (Jim Garrison)
Sally Kirkland (Rose Cheramie)
Ray LePere (Zapruder)
Steve Reed (John F. Kennedy)
Jodie Farber (Jackie Kennedy)
Columbia Dubose (Nellie Connally)
Randy Means (Governor Connally)
Edward Asner (Guy Bannister)
Jack Lemmon (Jack Martin)
Gary Oldman (Lee Harvey Oswald)
Sissy Spacek (Liz Garrison)
Brian Doyle-Murray (Jack Ruby)
Beata Pozniak (Marina Oswald)
Tom Howard (Lyndon Baines Johnson)
Joe Pesci (David Ferrie)

The inspiration to make *JFK* came from a chance encounter director Oliver Stone had in an elevator in Havana, Cuba, while he was there to receive a film award. A woman in the elevator handed him a copy of former New Orleans district attorney Jim Garrison's book, *On the Trail of the Assassins*, which described a vast conspiracy to kill President John F. Kennedy. Stone found the book fascinating, read it three times, and decided to make a movie using it as his primary source.

It was an unfortunate choice of source material. Garrison's main thesis was that a cabal of high ranking, right-wing government officials (among many, many others) conspired to kill Kennedy because they feared he would withdraw American troops from Vietnam after the 1964 presidential election. Garrison accused so many people of being in on the assassination (LBJ, the Pentagon, neo-Nazis, White Russians, the CIA, Texas oilmen, the Mafia, the FBI, anti-Castro Cubans) that one critic joked the only person who wasn't a suspect in the murder of JFK was JFK.

On the Trail of the Assassins detailed the case prosecutor Garrison brought against Clay Shaw, a wealthy native of New Orleans who had devoted his life to restoring landmark buildings in the city's Latin Quarter. The masterminds of the plot were all gay, Garrison contended, and the assassination of the president was a "homosexual thrill-killing," which failed to explain what "thrill" such disparate participants as the CIA and the Mafia got out of JFK's death. Garrison claimed Shaw was gay, Lee Harvey Oswald was an impotent bisexual, Oswald's getaway accomplice, a pilot named David Ferrie, was gay, and Jack Ruby, Oswald's assassin, was also gay. This is history as interpreted by John Waters.

Incredibly, both Garrison and Stone based their beliefs in part on the allegations of a woman named Delphine Roberts, who said she was in possession of a dead pigeon that had been sent to the president as a warning before his death. Roberts also claimed she communed with God, who showed her "the sacred scrolls that God himself gave to the Hebrews for placing in the Ark of the Covenant." Roberts was writing a book that would not only reveal the real the identity of President Kennedy's murderers, but would also tell the real "story of the Creation" of the world.

Garrison's case against Shaw quickly fell apart after journalists discovered the district attorney had used bribery and witness intimidation, which included a member of Garrison's staff threatening a teenager at gunpoint for taping a meeting at which the D.A.'s office tried to bribe the teen. Clay was acquitted of all charges in 1969 after a brief trial.

Garrison's credibility suffered another setback when medical records from his service in the National Guard during World War II revealed that doctors had recommended his discharge from the military because he suffered "severe and disabling psychoneurosis." Further investigations revealed Garrison's Mafia ties, with organized crime figures paying off his gambling debts and facilitating the sale of his home. Garrison was later tried and acquitted of bribery and intimidation.

None of these embarrassing revelations deterred Stone from accepting Garrison's conspiracy theories, and the director indicated his estimation of the former prosecutor's character by casting a handsome superstar often typecast as a heroic figure in films, Kevin Costner, to play Garrison. One critic felt that under Stone's direction, Costner resembled Jimmy Stewart's character in *Mr. Smith Goes to Washington*, a little guy who takes on the corrupt establishment.

Stone defended his heroic treatment of such an oily character. "I made Garrison better than he is for a larger purpose," Stone said. Cynics felt the director whitewashed Garrison because he wanted the audience to cheer for him and see the assassination through Garrison's eyes, however distorted that view was.

The main premise of *JFK*—that Kennedy was killed to keep us in Vietnam—was not borne out by information that was easily available to Stone's battalion of researchers. Two months before his death, the president told Walter Cronkite in a televised interview, "I don't agree with those who say we should withdraw." He reiterated his position by later telling TV anchorman Chet Huntley, "We are not there to see a war lost." Indeed, if an assassin's bullet hadn't stopped him, Kennedy planned to say in a speech during his fateful visit to Dallas that although the war may be "painful, risky, and costly . . . we dare not weary of the task." After JFK's death, Robert F. Kennedy confirmed his brother's commitment to prosecuting the war, saying the late president "felt he had a strong, overwhelming reason for being in Vietnam, and that we should win the war." When asked in an oral history interview if his brother planned to pull out of Vietnam, RFK said flatly, "No."

LBJ is also one of the many unindicted co-conspirators in the president's death. In the film, LBJ is quoted as telling the Joint Chiefs of Staff, "Just let me get elected, and then you can have your war," providing him with a motive, but no proof, for wanting JFK dead. The quote was accurate, but it was only evidence of LBJ telling people what they wanted to hear for political ends. Johnson hoped the military brass would press their conservative friends in Congress to back the president's liberal social legislation. To win over liberal members of Congress, LBJ contradicted his promise to the Pentagon, and told congressmen opposed to the war that he didn't give a "damn about a pissant little country" like Vietnam. That quote is *not* repeated in *JFK*.

JFK does repeat the well-known fact that FBI director J. Edgar Hoover loathed the Kennedys, particularly Bobby, then uses that enmity to make the unsubstantiated claim that Lee Harvey Oswald was an FBI informant and that the FBI participated in a cover-up after the assassination to hide its ties with Oswald.

Oswald was a very busy man, in the world according to Oliver Stone. He not only worked for the FBI, he also participated in covert intelligence operations for the CIA, which used the services of the equally busy New Orleans preservationist, Clay Shaw.

In *JFK*, a preposterous number of people seem to have been in on the plot to kill the president. The vast military-industrial complex, per the film, conspired to get rid of Kennedy because his plans to end the Vietnam War would decrease the power of the Pentagon and cut into the profits of war-related industries with fat government contracts.

Stone also put Fidel Castro on his hit list. The film speculates that, incensed with the CIA-Mafia conspiracy to assassinate the Cuban dictator (which was true), Castro ordered the president killed.

JFK's worst distortion, which was an outright fabrication, involved a scene in which a gay solider of fortune, David William Ferrie (Joe Pesci), confesses to Garrison that he trained Oswald and was financed by the wealthy Shaw, whose orders he was following. Ferrie also describes details of the plan to kill Kennedy and the CIA's involvement. In reality, Ferrie did spill his guts, but not to Garrison. In an interview with the *Washington Post*, the real Ferrie insisted he had never heard of Oswald until the assassination and new nothing of the plot. He never mentioned the CIA in his *Post* interview. *JFK* claims that Ferrie was later assassinated by Cubans linked to Shaw. An investigation into Ferrie's death showed that he died of natural causes.

JFK suggests that the media may have participated in a cover-up of the conspiracies for reasons the director failed to explain.

The media was not amused. *Newsweek* columnist George Will wrote, "Stone falsifies so much that he may be an intellectual sociopath, indifferent to the truth." In the wake of blistering attacks, Stone backtracked and insisted *JFK* was not meant to be a docudrama, but lamely explained it was a "countermyth" to the "myth" presented by the Warren Commission, which famously investigated dozens of conspiracy theories and came to the conclusion that Oswald acted alone.

More likely, Stone was serving the cause of drama rather than accountability. He needed to tell a good story, and more conspirators than a lone gunman meant more drama. And just as he felt compelled to idealize Garrison to give his film a hero, Stone, who was a big Kennedy fan, presented a romanticized view of the slain president, including home movies with JFK surrounded by a beautiful wife and adorable children. No mention is made of his well-known womanizing or his failed legislative agenda in domestic affairs. That would have lessened the tragic loss and diminished the emotional impact of the movie. Stone's attitude toward the president is symbolized by the name of his production company, Camelot Productions.

Most importantly, *JFK* provides the "why" that the Warren Commission's lone assassin theory does not. The president's senseless death is given meaning if he's portrayed as the victim of good intentions—pulling out of Vietnam—rather than the random act of purposeless violence by a frustrated loser.

In an attempt to tell a compelling story, Stone served art first and the truth a distant second. John F. Kennedy Jr. once explained why he refused to see the film. "I don't like the idea of my dad's death being presented as entertainment." Misleading and fabricated entertainment at that. Or as Joseph Roquemore said, "*JFK* makes Cinderella look like a BBC documentary."

Mississippi Burning (1988)

Directed by Alan Parker
Written by Chris Gerolmo

CAST

Gene Hackman (Anderson)
Willem Dafoe (Ward)

Frances McDormand (Mrs. Pell)

Brad Dourif (Deputy Pell)

Rick Zieff (Passenger)

Christopher White (Black Passenger)

Gladys Greer (Hattie)

Jake Gipson (Mose)

Mississippi in 1964 was not a good place to be black. Retaliating against efforts to register black voters (only 5.3 percent of blacks were registered to vote in Mississippi compared with 45 percent in Virginia), the Ku Klux Klan launched a reign of terror that included four shootings, 52 severe beatings, 250 arrests, and the burning of 30 black homes and 37 black churches.

Into this dangerous cauldron, the Council of Federated Organizations sent 1,000 activists, mostly white college students from the North, to register black voters in Mississippi. On June 21, 1964, the violence reached a climax when three civil rights workers—black Mississippi native James Chaney and white New Yorkers Andrew Goodman and Mickey Schwerner—disappeared after being held for several hours on a moving violation in the county jail of Neshoba County. Their burned out station wagon was found several days later, but the three men remained missing.

The incident seemed to epitomize the lawlessness and violence of the Deep South and prompted a dramatic response from the federal government. President Johnson ordered the reluctant, racist FBI director J. Edgar Hoover to send a battalion of FBI agents to the state to find the missing men and also mustered hundreds of sailors from the local naval base to join the search.

The three bodies of the slain activists, pumped full of bullets, were found two months later buried in an earthen dam. Three years after that seven Klansmen were found guilty of violating the victims' civil rights by a federal jury after local officials had refused to indict the men.

Mississippi Burning suggests it is presenting an accurate account of the murders and investigation during the opening of the film, when credits precisely locate the time and place of the story: "Mississippi, 1964."

And indeed, much of the story is drawn from evidence presented at the trial. The film accurately depicts the Klan pursuing and overtaking the station wagon driven by the civil rights workers, then shooting the first victim at point-blank range. Also accurately portrayed is a scene in which information supplied by a Choctaw Indian leads to the discovery of the missing car. In another dramatic and fact-based scene, a witness wearing a paper bag over his head to hide his identity identifies the perpetrators. The courtroom scene reproduced testimony lifted verbatim from transcripts of the trial. Michael Schwerner, one of the victims, sported a goatee, and so does the actor who played him. The role of a local sheriff was given to an actor who looked like the official and duplicated his mannerisms. The actual morgue at the University Medical Center where the bodies of the victims were taken served as a film location.

Mississippi Burning also correctly dramatizes the intimidation by locals of journalists from the North sent to cover the story. Many reporters said they feared for their lives. David Halberstam reported for a small-town newspaper in Mississippi in the summer of 1964 and said when the movie came out in December 1988, "There always seemed to be a pickup truck following me as I left a small town, threatening to bump me off the road." NBC cameraman Bill Delgado said someone rammed his car, then the driver threatened him with a knife. While shooting aerial footage in a helicopter, a farmer aimed a gun at Delgado. After that, the cameraman asked the network to transfer him to another beat.

Despite its attention to details, *Mississippi Burning* was immediately and universally lambasted as a grotesque distortion of history when it was released in December 1988.

Detractors complained that the film minimized the involvement of blacks in the murder case in particular and the civil rights movement in general. The main figures in the film are white: two fictional FBI men played by Gene Hackman and Willem Dafoe battling the Klan. Instead of being shown as the movers and shakers of the civil rights movement, blacks in the film are passive, mostly silent victims. Basically, a couple of white guys save "poor," "helpless" Southern African-Americans. Hackman is a local redneck FBI agent teamed with a by-the-book, uptight Northern agent (Willem Dafoe.) The plot and casting resemble the pairing of a nerdy Jimmy Stewart and redneck John Wayne in the similarly themed western *The Man Who Shot Liberty Valance*. Or as historian Harvard Sitkoff wryly summarized the theme: "Two white guys learn to work together and like each other."

British director Alan Parker was surprisingly frank when he conceded that complaints about the film's focus were justified and admitted that the story line was influenced by commercial considerations rather than historical accuracy.

"Our heroes are white," Parker admitted. "And in truth, the film would probably never have been made if they weren't." Parker maintained—erroneously—that the audience for the film would be mainly white, and a drama about white FBI crime-busters duking it out with the Klan would do better at the box office than a film about the black civil rights movement, which appears as almost an afterthought in the film. Parker's box-office theory was bizarre. One wonders what kind of research he found that suggested black movie-goers would not be interested in a film about the history of *their* civil rights movement.

Parker insisted he was merely reflecting a different kind of reality. White tragedies draw more attention than the misfortunes of blacks. "One of the perverse ironies of the case was that two white kids got killed and the whole of America was interested suddenly, because it wasn't just a black problem. This reality undoubtedly disturbed many black activists because it underlined a national hypocrisy," Parker said.

Not only activists were incensed by the film's white-makes-right mentality. *Chicago Sun-Times* editor Vernon Jarret fumed, "The film treats some of the most heroic people in black history as mere props in a morality play." Coretta Scott King, who was deeply immersed in the struggle the film was supposed to be about, wondered why so few black faces were visible on screen. "How long will we have to wait before Hollywood finds the courage and the integrity to tell the stories of some of the many thousands of black men, women, and children who put their lives on the line for equality?" the widow of Martin Luther King Jr. wanted to know.

The luckless director seemed damned when he didn't and damned when he did cast a black actor in a prominent role. The problem was the role Parker chose for the black cast member, that of an FBI agent. Critics were quick to point out that in 1964, the only black member of the FBI was the virulently racist J. Edgar Hoover's chauffeur.

The action the director and writer assigned to this fantasy G-man raised further hackles. According to a rumor he had heard, the director, over the objections of screenwriter Chris Gerolmo, wrote a fictionalized scene based on an incident where a member of the Mafia working for the FBI allegedly threatened a member of the Klan by sticking a gun in his mouth. Parker drastically changed the incident, and in the film, it's the black FBI agent who does the intimidating, and instead of a gun, he threatens the racist with castration by a razor he brandishes in the man's face. The scene seemed to pander to every Southern white racist's worst fears about what happens when blacks get "uppity."

Even in small matters of fact, the production seemed determined to put whites in the driver's seat—literally. In the film, white civil rights worker Michael Schwerner is shown driving the station wagon on the fateful night when he was stopped by Kenoba County sheriff's deputies. During a lecture at Queen's College, the film's producer, Fred Zollo, was interrupted by the sister of the black victim, James Chaney, who pointed out that her brother had been the driver of the car. Zollo lamely countered that *sometimes* Schwerner drove the car.

Historian Robert Brent Toplin claims, "Most of the FBI activity that dominates the second half of the movie is simply invented." The most outrageous invention may have been the way the case is solved in the film. After Dafoe's by-the-book FBI investigative methods fail, good ole bad boy Hackman seduces the wife of a sheriff's deputy and learns critical information from her which solves the case. The FBI did break the case, but its methods were more routine and less dramatic than a romantic seduction. A reward of $30,000 offered by the Bureau prompted informants to come forth with information the led to indictments of the murderers. The offer of reduced sentences also prompted some of the guilty to testify against their accomplices.

A year before the murders, 85,000 black Mississippians cast symbolic "freedom votes" to emphasize the power of their numbers and their commitment to enfranchisement. During the summer depicted in *Mississippi Burning*, black activists sent delegates to the Democratic National Convention to protest the lily-white composition of the official Mississippi delegation to the Convention.

Where were these thousands of black faces in *Mississippi Burning*?

Malcolm X
(1991)

Directed by Spike Lee
Written by Spike Lee, Alex Haley (book), Malcolm X (book)

CAST

Denzel Washington (Malcolm X)
Angela Bassett (Betty Shabazz)
Albert Hall (Baines)
Al Freeman Jr. (Elijah Muhammad)
Delroy Lindo (West Indian Archie)
Spike Lee (Shorty)
Theresa Randle (Laura)
Kate Vernon (Sophia)
Lonette McKee (Louise Little)
Tommy Hollis (Earl Little)
James McDaniel (Brother Earl)

If director Spike Lee had trouble nailing the "real" Malcolm X in his 1992 film about the slain black leader, it may be because there is no single Malcolm X. He was figure who continually evolved throughout his protean life—from pimp to prison convict to anti-Semite and black separatist to his questionable final incarnation as a proponent of a racial harmony that approximated the peaceful, Gandhi-like philosophy of his civil rights coeval, Dr. Martin Luther King Jr.

There are so many Malcolm X's to choose from, it was inevitable that even a kaleidoscopic portrait that showed many facets of an ever-changing human being would lead to charges of inaccuracies, distortions, fabrications, and omissions. If anything, Malcolm X was a Rorschach test and a mirror for anyone who examines him. He was also the Thomas Edison of self-reinvention.

Lee's dramatization of Malcolm's formative years, his conversion to Islam, his wife's role in his activism and the treatment of other contemporary black leaders all came under attack by political activists, biographers, those who knew him, and even theologians.

Lee's three-and-a-half-hour "personal epic" was based on *The Autobiography of Malcolm X*, co-written or ghostwritten depending on whom you ask, by Alex Haley, as well as on independent research commissioned by the producer, Marvin Worth. But just as the credibility of the autobiography had been questioned, the same doubts plagued the film. A huge-bestseller, Malcolm's autobiography is an ideological rather than a genealogical sequel to Haley's even bigger success, *Roots*. But

Malcolm X (1925–1965) at Queens Court, 1964. *Photo by Herman Miller, courtesy of the Library of Congress.*

critics and biographers insisted some of Malcolm's early roots had been fabricated or distorted to serve later political causes. Both the autobiography and the film suggest that Malcolm X's adult rage was fueled by a literally fiery childhood ignited by white racism. Repeating the story in Malcolm's memoir, the film depicts the Ku Klux Klan burning down Malcolm's childhood home in Lansing, Michigan, in 1929. But in Bruce Perry's *Malcolm X: The Life of a Man Who Changed Black America*, which was published a year before the release of the film, the author quoted Malcolm's mother and her sister-in-law, who insisted the fire never occurred! The film repeats the autobiography's claim that his father, an adherent of Marcus Garvey's 1920s "Back to Africa" movement, was pushed to his death in front of a streetcar by white racists, more fuel for his son's rage, but a 1992 CBS documentary reported that the cause of death remains unknown and mentioned speculation that Malcolm's father stumbled onto the tracks, and his death was an accident.

The film accurately depicts Malcolm's early adulthood in 1940s Boston as a pimp and a cocaine user and his abusive relationship with a white woman, but omits evidence that young Malcolm was also a male prostitute.

The film also downplays two important contemporaries and rivals in Malcolm X's life. Dr. Martin Luther King Jr.'s presence is limited to a few seconds of TV news footage of King's epochal 1963 March on Washington, a dirty joke told by an FBI wiretapper about King's compulsive womanizing, and King's acerbic comments on Malcolm's assassination. Film commentator Ray Greene speculated that the film's Martin Luther King Lite reflected the "ideological schism between the two black leaders over passive resistance and violent activism that continues to this day."

Airbrushed out of the film like a purged victim of a Stalinist show trial is the politically embarrassing disciple of Malcolm X, the Reverend Louis Farrakhan, whose racist and anti-Semitic diatribes make director Lee's intermittent white-baiting seem like a touchy-feely segment on *Oprah*. Farrakhan's Orwellian non-person status in the film is especially surprising since Lee included a long interview with Farrakhan in his book *By Any Means Necessary: The Trials and Tribulations of the Making of Malcolm X*.

One of the most important figures in Malcolm's life, his wife, Dr. Betty Shabazz, objected to her portrayal even though she served as a paid consultant to the project.

Perhaps reflecting current feminist views rather than 1960s male chauvinism, Angela Bassett's Betty Shabazz is an independent, self-assertive woman. Her screen portrayal seemed like wish fulfillment to the real woman. At the time of the film's release, Dr. Shabazz said, "I was not as assertive as she was. I always wanted to be assertive [but] I couldn't do that with Malcolm. There were so many of the sisters who felt God had put him on Earth for them, and so I just kind of held back."

The greatest controversy surrounding the film, as in the subject's life, is the great whodunit of his death in a Harlem ballroom in 1965. Was it the usual suspects these days in most political assassinations, the FBI or the CIA? A hit squad from the black separatist Nation of Islam, which Malcolm X defected from as he rejected its hatred of whites in favor of racial reconciliation? Elijah Muhammad, the leader of the Nation of Islam at the time? Even Malcolm X had an opinion on his assassination, which he predicted during a conversation two weeks before his death with *Village Voice* columnist Nat Hentoff, who quoted him as saying, "Whatever happens to me, it won't be Elijah [Muhammad]."

No one disputes that four members of the Nation of Islam were tried and convicted of the murder, but since no smoking gun ever connected Elijah Muhammad to the assassination, Lee didn't name him as the mastermind of a conspiracy. However, during an appearance at the University of Southern California, the director implied the fish stinks from the head. "The Nation of Islam is run like the military. . . . There's no way anyone in the Nation would have taken that upon himself and gone out and shot Malcolm X without orders," he said in a non-responsive answer to a USC student who blasted him for even implicating the rank and file in the murder, despite the convictions of four members of the Nation of Islam. Black Muslims were enraged by the film's mention of Elijah Muhammad's three illegitimate children, which Muslims deny because of Muhammad's puritanical sexual standards.

The CIA and FBI are the alleged perpetrators of so many assassinations, the two agencies at times seem to have killed everything except Kevin Costner's career. O. J. Simpson's attorney, Johnnie Cochran, said, "People believe overwhelmingly that he was killed by the FBI." And even a pillar of the white establishment, CBS, speculated in a 1992 TV documentary that 46,000 CIA and State Department documents, so far unexamined, may reveal the "government's real role in the assassination." Conspiracy buffs mention the documented fact that both the CIA and FBI kept Malcolm X under constant surveillance and so at the very least they must have had foreknowledge of the assassination and did nothing to prevent it. To his credit, Lee rejected the paranoid P.O.V. of another director, Oliver Stone, to whom Lee is often compared, and his film does not indict the CIA or FBI. Extensive research, he told incredulous and enraged USC students, proved to him neither agencies conspired to kill Malcolm X.

The doctrinaire apocrypha surrounding Malcolm X's mercurial life make a definitive biography on film or in print unlikely. The *New York Times'* Caryn James conceded defeat at the end of a long think piece on the difficulties: "Maybe the real story is impossible." But Lee's *Malcolm X* came close to knowing the unknowable Malcolm X, according to his widow. "It is totally impossible to portray his total life, his variances," Dr. Shabazz said," but the film "captures the essence of Malcolm quite well."

Perhaps we should be satisfied with "essence," which is more accurate than mythology or legend.

Ali
(2001)

Directed by Michael Mann
Story by Gregory Allen Howard
Written by Michael Mann, Stephen J. Rivele, Christopher Wilkinson and Eric Roth

CAST

Will Smith (Cassius Clay/Cassius X/Muhammad Ali)
Jamie Foxx (Drew "Bundini" Brown)
Jon Voight (Howard Cosell)
Mario Van Peebles (Malcolm X)
Ron Silver (Angelo Dundee)
Jeffrey Wright (Howard Bingham)

Mykelti Williamson (Don King)
Jada Pinkett Smith (Sonji)
Giancarlo Esposito (Cassius Clay Sr.)

Although *Ali*, the $100 million biopic of the greatest fighter of all time, was a box-office and critical failure, most reviewers agreed on one thing. Although Will Smith looks and talks nothing like Muhammad Ali, he nailed the champ perfectly. Smith performed a Robert De Niro/*Raging Bull* beef-up-type transformation, adding 35 pounds of muscle to his ectomorphic frame with the ironic result that he actually looked more muscular than his real-life counterpart did at the height of his boxing career. Smith also slowed down his rapid-paced talking style, developed over years as a rap artist, to re-create Ali's slow, whispery voice. The bright-eyed actor here is heavy-lidded and as enigmatic as Will Smith, movie star, seems open and accessible.

To pump up his ectomorphic frame for the title role in *Ali*, Will Smith gained thirty-five pounds and ended up looking more muscular than the former heavyweight champ.

Smith must have enjoyed reading the reviews, which praised the accuracy of his fight scenes, because he refused to use a stunt double, and every punch you see connecting with the star's $20 million-a-pic mug actually happened—and no doubt hurt like hell.

Ironically, while Smith's clout kept the boxing sequences hyperreal, he also used his power to sanitize a less flattering aspect of the One and Only's private life. Sounding more like the *National Enquirer*, the *Sunday Times of London* claimed that Smith cinematically castrated Ali. "Hollywood has white-washed the greatest black boxer of all time. The wildly adulterous sex life of the young Muhammad Ali has been erased from [the film], on the orders of Will Smith, its powerful star." The *Times* attributed this "ethnic cleansing" of Ali's messy love life to a puritanical streak in Smith, a well-known family man and not the womanizer Ali was. But the *Times* undercut its credibility when it said Smith's sanitizing of this aspect of the hero's life cost him a $5 million pay cut, because the absence of sex scenes meant more expensive scenes shot in Africa where the film's climactic Rumble in the Jungle against George Foreman had to be filmed to compensate for time lost in the sack.

George Russell, author of *Ali and the Women*, said that Ali's promiscuity got a G-rated treatment to "appease myth-makers and Oscar voters. Will Smith was right to argue that showing Ali as a serial womanizer would play into white prejudices, but it is a vital party of his story." But Russell makes the egregious claim that Ali's extensive vocabulary and famous rhymes ("The Thrilla in Manila") were learned from well-educated bedmates, "college-educated, smart women who gave him the vocabulary to become the vivid big mouth we remember so fondly today. It is dishonest to hide all this away."

The *Times* story ran before the film was screened for the press or Russell. While *Ali* was criticized for its one-dimensional portrayal of the champ's wives and lovers, "it doesn't shy away from illuminating a few of Ali's less endearing qualities. In his prime, the champ appears to have been a serial adulterer," wrote the *San Francisco Examiner's* reviewer, Joe Leydon.

Director/co-writer Michael Mann and four screenwriters also don't shy away from depicting how Ali dumped his first wife (played by Will Smith's real life wife Jada Pinkett Smith) because she failed to wear the proper dress and display demure behavior dictated by the Nation of Islam.

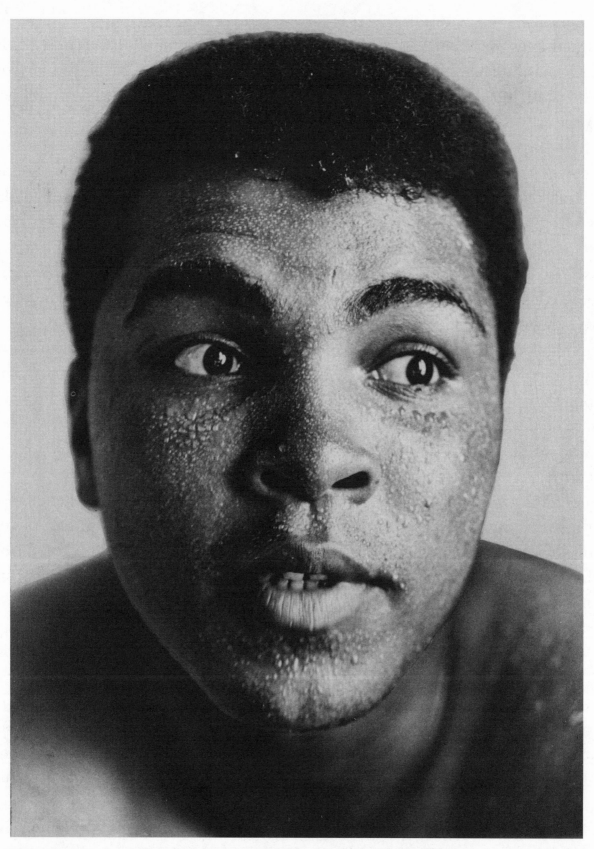

Muhammad Ali, a.k.a. Cassius Clay (1942–) in 1966. *Courtesy of the Library of Congress.*

Mann and his collaborators take off the gloves and set the record straight on Ali's relationship with the radical Nation of Islam, which has often been condemned as racist, and here is revealed as not at all radical regarding Ali's refusal to be inducted into the army. The U.S. government offered Ali a sweetheart deal: no fighting the Cong, just other boxing opponents in exhibition bouts. All Ali had to do was put on a military uniform. While it's well known that Ali refused to be drafted during the Vietnam War ("I ain't got no fight with the Viet Cong; they never called me nigger") and because of that lost his heavyweight title, it's much less known what the film depicts—that the Nation of Islam suspended Ali because he refused to be inducted into the army.

The film shows that on other issues, Ali accepted the teachings of his church, an unflattering fact that lessens accusations that the filmmakers presented a one-dimensional saint. Perhaps most disheartening is the revelation that Ali snubbed his mentor, Malcolm X (Mario Van Peebles, whom some critics faulted for looking more like a male model—which Van Peebles used to be—than the radical black martyr), on the orders of the leader of the Nation of Islam, "the honorable" Elijah Muhammad. The *Washington Post* faulted the film for presenting Malcolm more as Ali's sweet-souled career guidance counselor than the firebrand and object of white fear and loathing he was.

Critical praise for Jon Voight's dead-on impersonation of ABC sportscaster Howard Cosell was almost universal and included a best supporting acting Oscar nomination. *Ali* reveals a little known fact about the vicious public feud between Ali and the obnoxious sportscaster. In private, they were such great friends Ali actually made Cosell's career by granting him exclusive interviews. Their on-air squabbles owed more to professional wrestling than personal enmity. The *Chicago Sun-Times'* Roger Ebert wrote, "Ali's most authentic relationship in the film seems to be with Howard Cosell."

Like most of Ali's wives and girlfriends who go missing in action, one of the most influential people in the champ's life, his trainer Angelo Dundee, who was there from the beginning of his career, goes missing in plain sight. Or as the *Washington Post* perfectly described it, the brilliant actor Ron Silver, who plays Dundee, "is in virtually three-fourths of the scenes, yet says but three-fourths of a single sentence." Ali's "court photographer," Harold Bingham, who shot most of his fights and served as a confidant, is reduced to an extra's role here.

Many of the omissions in the film may be due to the fact that Ali's life was so rich, not as the greatest fighter of all time but as a political symbol, bully pulpit and whipping boy for a public that didn't like uppity blacks. Ali was the ultimate uppity black. Wisely, the filmmakers chose to dramatize only 10 years of the champ's life, from his 1964 win over Sonny Liston to his Rocky-like comeback when he beat George Foreman, eight years his junior, in Zaire in 1974.

The two fights neatly bracket a life that was anything but neat, a hero with a weakness for women and a religion that almost despised them. Ten years in the life of what some have called the most famous man of his time just may not have been enough to tell his story, although it did provide two and a half hours of screen time. Critics have said only a miniseries could do justice to the champ's complex life, and others claim the documentary *When We Were Kings* came closer than this fictionalized account.

The Elizabethans believed the eyes were the window to the soul. Ali's heavy-lidded gaze seems to underline Roger Ebert's claim that "Ali remains an enigma."

The Hurricane
(1999)

Directed by Norman Jewison
Written by Armyan Bernstein, Dan Gordon, Rubin "Hurricane" Carter (book), Sam Chaiton (book), Terry Swinton (book)

CAST

Denzel Washington (Rubin "Hurricane" Carter)
John Hannah (Terry Swinton)
Deborah Unger (Lisa Peters)
Liev Schreiber (Sam Chaiton)
Vicellous Reon Shannon (Lesra Martin)
David Paymer (Myron Bedlock)
Dan Hedaya (Det. Vincent Della Pesca)

Harris Yulin (Leon Friedman)
Rod Steiger (Judge H. Lee Sarokin)

The most inexplicable thing about *The Hurricane* was the decision to dump a true, absorbing legal drama and replace it with a largely concocted soap opera pitting a single bad white guy against a bunch of noble white folk who rescue a poor black guy, middleweight boxing contender Rubin "Hurricane" Carter (Denzel Washington), who was sentenced to prison for murders he did not commit. An attorney who defended Carter blasted the film for "taking the easy way out of a complex story by creating a soap opera."

The facts in the case were substantial enough to provide enough plot fodder for an entire season of *Law & Order*.

The facts, most of which didn't make it into the movie, are these: On a summer night in 1966, two black men invaded a Paterson, New Jersey, bar and opened fire, killing three white people. A witness said he saw two black men leaving the bar in a white car with out of state license plates. The police theorized that the killings were revenge for the recent murder of a black tavern owner by a white man in Paterson.

A few hours after the murder of the whites, the police picked up Carter and a friend, John Artis, in Carter's white Dodge van. They also claimed they found a shotgun and a bullet in the car.

Except for their race, neither Carter nor Artis resembled eyewitness descriptions of the killers, and after both men passed lie detector tests, the police released them.

Three months later, Carter and Artis were indicted for the murders based on the testimony of two men who admitted they were in the middle of committing a burglary when they claimed they saw Carter and Artis emerge from the Paterson bar carrying weapons.

Prosecutors offered no motive for the murders, and based solely on the testimony of the two burglars, Carter and Artis were sentenced to life in prison. The all-white jury reached its verdict during a tense period of race riots in New Jersey. Carter rotted in prison for the next four years (literally in one sense, when his teeth rotted away due to the lack of dental treatment). Then Fred W. Hogan, an investigator for the New Jersey public defender's office, inspired by Carter's prison-penned autobiography, took up his case with the help of a freelance writer, Richard Solomon.

In 1973 Hogan located the two burglars whose testimony had convicted Carter and got them to admit they had made up their story in return for the offer of lenient sentences for their own crimes, plus a cash reward of $10,000. Based on the new evidence, the New Jersey Supreme Court overturned Carter's conviction, but the dogged prosecutors decided to retry the two men, this time offering a new theory that their actions were revenge for the murder of the black tavern owner, a claim never brought up at the first trial. After nine months of freedom, Carter was convicted again and returned to prison, deserted by his celebrity supporters, including Bob Dylan, who wrote a hit song about the case. But Carter and Artis' defense lawyers didn't abandon their clients, and for the next 10 years they worked for free to clear the two men.

Finally in 1985 a New Jersey judge ruled that the second case had been fatally tainted by the injection of an unproved and racist theory that Carter and Artis had acted out of revenge and the perjured testimony of the burglars. Carter and Artis remained in prison for another three years until the U.S. Supreme Court upheld the lower court's decision. They were finally freed in 1988.

The Hurricane omits almost all of this fascinating drama of a corrupt judicial system in which racist prosecutors were willing to fabricate testimony to get a conviction. (The startling fact that the police planted the incriminating bullet and shotgun in Carter's van never made it into the script.) In the film, the two pivotal trials and all their exculpatory details are compressed into a single scene where Carter is sentenced!

Hogan, who found the burglars and got them to recant, isn't portrayed in the film despite his crucial role in the real life drama. At a book-signing party after his release, Carter pointed to Hogan and said, "There must be a beginning and the beginning is you." Carter's battalion of lawyers are reduced to minor roles.

Instead, the film places almost all the credit for the hero's release on the members of a Canadian commune, who are depicted as doing all the investigative work that led to the overturning of Carter's conviction. In fact, while the commune did a great deal of paralegal work on Carter's appeals, saving the defense attorneys thousands of dollars, the commune found none of the evidence that exonerated him, nor were their lives ever threatened by a fictional villain as depicted in the film.

Worse, instead of portraying the corruption that infected many members of New Jersey's prosecutor's office and judiciary, the film substitutes a completely fictionalized lone villain, a racist police detective (Dan Hedaya), who has been pursuing Carter since he was 11 and is responsible for his conviction as an adult.

The affluent white commune members who lived outside Toronto were introduced to Carter by an illiterate black Brooklyn youth they had informally adopted. The film accurately dramatizes the genuine affection that developed between the youth, Lesra Martin, now an attorney in Canada, and the imprisoned boxer.

The emphasis on the Canadians' role was due to the fact that the screenwriters, Armyan Bernstein and Dan Gordon, based their script on *Lazarus and the Hurricane*, written by two commune members and published in 1991. The result was that in the film version, rich bleeding heart liberals save Carter, not his dogged defense team. The film also lays all the blame on a single white racist instead of indicting an entire corrupt judicial system.

The Hurricane ends with Carter giving an impassioned courtroom speech and implies that this speech freed him. Carter never made such a speech, and he was freed as a result of a U.S. Supreme Court decision—not by his own eloquence.

The film also makes some minor and major omissions to boost the heroic nature of Carter and his Canadian supporters. *The Hurricane* presents Carter as an upstanding citizen at the time of his arrest when in truth he had previously served four years in prison for three burglaries and assault.

The ultimate fate of his relationship with the commune never made it on to the screen. After his release, Carter denounced the Canadians for using him as their "trophy horse" to raise funds not for his defense but for their commune. The film also fails to mention that Carter married the leader of the commune and then divorced her after becoming disenchanted with the group. Lesra Martin, the commune's black surrogate son, was expelled from the group for dating a woman his surrogate family, which had cult-like elements, did not approve of.

The Hurricane also distorted the Hurricane's boxing record. Former middleweight champ Joey Giardello sued the film's creators for defamation for including a sequence in which Carter "relentlessly pummels" Giardello, despite the fact that Giardello won the fight! Giardello settled the suit after unsuccessfully trying to have Universal, which produced the film, insert actual footage of the 1964 title bout.

After the film's release investigative journalist Selwyn Raab, whose reportage helped revive interest in Carter's case while he languished in prison, denounced the film as a "fairy tale" and "history contorted for dramatic effect" in an article in the *New York Times*. Screenwriter Bernstein dismissed the complaint as "an opinion piece by a man who was upset by being left out of our film," which indeed Raab and his enormous contribution to the case were, as were investigator Fred Hogan and much of the Carter defense team.

One of the neglected defense attorneys, Lewis M. Steel, felt *The Hurricane's* distortions and omissions had a much greater significance than being just another example of Hollywood simplifying and fictionalizing a true story for the sake of telling an even better one. Steel felt that while viewers of another highly fictionalized film, *JFK*, went to the theater knowing enough information about the president's assassination to form their own opinions about the preposterous conspiracy theories expounded in the film, for most people, their only information about the lesser known Rubin Carter came from a movie that was more fiction than reality.

The Hurricane, by ignoring the corrupt, racist judicial system that railroaded Carter twice, also missed a historic opportunity to shed some light on another case that continues to mystify white America, the O. J. Simpson trial.

In an Op Ed piece in the *Los Angeles Times*, Steel wrote, "If *The Hurricane* had shown what happened, many more people might have come to understand why the predominantly black jury in the O. J. Simpson case was so quick to acquit him and why so many black Americans applauded that decision."

Blow
(2001)

Directed by Ted Demme
Written by David McKenna and Nick Cassavetes
Based on the book by Bruce Porter

CAST

Johnny Depp (George Jung)
Penélope Cruz (Mirtha Jung)
Ray Liotta (Fred Jung)
Franka Potente (Barbara Buckley)
Rachel Griffiths (Ermine Jung)
Paul Reubens (Derek Foreal)
Jordi Mollà (Diego Delgado)
Cliff Curtis (Pablo Escobar)

The title of Bruce Porter's biography of cocaine dealer George Jung, *How a Small Time Boy Made $100 Million with the Medellin Cocaine Cartel and Lost It All*, on which the film *Blow* is based, provides an accurate summary of the film's plot and theme. George Jung's life was the flip side of the classic Horatio Alger story, a rise from rags to riches—except this particular Horatio goes back to rags—or more accurately a prison uniform. Jung is currently incarcerated at the Federal Corrections Institute in Otisville, New York, and won't be released until 2014 when he's 72.

The filmmakers, director Ted Demme and screenwriters Nick Cassavetes and David McKenna, interviewed Jung extensively in jail and apparently were so seduced by his charm that they decided to give a heroic treatment to the story of an imprisoned felon. In fact, Dominic Streatfeild, while researching his book *Cocaine*, traveled all the way from his native Britain to visit Jung in jail and pronounced him "charming . . . Because of his natural ebullience and because his story is so extraordinary, people gravitate towards him." That's definitely what happened to Demme and Co.

Jung's story is not only extraordinary but also seductive—at least the rags to riches part. The back to rags ending is not.

The filmmakers take a psychoanalytic approach to Jung's life. He is the product of his childhood in Weymouth, Massachusetts. His father (Ray Liotta) was an amiable working stiff who played by the rules, worked hard and ended up broke and emasculated by his wife (Rachel Griffiths) for not being a good provider. Young

Johnny Depp and Penelope Cruz mug for the camera as 1970s cocaine kingpin George Jung and his Colombian wife, Mirtha.

George learns this lesson early: honest hard work doesn't pay. Maybe crime does. And it does . . . for a while.

George drops out of college and moves to El Lay in the early 1960s, a paradise of free love offered by beautiful women all fueled by marijuana, which George becomes a small-time, then big-time peddler of. He's making a lot more money than his poor father ever did and having a ball at the same time. Life is good until 1974, when he's busted for pot possession and goes to jail, where he meets small-time Colombian drug dealer Carlos Lehder, whose name in the film has been changed to Diego Delgado (Jordi Mollà), perhaps for legal reasons or fear of a mob wipeout. It proves to be a life- and career-altering connection. Released from prison, the two men team up as small-time coke dealers, then Delgado introduces him to Pablo Escobar (Cliff Curtis), leader of Colombia's Medellin cartel . . . and a star is born.

In the film, Jung's voice-over brags, "If you snorted cocaine in the late 1970s and early 1980s, there was an 85 percent chance it came from us." *Cocaine's* author Dominic Streatfeild says, "This is not strictly true. It is a fact that in the late Seventies George and Carlos Lehder [Diego Delgado in the film] pioneered a wholesale cocaine pipeline to the United States. However, just a year after the transfer of the first large load (250 kilos, flown into the U.S. via the Bahamas in 1977), [Delgado] dumped George and went off on his own."

The real Jung was not in fact the huge drug kingpin *Blow* deliriously makes him out to be, but its portrayal of his lifestyle during those heady years, however inaccurate, does give you, well, a rush.

In a seductive montage, the Horatio Alger portion of Jung's life is dramatized in giddy detail: a palatial home, seven sportscars, millions in the bank and a supernally lovely Colombian wife, Mirtha. (Played by the supernally lovely Penelope Cruz, the sexiest woman alive. Just ask Tom Cruise.) "We were young, rich, and in love. We had it all," Jung's voice-over exults. Film critic Cosmo Landesman condemned this feel-good take on the "high life" as "amoral schmaltz," its heroes "sentimentalized as out-law heroes." *Time* magazine lamented *Blow*'s "moral confusion." *New York* magazine noted that while the film is glamorizing Jung's life, it omits the devastation his "career" in cocaine wreaked on America's inner cities when his product metastasized into crack. "There is no mention of such damage in *Blow*," *New York* said.

While neglecting the plight of the inner cities, which is another film anyway, *Blow* accurately conveys the damage cocaine addiction did to Jung's life and marriage. Early on, Penelope Cruz's Mirtha is an ethereal goddess who dumps her Colombian drug dealer husband for American drug dealer Jung. Gradually, she matches her husband snort for snort and lives up to his creepy boast, "I snorted 10 grams of coke in 10 minutes." Soon, Mirtha becomes a coke-addled harpie, and the filmmakers again indulge in psychoanalysis by having Mirtha emasculate George when his business goes bust and they run out of money. In a union Freud would have been proud of, George has married his money-obsessed mother (or a Latin spitfire facsimile of mom).

After serving several terms, George gets out of prison desperate to make enough money to pay child support so he can see a daughter he adores. He decides to make one last drug deal, then retire as a doting poppa. Unfortunately, the "customers" he picks to sell his last score to are undercover narcs, and Jung goes back to the slammer until 2014.

Critics faulted the film for sentimentalizing George's life and trying to turn him into a tragic figure at the end because his adored daughter (understandably) declines to visit her felon-father in prison.

Film critic Barbara Ellen wrote of the film's moral failure and omissions, "Ultimately, [*Blow*] comes across like some ultra-trendy social worker who wants to avoid censure and judgment of Jung at all costs. We are never allowed to get close to Jung's dark, selfish, ruthless side, but if he hasn't got one, he's the first ex-drug smuggler and addict who hasn't."

In some ways, *Blow*'s narrative re-creates the arc of ingesting uppers: a giddy high followed by a horrible crash, euphoria turning into dysphoria, as rehab counselors like to say.

Or as *Cocaine*'s Streatfeild described the life of George Jung, "It's the American Dream, played the way it would be if Horatio Alger had maintained a serious amphetamine habit."

Nixon
(1995)

Directed by Oliver Stone
Written by Stephen J. Rivele, Christopher Wilkinson, Oliver Stone

CAST

Anthony Hopkins (Richard M. Nixon)
Joan Allen (Pat Nixon)
Powers Boothe (Alexander Haig)
Ed Harris (E. Howard Hunt)
Bob Hoskins (J. Edgar Hoover)
E. G. Marshall (John Mitchell)
David Paymer (Ron Ziegler)
David Hyde Pierce (John Dean)
Paul Sorvino (Henry Kissinger)
Mary Steenburgen (Hannah Nixon)
J. T. Walsh (John Ehrlichman)
James Woods (H. R. Haldeman)
Brian Bedford (Clyde Tolson)
Kevin Dunn (Charles Colson)
Annabeth Gish (Julie Nixon)
Edward Herrmann (Nelson Rockefeller)
Madeline Kahn (Martha Mitchell)
John Diehl (Gordon Liddy)

Washington Post reporter Bob Woodward should know, since he was there, when he claims that half of Oliver Stone's biopic on Richard Nixon was based on the record; the other half was a combination of speculation and "borderline slander," according to the man who broke the Watergate story.

Woodward called *Nixon* an attempt at "cinematic psychoanalysis" and quipped that the late president got the analyst he deserved, Oliver Stone, because both men were paranoid.

How paranoid? Perhaps the most outrageous hypothesis Stone presents is that Nixon, during his years in the wilderness after losing the 1960 presidential race, planned to assassinate Fidel Castro. The attempt enraged the Cuban dictator, but instead of killing Nixon, Castro for reasons never supplied by the director wreaked his revenge by ordering Kennedy's assassination. The big question—why White House operatives burglarized Democratic Party headquarters in the Watergate complex during the 1972 presidential race—has never been answered by historians despite countless books on the subject, including the memoirs of the burglars and the White House officials who covered up the break-in. Oliver Stone loves to answer history's big questions, and when he doesn't have the proof, he uses the excuse that film is a medium of fiction, so his answers don't have to be true. Never let the facts get in the way of a good story indeed.

In *Nixon*, Stone's answer to the big question reflects the historical consensus that the president didn't order or know about the break-in, but instead of distancing himself from the burglars, he actively engaged in covering up their crime. Watergate conspirator Bob Haldeman supported Stone's premise when he wrote in his autobiography that Nixon was surprised when he learned of the burglary, but immediately set about managing the cover-up from Day One.

Like the fools of the famous saying, Stone rushes in with an explanation for Nixon's post-burglary behavior where historians have been unable to tread. According to Stone, one of the burglars, Howard Hunt, was also involved in the CIA's plot to kill President Kennedy, and Nixon feared the CIA's culpability would be revealed by Hunt. Hence, the $100,000 bribe Nixon offered Hunt for his silence, which is part of the historical record.

Stone and his co-writers get many things right: illegal wiretaps justified by Nixon on national security grounds, the bribes paid the burglars, and the burglary of the office of the psychiatrist of Daniel J. Ellsberg, who leaked the Pentagon Papers to the press.

The director's portrait of the president's personal life is distorted for melodramatic purposes. Stone's Nixon (Anthony Hopkins uncharacteristically chewing up the scenery) is a potty-mouthed drunk trapped in a hellish marriage. The director's depiction of Nixon's dysfunctional relationship with his wife was called "sick" and "near slander" by one critic.

Nixon didn't deserve his reputation for an obsessive use of obscenity, which arose from all those "expletive deleted" in transcripts of the White House tapes. Nixon biographer Stephen Ambrose, no fan of the president, claimed that the deletions contained G-rated curses like "hell" and "damn" and that Nixon sounds embarrassed while making the mild oaths.

His alcoholism was not based on fact but his inability to hold his liquor. One drink put him under the table, or as Watergate conspirator John Ehrlichman said, "One drink can knock him galley-west if he's tired." Nixon was aware of his susceptibility to alcohol and took care to drink moderately if at all.

After so many distortions and fabrications, Bob Woodward believed that Stone ironically stumbled upon the truth about Nixon with the film's depiction of such a flawed human being. "The point is simple: America had the wrong person as president. Nixon was not suited to the office. It's not just the criminality, the insularity, the almost total absence of a higher purpose. It was the sheer inadequacy of the man, who could not order his own life, much less the life of the country," Woodward said.

Missing
(1982)

Directed by Constantin Costa-Gavras
Written by Constantin Costa-Gavras, Donald Stewart, Thomas Hauser (book)

CAST

Jack Lemmon (Ed Horman)
Sissy Spacek (Beth Horman)
Melanie Mayron (Terry Simon)
John Shea (Charles Horman)

In *Missing,* Sissy Spacek plays the wife and Jack Lemmon the father of left-wing journalist Charles Horman, who disappeared in Chile during a military coup that the film alleges was facilitated by the U.S. State Department and resulted in the murder of Chile's Marxist president Salvador Allende.

Did the U.S. government help overthrow Chile's Marxist president Salvador Allende Gossens in 1973 and conspire in the murder of leftist freelance journalist Charles Horman by the right wing regime of General Augusto Pinochet after he discovered evidence of U.S. involvement in the Allende coup? Then, did U.S. embassy officials in Chile try to cover up the murder when Horman's father, Ed, went there to discover the cause of his son's death?

Missing dramatically answered those questions in the affirmative. The alleged culprits, including the U.S. ambassador at the time, begged to differ and filed a $150 million lawsuit against *Missing*'s director, Constantin Costa-Gavras; Thomas Hauser, the author of the book on which the film was based; the book's publisher; and Universal, which released the 1982 film.

The U.S. State Department took the unusual step of issuing a three-page statement denying the allegations and implications of the film shortly before its release, in particular the charge that the State Department obstructed Ed Horman's search for his son's murderers: "The Department of State undertook intensive and comprehensive efforts to locate Charles Horman from the moment it was learned that he was missing, to assist his relatives in their efforts to locate him and also to learn the circumstances of his disappearance and death." Tellingly, the State Department rebuttal did not address *Missing*'s more explosive accusation, that the U.S. government colluded in the murder of President Allende by his successor, General Pinochet.

A U.S. Senate committee that spent a year investigating the matter and had access to secret files of the CIA and the State and Defense Departments in 1975 found no evidence of U.S. involvement in either Allende's or Charles Horman's death, which was confirmed in a series of reports by the *New York Times'* Pulitzer-Prize-winning reporter Seymour Hersh. But Congress did find that the U.S. had tried to prevent the election of Allende in 1970 by funding opposition newspapers and unions during the presidential campaign that put Allende in office. Political columnist Jeffrey Hart bluntly assessed the merits of *Missing*: "Costa-Gavras simply invented or intuited the whole thing and is now passing his fancies off as facts."

The director pleaded the usual Fifth of filmmaking, that he hadn't made a documentary. But his argument is undercut by the film's opening statement: "This film is based on a true story. The incidents and facts are documented."

These facts were not disputed: In 1972, Charles Horman, a Harvard-educated freelance writer and documentary maker, and his wife, Joyce, arrived in Santiago, Chile, where he planned to write about the new Marxist regime of Dr. Salvador Allende. The Hormans were in a Chilean seaside resort on September 11, 1973, when a military coup overthrew Allende, murdered him, and installed the right wing General Augusto Pinochet. Six days later, after the Hormans had returned to Santiago, men wearing military uniforms entered the Hormans' home, seized Charles, and took him to the national stadium, where other left-wing political prisoners were being held. Four weeks later, the new government revealed that Horman had been shot and killed. Horman's father, Edmund, a conservative New York businessman who disagreed with his son's radical politics, went to Chile and began his assault on the U.S. embassy in an attempt first to find his son, then unravel the cause of his son's death.

Everything that followed in the film was hotly contested by Horman and what became his bitter nemesis, the U.S. State Department. Edmund Horman, played by Jack Lemmon, is stonewalled by American diplomats who pretend to help while knowing all along that the Chilean government has murdered his son. Nathanael Davis, who was U.S. ambassador to Chile at the time, denied U.S. government knowledge of Charles' death when his father arrived in Santiago, and Davis told Horman that his son was probably in hiding. Although Davis was not identified in the film by name, he was one of the plaintiffs in the $150 million libel suit filed (and later dismissed) against the filmmakers and the author of book on which the film was based.

Ed Horman, however, through the Freedom of Information Act, found a cable from Davis to Secretary of State Henry Kissinger, dated one day before Horman's arrival in Santiago, in which Davis mentioned eyewitness accounts of neighbors who saw Charles Horman taken away by Chilean soldiers. No documents surfaced, however, that the U.S. participated in or condoned the seizure of Horman.

Charles Horman kept a diary that recounted his meeting with several U.S. military officials who told him that the U.S. had participated in Allende's overthrow. A few days later, Horman became one of the estimated 30,000 who disappeared during Pinochet's reign of terror.

In *Missing*, Costa-Gavras and screenwriter Donald E. Stewart not only fail to mention Ambassador Davis by name, but the Latin American country where the action takes place also remains unidentified. Cynics might feel the omissions were an unsuccessful attempt on the part of the filmmakers to avoid a lawsuit, but students of Costa-Gavras' films might conclude that the director, who eviscerated repressive regimes in Z and *The Confession*, tried to turn *Missing* into a generic indictment of the government-sponsored murders that took place in several Latin American countries, Argentina being the most notorious example of such.

Some felt that by casting the No. 1 Nice Guy of American cinema, Jack Lemmon, in the role of Ed Horman, the director stacked the deck in favor of those who blamed the U.S. for many of Chile's woes. Others complained that not only were Allende and his Marxist beliefs left out of the film, but also missing in *Missing* were the extralegal measures Allende used to nationalize private industries and expropriate privately owned land, which helped bring on his downfall and murder.

New York magazine's David Denby felt that by omitting the political context in which Charles Horman was killed, Costa-Gavras, despite all his left-wing baggage, ended up with an old-fashioned melodrama "about a sweet boy who gets picked on and the insensitive old papa who melts into humanity by admitting his love for that boy." Great psychodrama perhaps, but a deracinated political one.

Silkwood
(1983)

Directed by Mike Nichols
Written by Alice Arlen, Nora Ephron

CAST

Meryl Streep (Karen Silkwood)
Kurt Russell (Drew Stephens)
Cher (Dolly Pelliker)
Craig T. Nelson (Winston)
Diana Scarwid (Angela)

On the night of November 13, 1974, Karen Silkwood was on her way to a meeting with a union official and a *New York Times* reporter with evidence she claimed would show her employer, the Kerr-McGee Nuclear Corp. in Cimarron, Oklahoma, was manufacturing defective plutonium fuel rods that could cause a disaster worse than Three Mile Island. But before she could meet the official and the reporter, Silkwood's car crashed into a concrete culvert going 45 mph. That much everyone involved in the story that became *Silkwood* agreed upon. The rest of the story generated enough controversy to take the case all the way to the Supreme Court.

As Karen Silwood, Meryl Streep searches for evidence that her employer, Kerr-McGee Nuclear Corp., is manufacturing defective plutonium fuel rods that could cause a disaster worse than Three Mile Island in *Silkwood*.

An autopsy revealed that Silkwood's bloodstream had large amounts of the illegal barbiturate Methaqualone (Quaaludes) and a small amount of alcohol, plus more of the powerful sedative undigested in her stomach. The Oklahoma Highway Patrol declared the accident a "classic one-car crash." The film hinted that a second car may have run Silkwood off the road and showed headlights approaching her Honda Civic just before the crash. Attorneys for Silkwood's estate, which won a $10.5 million award from Kerr-McGee that was upheld on appeal to the Supreme Court, argued that fresh dents in Silkwood's rear bumper showed she had been rear-ended. However, the *New York Times* quoted a tow-truck driver who said he had made the dent when he towed Silkwood's car.

A week before her death or murder, Silkwood (Meryl Streep) and her apartment were found to have been contaminated with plutonium. Kerr-McGee claimed she poisoned herself to draw attention to her claim that the manufacturer was covering

When she's not comforting her lesbian roommate (Cher, right) Meryl Streep's Karen Silkwood tries to expose unsafe conditions at the nuclear power plant where she works in *Silkwood*.

up defective fuel rods. Silkwood's lead attorney, Daniel Sheehan, argued successfully in court that the form of plutonium found in food in Silkwood's refrigerator was kept in a locked vault that only Kerr-McGee's higher ups had the key to.

No incriminating documents on defective fuel rods at the plant were found in Silkwood's car after the crash, which Kerr-McGee cited as proof the documents never existed. Sheehan vehemently denied that contention: "That is bullshit! It's hard to imagine them saying something like that." Sheehan said there were taped telephone calls of Silkwood reading excerpts from the documents to Steve Wodka, an official at her Oil/Chemical and Atomic Workers union, who was with the *New York Times* reporter Silkwood had arranged to meet on the night of her death. "There is sworn testimony put into the trial of people who were there at the Hube Cafe who saw the documents, who she talked with about the documents," Sheehan said. Sworn testimony by the director of personnel for Kerr-McGee revealed that the company removed documents from Silkwood's car after telling the Oklahoma Highway Patrol they needed to check them for radiation. The on-screen text, or "crawl," at the end of the film only says no documents were found.

Although Kerr-McGee denounced *Silkwood* after its release, calling it a "highly fictionalized Hollywood dramatization scarcely connected to the facts," the company may have gotten off lightly. Sheehan noted that the film failed to mention the collaboration between the corporation and Oklahoma police, which included electronic surveillance of Silkwood and her boyfriend, plus wiretaps of her phone. Or as the director of the Silkwood Fund, Sara Nelson, said, "The facts were much worse than portrayed in the film."

The Atomic Energy Commission did clear Kerr-McGee of one allegation the film made. In one scene, Karen discovers a supervisor at the plant touching up an X-ray that shows faulty welds in the fuel rods, but the Commission said the supervisor was touching up dust spots to avoid the trouble of retaking the photos—not trying to hide dangerous flaws in the rods.

Some accused the film of trying to capitalize on the box-office success of a similar-themed thriller about a fictional meltdown, *The China Syndrome*. But *Silkwood*'s nuclear bogeyman was a hollow man, according to an executive at the Washington State breeder reactor where the allegedly damaged rods were shipped. In the film, a union official tells Silkwood, "You put one of your defective fuel rods into a breeder reactor, for all we know the whole state could be wiped out." For all they knew, they knew nothing, said Daniel Simpson, a vice president at Westinghouse-Hanford, the company that operates the reactor in Washington State. "The effect of the failure of a faulty fuel rod is essentially nil. Even a number of failures could never cause criticality," i.e., a chain reaction that would wipe Washington off the map.

Although some critics complained that *Silkwood* tried to turn a dim-bulb, pill-popping blue collar worker into the Joan of Arc of the anti-nuclear movement, those close to Karen Silkwood felt the film had portrayed her too harshly. Silkwood never abandoned her three children, as the movie claimed, nor was she the dumb Okie it presented. Her father, Bill Silkwood, said she was "a whole lot smarter, more intelligent than they showed her in the movie," noting that Karen had been a National Honor student and had won a college scholarship.

The real Silkwood lived in a modern apartment, not the ramshackle rural house in the film. Her roommate, Dolly Pelliker, played by Cher, has a lesbian relationship with a mortuary makeup artist who never existed and whose ghoulish profession may have been injected to add to the grim tone of the film. Ellis was not happy with her screen incarnation, and it had nothing to do with the lesbian relationship, although Ellis refused to discuss her sexual orientation in interviews. She did object to the film's implication that she "snitched on Karen to the company." When her dialogue in the script was read to her over the phone, Ellis said, "I threw up halfway through," but the studio had paid her $67,000 for the rights to her story "so they can defame my character any way they want." Silkwood's father insisted Ellis never lived with his daughter and her boyfriend.

Meryl Streep, the screen's best chameleon and mimic, got Silkwood's look right, but her voice wrong, according to Silkwood's real-life boyfriend, Drew Stephens (Kurt Russell) and Streep herself. Stephens recalled his first meeting with the actress. "Meryl came in wearing a pair of plaid slacks—like ones Karen had . . . The mannerisms were all there." But Streep, who has perfectly duplicated accents ranging from the Polish-German of a Holocaust survivor to an Australian mother accused of murdering her children, gave up trying to imitate Silkwood's Oklahoma drawl after hearing a tape of her phone conversation with a union lawyer. "Her voice was quite a lot lower than mine, and she spoke r-e-a-l slow. I listened to it again and . . . then I stopped listening to it . . . it was wrong dramatically for the movie," Streep said.

The most dramatic omission of *Silkwood* may also be the scariest. Claims by conspiracy buffs that the CIA killed Silkwood to hide the removal of plutonium from the Kerr-McGee plant that the agency funneled to foreign allies were not brought up in the film and dismissed by the filmmakers as preposterous. Or were they?

Art Angel, another attorney for the estate, said, "As of the day of the trial, four years after the closing of the plant, 18.6 kilograms [40 pounds] of plutonium still remain unaccounted for."

Still proclaiming the safety of its operations, Kerr-McGee closed the Cimarron, Oklahoma, plant two years after Silkwood's death.

In the Name of the Father
(1993)

Directed by Jim Sheridan
Written by Terry George, Jim Sheridan, Gerry Conlon (book)

CAST

Emma Thompson (Gareth Peirce)
Daniel Day-Lewis (Gerry Conlon)
Pete Postlethwaite (Giuseppe Conlon)

In 1974, bombs went off in two pubs in Guildford, south of London, killing five and injuring 64. In the hysteria that followed, Britain passed the draconian Prevention of Terrorism Act, which allowed suspects to be held for seven days without representation by an attorney. Gerry Conlon, a young petty thief from Belfast, and four buddies were arrested, a confession was beaten out of them by police, and they were sentenced to life in prison. After 15 years of confinement, their case was taken up by crusading attorneys, among them Gareth Peirce, who gained their release. An appeals court freed the Guildford Four in 1989 after finding the police had withheld exculpatory evidence.

That part of *In the Name of the Father*'s story is agreed upon by all sides in the tortured history of "The Troubles" in Northern Ireland, which since 1969 have pitted Catholics against Protestants and the British military that tries, more often than not unsuccessfully, to keep the peace between the warring sides.

The rest of the story, as dramatized in the film, makes *Rashomon* seem like a linear narrative, enraged British audiences, and delighted Americans enough to earn *In the Name of the Father* seven Oscar nominations, including best actress for Emma Thompson, who played defense attorney Gareth Peirce.

British film critics roasted the film for a slew of omissions and fabrications, from the petty to the ludicrous. For starters, the real life Peirce only had a minor role in freeing the Guildford Four. That honor goes to Alastair Logan, who doesn't appear in the film except for a quick thank-you note in the closing credits. On the ludicrous side, Peirce, a solicitor, is shown wigless and screaming at a judge in the Old Bailey (the screenwriters lifted the judge's dialogue from court transcripts but invented Thompson's), despite the fact that such bad behavior would never be tolerated and more important, only barristers (trial lawyers in the U.S.) wearing wigs are allowed to represent defendants, not solicitors. That wiggy complaint is a minor misstep and doesn't undercut the innocence of the Guildford Four, which even the most strident Protestant nationalists on both sides of the Irish Sea do not dispute. But to add drama, the film fabricates a scene in which Peirce finds a police document, withheld from the original trial, which corroborates Conlon's alibi that he was somewhere else on the night of the bombings. The much less dramatic reality was that a government official uncovered the document and turned it over to the court and the defense team. Co-screenwriter Terry George was flat out wrong when he wrote in a letter to the *Los Angeles Times* that although Peirce did not find the exonerating evidence in the police archives, as she does in the film, she did discover it while examining police documents at home in bed!

The film also creates a fictional cellmate named Joe McAndrew, an IRA member, who confesses to Conlon in prison that he planted the bombs that sent Conlon to prison. In reality, the IRA publicly announced that they, not the Guildford Four, had bombed the pubs, but because the plight of unjustly imprisoned Irish Catholics served their purposes, the IRA undercut its announcement by refusing to identify the real perpetrators.

The saddest victim in this miscarriage of justice was Giuseppe Conlon, Gerry's kind-hearted da', who leaves Belfast for England to find his son a good lawyer after Gerry's arrest. Instead, the elder Conlon is arrested, convicted of the bombings and sent to prison, where he dies of a heart attack before the release of the Guildford Four.

Director and co-writer Jim Sheridan dismissed the film's political and judicial inaccuracies by saying he sought a greater "emotional honesty" and that the real subject of the film was the relationship of a father and son and the son's maturation from petty criminal to political activist and autobiographer. (The film is based on Conlon's account, *Proved Innocent*.) But critics said the director even got that story wrong. They pointed out that Gerry and Giuseppe never shared a cell, as they do in the film, and Giuseppe spent most of his incarceration in another prison. Screenwriter Terry George insisted that for the last year and a half of his sad life, Giuseppe occupied the cell next to his son's, and they spent every day together until the father's death.

The dramatic turning point in Gerry Conlon's evolution from sleazy thug to virtuous martyr is provided by a fictional character, McAndrew, in a fictional scene. Using a homemade blowtorch, McAndrew sets a prison guard on fire. While the guard writhes in agony, Conlon experiences a spiritual rebirth and extinguishes the flames with a blanket. Incendiary melodrama but pure fantasy. An embarrassing voice of reason and reality, Gerry's uncle, Sean Smyth, insisted after the film's release, "The truth is that Gerry Conlon had very little time for his father." Conlon's aunt, Anne Maguire, loved the film, even though she found it more fiction than fact. "It's a good film, well acted and everything. But I think if they'd put more of the true facts [*sic*] in, it would have been a much more powerful film."

While the politically neutral story of the two Conlons' cell-side rapprochement drew critical acclaim on this side of the Atlantic ("The film's power lies in its exploration of the relationship between Gerry Conlon and his father Giuseppe. Daniel Day-Lewis gives Gerry's confusion and political awakening and disillusionment gritty authenticity. Yet the picture's heart lies with Giuseppe, the simple moral man given strength by the English actor Pete Postlethwaite."—the *Wall Street Journal*), appalled critics on the other side of the pond felt Americans had been psychologically hoodwinked. The *Sunday Times of London* was not emotionally seduced by the film's refried Freud and said, "Americans like to bring all politics down to Oedipal struggles and 'the politics of the *poisonal*.' It's no wonder they wet themselves in their hundreds at this touchy-feely field day."

Ironically, both sides of this argument and struggle are probably right. The Troubles in Northern Ireland are equally personal and political—as impersonal as the anonymous bombings of civilians and as personal as the innocent victims who suffer death or mutilation when they occur.

All the President's Men (1976)

Directed by Alan J. Pakula
Written by William Goldman, Carl Bernstein (book), Bob Woodward (book)

CAST

Dustin Hoffman (Carl Bernstein)
Robert Redford (Bob Woodward)
Hal Holbrook (Deep Throat)
Jason Robards (Ben Bradlee)

The demands of story telling and appealing to the broadest possible audience for commercial success mean that film is by nature a reductive medium. A cast of thousands looks terrific in crowd scenes, but when depicting a highly complex historical event involving dozens of players, it's much easier to simplify the complexities by condensing a multitude of participants into a few heroes who are easy to identify with and root for. Just as *Mississippi Burning* suggested that the civil rights movement boiled down to a couple of white guys busting heads to crack a murder case, *All the President's Men* was just as reductive in having the Watergate scandal solved by two obscure reporters at the *Washington Post*, Bob Woodward and Carl Bernstein.

The film begins on the pivotal night of June 17, 1972, when burglars hired by the White House broke into Democratic Party headquarters in the Watergate complex in Washington, D.C., and ends two years later as the *Washington Post* wraps up its reportage, bringing down the Nixon administration and sending several of the President's top officials to prison. A coda depicting newspaper stories on the screen reveals the fate of the Watergate conspirators, leaving the impression that their fall was the sole result of intrepid investigative reporting by the no longer obscure Woodward and Bernstein.

A huge gap of time and events between the end of the film and the coda leaves out all the major government figures who actually put the conspirators in jail and kicked Dick Nixon out of office.

Also unrepresented was Senator Sam Ervin, whose committee held the first hearings on the break-in and uncovered the incriminating Oval Office tapes—the real reason Nixon resigned the presidency. Also on the M.I.A. cast list: Representative Peter Rodino, whose committee voted to impeach the president; Archibald Cox, the special prosecutor sacked by Nixon for being too persistent in his investigation of the White House's crimes; and Judge John J. Sirica, who forced the burglars to talk and

Some critics complained that *All the President's Men* implied that two *Washington Post* reporters, Carl Bernstein (Dustin Hoffman, left) and Bob Woodward (Robert Redford), brought down the Nixon White House without help from others.

Nixon to surrender the tapes. The contribution of Pulitzer-Prize-winning reporter Seymour Hersh, whose stories in the *New York Times* also helped bring down the president, is similarly ignored. Attorney General John Mitchell only "appears" in a "cameo" as a voice on the telephone. And the most important figure in the story, Nixon, is only seen on a TV set in the *Washington Post*'s newsroom.

The director's prejudice in favor of the press at the expense of the executive branch, good guys and bad, is reflected in such subtle things as lighting. The *Washington Post* newsroom is drenched in both artificial light and sunlight, a glowing font of truth and righteousness. Despite its image as a sunny Southern capital, Washington in the film is largely filmed at night and its denizens are seen to operate in a sepulchral darkness of covert crimes.

Woodward and Bernstein deserve heroic treatment; they kept the story alive when the public and the rest of the press, afraid of scaring off its sources, ignored the Watergate break-in and cover-up. A Gallup poll in December 1972, a month after Nixon's election, revealed that 48 percent of the public was unaware of the Watergate burglary!

While the director's focus was skewed for drama and simplicity, one situation was an outright fabrication designed to heighten the tension. In the film it's suggested that Woodward and Bernstein are being bugged and that their lives are in danger. A rebuttal comes from a dubious source: convicted Watergate conspirator Charles W. Colson, who said, "*All the President's Men* is steeped in a paranoia as deep as that which I witnessed inside the embattled White House." There was not a shred of evidence, Colson maintained, that either Woodward or Bernstein had been bugged or threatened.

Some of the film's paranoia was based on fact, or as Henry Kissinger once noted, "Even paranoid people have enemies." *Post* editor Ben Bradlee claimed that the Nixon White House pressured the Federal Communications Commission to reject the paper's application to renew the licenses of its six radio and TV stations, and a few years later, a transcript of Nixon's secret White House tapes revealed that he had done just that—to no avail.

While director Alan J. Pakula and screenwriter William Goldman distorted the overall picture, they got the details right with a passion that can only be called anal-retentive. Robert Redford famously hung out with his film character, Bob Woodward, for weeks, learning and imitating the shy reporter's mannerisms. Dustin Hoffman did the same with his *Doppelgänger*, Carl Bernstein, although the two men did not enjoy the close relationship that developed between Woodward and Redford. Every frame of the newsroom scenes is crammed with accurate detail. The film's production designer spent time in the *Post's* newsroom and used the original blueprints to create a 35,000-square-foot set on a soundstage in Burbank, California. The set, costing nearly half a million dollars, was money well spent because when Bradlee visited the Burbank location, he said he felt he was still in Washington. The production designer also conferred with the interior decorators who furnished the *Post's* headquarters. The huge set contained 200 reporters' desks supplied by the same company used by the *Post*. The movie desks were painted the same color as the originals, six and a half PA Blue and 22 PE Green. Although the film was released in 1976, the production designer managed to find 200 1972 calendars for the desks, and the date of the event depicted in the film was circled on the calendars. Telephone directories and newspapers (with the appropriate date) from 1972 were also used as props. The production designer managed to scavenge 270 cartons of papers from the real newsroom containing letters, pamphlets, newspaper clippings, mimeograph sheets, carbons, and reporters' notes. These were all sent to Burbank, where they were unceremoniously dumped in the trash cans next to the 200 desks.

The film's obsession with accuracy extended beyond the cluttered *Post* offices. The Watergate burglary scene was filmed at the Watergate complex. The burglars' walkie-talkies in the film were the same model used by the real culprits. The burglars used Howard Johnson's as a stakeout across from the Watergate building, and so did the film. And in a case of perfect type-casting, the security guard who discovered the unlocked door that led him to the burglars, Frank Willis, reprised his role in the film.

With the casting of a matinee idol like Redford, the film telegraphs who the good guy is, even though his partner, the other good guy, was played by the nebbishy Hoffman. Despite their heroic treatment of Woodward and Bernstein, the film's creators didn't omit some of the investigative reporters' more unsavory actions in pursuit of the story. *All the President's Men* clearly embraces the philosophy that the ends justify the means. Some of the investigative means Woodward and Bernstein use in the film include talking to members of a grand jury, which is illegal, obtaining the credit card records of Watergate conspirator Donald Segretti, and also illegally obtaining phone records that tied burglars to the president's reelection committee, which had the redolent acronym CREEP.

All the President's Men got all the details right, but distorted and shrank the larger picture, which was ironically best summed up by the heroes' boss, *Post* editor Ben Bradlee, who said, "Journalists belong in the audience, not on the stage."

But the siren song of glorification on the big screen won over even the naysayers. Despite his philosophy, Bradlee cooperated closely with the making of the movie. It was a fruitful collaboration. The actor who heroically portrayed Bradlee, Jason Robards Jr., won the best supporting actor Oscar for his efforts.

The People vs. Larry Flynt
(1996)

Directed by Milos Forman
Written by Scott Alexander, Larry Karaszewski

CAST

Woody Harrelson (Larry Flynt)
Courtney Love (Althea Leasure)
Edward Norton (Alan Isaacman)
Brett Harrelson (Jimmy Flynt)
Donna Hanover (Ruth Carter Stapleton)

Mary McCarthy once said of fellow author Lillian Hellman, "Every word she writes, including 'and' and 'the,' is a lie." Critics (but not most film critics) of *The People vs. Larry Flynt* felt almost the same way about the film's deification of *Hustler* magazine publisher Larry Flynt.

Where to begin? Let's start with the title, which refers, inaccurately, to the famous 1988 Supreme Court case Flynt won against the Reverend Jerry Falwell. Flynt's acquittal is presented as a victory for free speech, but it was not a First Amendment case; it was a libel suit, brought by the fundamentalist televangelist after *Hustler* published a cartoon of the reverend having sex with his mother in an outhouse. Falwell claimed the cartoon had caused him emotional distress and was not attacking Flynt's right to publish *Hustler*, as implied in the film. Hanna Rosin wrote in *The New Republic* that Flynt made a bad poster boy for free speech and the battle against censorship: "Flynt didn't go to court to stop the totalitarians from starting down the slippery rope of censorship. He went to court to protect his bank account. In doing so, he accidentally protected the right of free speech."

Kentucky-born Flynt represents the flip side of the American dream, success seen through a glass darkly. Showing early entrepreneurial spirit, 10-year-old Larry appears in the film selling moonshine to an alcoholic in the backwoods of Kentucky. (The real Flynt bought commercially produced liquor, outlawed in his "dry" area of

Kentucky, from a neighboring "wet" area.) Flash to the young man operating a chain of successful strip clubs in Cincinnati who decides to publish a newsletter for club-goers, which evolves into the enormously successful glossy *Hustler* magazine.

Lawsuits against *Hustler* on obscenity charges attempt to put his porn empire out of business. While Flynt is defending a case in Georgia, a right-wing sniper wounds him and his attorney, paralyzing Flynt for life and putting him in his $85,000 gold-plated wheelchair. Excruciating pain leads to an addiction to intra-venous painkillers. To show her "support," his wife, Althea Leasure, a bisexual ex-stripper who's as sexually voracious as her husband, shares her husband's drug cache, and also gets addicted. She drowns in her bathroom jacuzzi before her AIDS-ravaged body gives out on its own. Oh, and in mid-film, Flynt briefly be-comes a born-again Christian under the influence of Jimmy Carter's evangelist sis-ter, Ruth Carter Stapleton.

A supreme ironist, director Milos Forman was not attracted to the irony of a pornographer becoming a free-speech hero. Having survived two totalitarian regimes while losing his parents to Nazi death camps, Forman fled his native Czechoslovakia after government censors suppressed his classic 1967 farce, *The Firemen's Ball*, and emigrated to the U.S. The director turned Flynt's tawdry bio-tale into a bully pulpit against censorship.

He explained his fascination with Flynt by saying, "I've lived long enough in to-talitarian regimes, in a society where censorship was rampant and freedom of the press was abolished. I know what kind of a devastating effect that has, how it chokes creativity in all fields. This country has never lived under a totalitarian regime, so we have a tendency to take freedom of speech for granted."

Film critics bought Forman's take on Flynt and bought the film about him—big time. The *New York Times*' Frank Rich hailed it as "the most timely and patriotic movie of the year" when it debuted on Christmas Day in 1996. Five Golden Globe nominations followed, and the film seemed a shoo-in for an Oscar sweep. The South-ern California branch of the ACLU gave Forman its Torch of Liberty Award for up-holding First Amendment values.

Then a funny thing happened. A member of the media actually picked up a copy of *Hustler* and looked at what was inside. (Forman mystifyingly confessed that he had never looked at the magazine!) In an Op Ed piece in the *New York Times* two weeks after the film's release, feminist Gloria Steinem denounced Flynt and *Hustler* as misogynist and racist. "*Hustler* [in the film] is depicted as tacky at worst, and maybe even honest for showing full nudity. What's left out are the magazine's images of women being beaten, tortured and raped, women subjected to degradations from bestiality to sexual slavery."

The film did portray *Hustler*'s content as a brave effort to break social taboos and dramatized Flynt's tasteless but harmless tweaking of upper-class sensibilities while presenting him as an Everyman with every dirty picture imaginable. "Tacky" in Steinem's term. The film mentions *Hustler*'s spread of nude photos of Jacqueline Onassis, an X-rated cartoon of Dorothy and the Tin Man ("Dorothy!" a rightwing censor fumes in the film), and interracial couples. What the film doesn't show, and what Steinem and other critics who jumped on her bandwagon were happy to share with fans of the film who, like the director, didn't read *Hustler*, was a catalogue of human degradation and an obsession with excrement and well-endowed black men.

The words of the *New York Times*' Frank Rich—"What makes this movie so effective is that it doesn't sentimentalize or airbrush Larry Flynt"—must have come back to haunt him when he read Steinem's description of *Hustler*'s actual content in the pages of his own newspaper.

Absent from Forman's presentation of Flynt as a fuzzy, cuddly pornographer were graphic images, like those in the magazine, of women being gang-raped on a pool table, a naked woman in handcuffs who is shaved, raped, and killed by guards in a concentration camp, and *Hustler*'s popular cartoon figure "Chester the Molester," a pedophile whose creator, Dwain Tinseyl, was convicted of molesting his daughter. Steinem's concerns derived from personal and public motivations. A few months after *Hustler*'s depiction of gang rape on a pool table, a real-life copycat version occurred in a New Bedford, Massachusetts, pub. *Hustler* responded to the attack by featuring a postcard of a woman on a pool table with the caption: "Greetings from New Bedford, Mass. The Portuguese Gang-Rape Capital of America." After she wrote an earlier critique of the magazine, Steinem found herself in *Hustler*'s dog house with her face on a "Most Wanted" poster and a photo spread which depicts her sexual mutilation. Given *Hustler*'s power to generate copycat atrocities, Steinem's piece in the *Times* was more than an abstract argument about porn's political incorrectness and represented a *cri de coeur*, her fear that some psycho might act out Flynt's magazine mutilation of her.

Steinem was writing in a family newspaper and her description of the real *Hustler*, unseen in the film, had to be G-rated. But the *New Republic,* which caters to an adult readership, catalogued *Hustler* horrors in a way almost as triple-X-rated as the magazine itself. The *New Republic's* Hanna Rosin summed up Flynt's point of view: "*Hustler*'s preferred sex toy is a pile of shit." Then Rosin described pictures in the magazine of women smeared with excrement and another woman's rear end with diarrhea dripping down her leg.

Hustler's racism, apparently unknown to the left-leaning intelligentsia who praised the film, may be more shocking than its misogyny. Blacks in the magazine speak in stereotyped ebonics and wave preposterously large penises. One cartoon showed black activist minister Louis Farrakhan eating watermelon while spying on two white women having sex.

Forman left *Hustler*'s ugly side out of the film. Ironically, for a man who suffered censorship as a director in Stalinist Czechoslovakia and denounces it in the film, Forman engages in a great deal of self-censorship in *The People vs. Larry Flynt* by sanitizing his hero.

With no sense of irony, however, Forman responded to his critics and explained why he avoided the truly dark side of Larry Flynt: "Biopics are boring . . . Censorship is bad enough, but even worse is the self-censorship which it provokes. Because you start to tamper with your own honesty."

Forman tampered with it a lot. He romanticizes Flynt's tragic love for his dead wife while making no mention of Flynt's previous four marriages. And in the film's supreme moment of unintended irony, while Flynt discusses the magazine's brave decision to photograph women totally nude at a time when it was presumed to be illegal, the film blurs the crotch shot of one of the magazine's models, something the real Larry Flynt would never have done.

The attacks against the film's airbrushed omissions became personal when Flynt's daughter, Tonya Flynt-Vega, publicly claimed her father had sexually molested her. Absent from the film is the Christmas card her absentee, deadbeat dad sent her and her destitute mother. The card contained $500 and a cartoon of Santa exposing himself to a little girl, a sad Ghost of Flynt-Vega's Christmas Past.

"This movie makes *Hustler* into a coffee-table magazine," his daughter said. "It lifts my father up as some kind of American hero, like Bonnie and Clyde. He's very manipulative, and he's just bought himself a respectable place in history."

Not quite. Here's the epilogue to the canonization of Larry Flynt, which the supreme ironist Milos Forman might have enjoyed—except it happened to him. After Steinem's Op Ed attack, Hollywood's liberal elite fell in with the feminist line. After her piece ran in the *Times* on January 10, 1997, *The People vs. Larry Flynt*, which did terrific business in limited release, went into a tailspin and disappeared from theaters within weeks, although industry reporters believed it bombed in the boonies due to lack of interest in the subject matter—free speech—and not because of revulsion toward the film's R-rated porn. Reporters bolstered their argument by noting that the film continued to do well in big cities while failing to play in Peoria. But the expensive movie, all agreed, was a major commercial disappointment, grossing only $20 million.

It got worse. Touted as a sure-fire Oscar magnet, *The People vs. Larry Flynt* ended up receiving only best actor (Woody Harrelson) and best director nominations after an anonymous opponent took out a full-page ad in *Daily Variety* during the middle of Oscar voting. The ad featured the ironic Oscar solicitation "For your consideration . . .," followed by a complete reprint of Steinem's denunciation in the *New York Times*.

And worst: When Oscar-nominated Forman got out of his limo at the Academy Awards, "fans" booed and spat on him. He didn't win the Oscar either.

A Civil Action
(1998)

Directed by Steven Zaillian
Written by Steven Zaillian, Jonathan Harr (book)

CAST

John Travolta (Jan Schlichtmann)
Robert Duvall (Jerome Facher)
Tony Shalhoub (Kevin Conway)
William H. Macy (James Gordon)
John Lithgow (Judge Walter J. Skinner)
Kathleen Quinlan (Anne Anderson)

Writer-director Steven Zaillian had a tough assignment—turn Jonathan Harr's 1995 best-seller, *A Civil Action*, about two corporate polluters who may have caused the death of five children, into a movie. Zaillian had adapted and won a best screen-writing Oscar for another difficult book based on fact, *Schindler's List*, but *A Civil Action*'s story was arguably more daunting and the material was not promising. The writer had to turn a sleazy, ambulance-chasing attorney, Jan Schlictmann, into a hero despite the fact that Schlictmann botched his case against the polluters, W.R. Grace and Beatrice Foods, one of whom was acquitted while the other settled with a paltry payment to the victims' families and no apology.

There were no real winners in the case, which began in 1971, when three-and-a-half-year-old Jimmy Anderson of East Woburn, Massachusetts, developed leukemia and died. In 1979, the *Woburn Daily Times* reported a possible cause of Jimmy's death: two wells that supplied the town's drinking water had been shut down after they were found to be polluted with the carcinogen trichloroethylene, an industrial solvent dumped in the 1960s on the grounds of a tannery jointly owned by Beatrice Foods and W.R. Grace. Five children in East Woburn later died of leukemia.

In 1982, Jan Schlictmann, a partner in a tiny Boston law firm, filed a $100 million lawsuit on behalf of the families of the children against W.R. Grace and Beatrice. During the trial, Schlictmann rejected a $20 million offer to settle the case, certain he could get much more at trial. Beatrice and W.R. Grace argued that there was no direct link between trichloroethylene and leukemia. Schlictmann hired expensive scientific experts, which made his legal costs soar to $2.6 million. One of the experts erroneously testified on how the toxins had entered the drinking water. Beatrice was acquitted of the charges, and W.R. Grace settled for $8 million, which after expenses and Schlictmann's cut of $2.2 million left the families with only $450,000 each. The $20 million cost of litigating the case ruined Schlictmann, who lost his home and Porsche. He ended up living in a shabby apartment and was dropped from a magazine's list of Boston's most eligible bachelors.

Zaillian's task of ennobling Schlictmann was helped by the casting of John Travolta, who brought his patented charisma to a flawed character, but the screenwriter was still saddled with grotesque dialogue from the book, which he faithfully put in Travolta's mouth, including a scene where the "hero" says, "I can appreciate the theatrical value of several dead kids," as he conjures up the zillion dollar award he hopes to win for the parents of those "several dead kids."

The penultimate scene is a real downer, showing Travolta in his dingy bachelor apartment, no longer one of the town's most eligible bachelors. But Zaillian seemed so desperate for a happy ending that he fudged the facts of the trial's aftermath. A crawl appears at the end of the film and says in part, "Faced with the prospect of returning to court, [W.R. Grace and Beatrice] agreed to pay their share of the $69.4 million in cleanup costs—the largest, most expensive of its kind in New England history." Viewers leave the theater with the feel-good impressions that long-suffering East Woburn has finally been cleaned up.

Not quite. The crawl failed to mention that the EPA gave the two perpetrators 50 years to clean up the toxic site. The luckless residents of Woburn still can't drink tap water to this day. The *New Republic* called the EPA's leisurely cleanup order "a testimony to government impotence; it will take decades before the groundwater is clean enough to drink."

The story gets sadder. The fudged happy ending may have been a result of the fact that the film was produced by the compulsively cheerful Disney, which wanted an upbeat finale whatever the cost, including the truth. The studio's participation in the film's content had other questionable elements. Fearing a lawsuit, lawyers for Disney had Zaillian fax the crawl to Grace, which was allowed to edit it. Zaillian admitted, "They [Grace's attorneys] wanted the wording to be very precise. They'd ask me what I wanted to say. I sent it to them. They'd review it, and sometimes they'd say it's fine, and sometimes they wanted a word or two changed."

Anne Anderson, whose son Jimmy's death in 1972 launched the case, believed Schlictmann botched the trial and resented the sympathetic portrayal of an attorney decimated by *his* loss of home and car, while the victims lost their children. "I'm sorry, but I can't feel sorry for Jan as he goes off to replenish himself in Hawaii," where Schlictmann went to lick his wounds after the trial.

Adding insult to injury, W.R. Grace still denies that trichloroethylene and other toxins it dumped in East Woburn ever made it into the town's wells and drinking water.

The Perfect Storm
(2000)

Directed by Wolfgang Petersen
Written by William D. Wittliff, Sebastian Junger (book)

CAST

George Clooney (Capt. Billy Tyne)
Mark Wahlberg (Bobby Shatford)
Diane Lane (Christina Cotter)
Karen Allen (Melissa Brown)
Mary Elizabeth Mastrantonio (Linda Greenlaw)
John C. Reilly (Dale "Murph" Murphy)
Michael Ironside (Bob Brown)

Big-budget movies almost always have happy endings. The huge cost of making these films requires the largest possible audience to turn a profit, and it's axiomatic that people like to leave the theater with a warm and fuzzy feeling inside, which you don't get from a downer ending. Director Wolfgang Petersen and screenwriter Bill Wittliff had a big problem when they tried to turn Sebastian Junger's 1997 nonfiction best-seller, *The Perfect Storm*, about the crew of a Massachusetts swordfish boat, the *Andrea Gail*, that collided with three converging storms in 1991, into a blockbuster with a budget of $140 million. Anyone who had read the immensely popular book—and spoilsport film critics informed those who hadn't—knows that the entire six-man crew dies at the end. It's hard to make a popcorn movie about death.

Author Sebastian Junger fretted that Petersen would inject a happy ending into his tale, but the director assured him he would stick to the facts. "I was worried that not wanting to kill off a big-name actor, they would have some of the *Andrea Gail* crew survive. [The director] had no intention of departing from the book, he told me."

Petersen, however, had an elastic concept of the "truth." The film version does kill off the entire crew of the *Andrea Gail*, including the big-name actor George Clooney, who captains the boat. But moviegoers had to be appeased—not to mention stockholders at Warner Bros., which had ponied up $140 million. So Petersen and Wittliff fleshed out footnotes in the book about other ships caught in the storm whose crews did survive, and gave them equal time with the main event, the *Andrea Gail's* disappearance with all crew lost.

As the *Andrea Gail* is about to go under, the director intercuts scenes that were only footnotes in the book, about the sailboat *Satori*, which is rescued during a thrilling sequence in which a Coast Guard helicopter crew leaps into the sea and saves the *Satori* crew. For more drama, the helicopter has to ditch at sea after running out of gas, which never happened. As a counterpoint to the loss of the *Andrea Gail's* crew, those on the *Satori* survive. The final effect, according to the *New Times'* Robert Wilonsky is that "Petersen and Wittliff *have* given a downer tale a happy near-ending. The crew of the *Andrea Gail* may disappear beneath the sea, but all is not lost to the graveyard. We can leave the theater satisfied that at least some have survived." A lot of people left the theater feeling good and then spread the word, with the result that that *The Perfect Storm* became the No. 2 hit of the year (after the sequel to *Mission: Impossible*) with a box-office take in the U.S. of $179 million.

Despite a contented public, critics found fault with the film's cardboard characters, melodramatic additions and exclusions, and special effects that looked fake despite the enormous amount of money lavished on them. Sharks, moviemakers' favorite villains of the deep since *Jaws*, attack the *Andrea Gail*, although another boat suffered the attack in the book. Critics complained that the sharks and the rest of the seagoing "cast" looked "cheesy," per *Rolling Stone*'s Peter Travers, who said of the swordfish the *Andrea Gail* braves the storm to catch: "The inert fishies here look like refugees from frozen foods (actually, they're animatronic creatures with what appear to be motorized tail fins that flap wanly on cue.)" *Rolling Stone* also felt the digitized ocean, the main "character" in the film, looked, "well, digital—pristine, processed and lifeless, while the high seas didn't look like the waters off the coast of Newfoundland where the *Andrea Gail* went down but like a studio water tank," which is where George Lucas' Industrial Light and Magic created a computerized—and unconvincing storm. *The Independent* in London thought the waves looked "cartoonish" and reminded critic Gilbert Adair of the animated tsunamis that overwhelmed Mickey Mouse in "The Sorcerer's Apprentice" sequence of *Fantasia*.

The real Captain Billy Tyne, played by George Clooney, had an interesting, dramatic life off ship counseling drug addicted teens, but the director omitted that back story in favor of a fictional romance between Tyne and the female captain of another ship (Mary Elizabeth Mastrantonio). Tyne's motive for taking on the storm, unmentioned in the book, is fictionalized and presented as a challenge to his manhood when the *Andrea Gail*'s owner criticizes him for not bringing in enough swordfish. Tyne retorts with macho bravado, "I'm gonna bring you more fish than you ever dreamed of." The incident where a crew member of the *Andrea Gail* is dragged through the ocean with a hook in his hand also occurred in the book, but on another vessel mentioned in a footnote.

Meteorologists even quibbled with the title of the book and film, whose "perfect" label was meant to be an ironic substitution for "worst." University of Washington meteorologist Cliff Mass insisted that the champ was the Columbus Day storm that hit Northern California and British Columbia in 1962, if you define "worst" by Mass' measure of damage and destruction. But Junger countered that he didn't mean to equate perfect with worst and that the storm in his book does rank as the worst if you go by wave height. In that case, Junger's 1991 storm wins with 100-foot waves, the highest ever recorded, according to research meteorologist Val Swail of Environment Canada.

A fish story with pixilated waves, mechanized fish, and a romance as artificial as the special effects—pun-loving critics couldn't resist calling the film an "Imperfect Storm," but audiences disagreed and stormed overflowing theaters.

Boys Don't Cry (1999)

Directed by Kimberly Peirce
Written by Kimberly Peirce, Andy Bienen

CAST

Hilary Swank (Teena Brandon)
Chloe Sevigny (Lana Tisdel)
Peter Sarsgaard (John Lotter)
Brendan Sexton III (Tom Nissen)
Alicia Goranson (Candace)
Jeanetta Arnett (Lana's Mom)

Although *Boys Don't Cry* earned terrific reviews and a best actress Oscar for Hilary Swank, who played a small town Nebraska woman murdered for passing herself off as a male, some of the real life people in the film cried foul. One sued.

Boys Don't Cry tells the nightmarish story of Teena Brandon, who changed her name to Brandon Teena, dressed like a man, and fell in love with a high school student named Lana Tisdel in Falls City, Nebraska, in 1993. When two friends, if that's the right term, learned of Teena/Brandon's deception, they raped and killed Teena and two of her roommates.

A few days before the film's release in October 1999, lawyers for Lana Tisdel tried to have her name removed from the film, an impossibility, or stop its release. After the film opened, Tisdel's attorneys hit the producer, Fox Searchlight Pictures, with a slander suit. Although the actress who portrayed her in the film, Chloe Sevigny, went on to win an Oscar nomination for best supporting actress, Tisdel was not happy with her screen incarnation. She had good reason not to be.

In her suit, Tisdel claimed that the movie referred to her as "lazy, white trash and a skanky snake" and falsely implied she had sex in exchange for alcohol and used hallucinogens. The film also placed Tisdel at the scene of the murder, which she felt gave the impression she had been an accessory to her lover's shotgun slaying, although in reality she had been asleep in the murderers' car at the time. The film created a mixture of anger and fear in Tisdel, who said she received death threats from Teena's mother because of her apparent participation in the murder. Tisdel also blamed the film for getting her fired from her factory job.

The wording of Tisdel's lawsuit suggests that fear of reprisal and homophobia fueled the suit. Tisdel strongly objected to a scene where she and Teena undress each other and make love. Her suit tried to set the record, uh, straight: "Further, [the film] falsely depicts Ms. Tisdel as being unfazed by the discovery that the object of her sexual desire whom she believes was a male, was in actuality a female transvestite and/or transsexual who is later murdered." Tisdel's claim was backed up by Aphrodite Jones, who wrote the definitive nonfiction book about the case, *All She Wanted*. Jones confirmed that Tisdel ended the relationship, which the film portrays as warm and protracted, as soon as she learned Teena's true sexual identity. Tisdel told Jones she only had sex with Teena once, and that she was drunk at the time. The film also dramatizes the couple's plans to elope. The lawsuit said, "[The film] goes to great lengths to portray a modern day gender bending Romeo and Juliet relationship that simply did not exist as depicted. There was never any proposal of marriage made to Ms. Tisdel."

The depiction of the residents of Falls City as redneck, murderous homophobes was for some reason blamed on Tisdel, or in the slander suit's words, "[It is] objectionable to plaintiff and to a reasonable person of ordinary sensibilities in that the plaintiff has and will be scorned and/or abandoned by her friends and family . . . [Tisdel has] been and will be exposed to contempt and ridicule." Considering the fate of her late boy/girlfriend, Tisdel had good reason to be very afraid of a backlash from local vigilantes. The film only inflamed the climate of homophobia in Falls

City; for example, a fictional character warns Teena, "They hang faggots out here." However, author Aphrodite Jones, who spent a lot of time in Falls City interviewing residents for her 1994 book, didn't feel the film had overemphasized the town's endemic bigotry, and Tisdel was not exaggerating the danger the film had placed her in. "Falls City is a very conservative, racist, and homophobic place. For the town to be reminded that [Tisdel] was in a lesbian relationship—that makes her a target," Jones said.

The suit's overall complaint was that "Miss Tisdel believes the film casts her in a false light." Although the film's Lana is open-minded and loving even after she discovers Teena's gender, the rest of the portrait is less than picture pretty. In real life, both of Lana's parents were on welfare, and the film portrays her mother as an alcoholic, homophobic harpie. In the film, Lana does lots of drugs and leads a purposeless life with a dead-end job in a factory.

Adding injury to insult, Fox Searchlight had failed to pay Tisdel for the use of her name, the suit contended. In addition to slander and invasion of privacy, Tisdel sued for unauthorized use of her name.

Although her lover's story did not, Tisdel's had a happy ending, if you don't count her ticked off acquaintances in Falls City. Four months after filing suit, she settled with the studio without disclosing the terms. It's amazing how a presumed large cash payoff can change one's film critique. When the suit was settled, Tisdel raved about the star of the film that had caused her so much fear and distress. "I would also like the public to know how realistic I found Hilary Swank's portrayal of Brandon. She captured the real Brandon," Tisdel said. Interestingly, Tisdel made no comment about the other Oscar-nominated actress, Chloe Sevigny, her film avatar.

For such an otherwise liberal minded drama, *Boys Don't Cry* omitted an important real life character, who was also murdered that night. In the film, Teena and her female roommate are shot at point blank range by two drunken friends, one of whom was a jealous ex-boyfriend. In real life, there was a third murder victim, the black boyfriend of Lana's sister, Leslie.

Leslie Tisdel was not happy about her neglected boyfriend, whose story may have been almost as compelling as the protagonist's. She said, "I frown on that. They're just looking at Brandon Teena, and they're not wanting to think about anybody else. It's like, 'There were two other victims? Who cares?'"

Author Aphrodite Jones, who did include the black man, Philip Devine, in her account of the triple slayings, also regretted his exclusion from the film. "Philip was someone who climbed mountains on one leg, literally, in his lifetime, and he was a good soul."

The director, Kimberly Peirce, pleaded economy rather than indifference. The inclusion of Devine would have also necessitated adding his girlfriend, Leslie Tisdel, to the story, and the director felt there were already too many *dramatis personae* in the drama. "I already had seven main characters. I didn't have room for Lana's sister," Peirce said.

There was a more surprising omission that had nothing to do with economy of casting. JoAnn Brandon, Teena's mother, complained that the film filed to mention an important psychological factor that may have led to what the film called the "gender crisis" that prompted Teena's tragic masquerade. Mrs. Brandon revealed that her daughter had been sexually molested as a young girl and had told her mother that she chose to live as a man "so no other man could touch her." Mrs. Brandon was also furious when Swank thanked her dead daughter in her acceptance speech at the Academy Awards.

The Insider
(1999)

Directed by Michael Mann
Written by Eric Roth, Michael Mann, Marie Brenner (magazine article)

CAST

Al Pacino (Lowell Bergman)
Russell Crowe (Jeffrey Wigand)
Christopher Plummer (Mike Wallace)
Diane Venora (Liane Wigand)

Philip Baker Hall (Don Hewitt)
Michael Gambon (Thomas Sandefur)

No one, it seems, was pleased with *The Insider* except the critics, who hailed it as one of the year's 10 best in 1999, and the Academy of Motion Pictures Arts and Sciences, which gave the actor who played the film's hero, Russell Crowe, a best actor nomination.

Based on a true story about corruption in the tobacco industry (surprise!) and corruption and cowardice among respected journalists (genuine surprise), *The Insider* managed to antagonize just about everyone the film depicted.

Crowe played whistle-blower Jeffrey Wigand, the $300,000-a-year vice president for research and development at the Brown & Williamson Tobacco Corp. Wigand was fired in 1993 for allegedly being a general pain in the neck to work with. Brown & Williamson would find Wigand an even bigger pain once he became an ex-employee. Wigand claimed the real reason he was fired had nothing to do with his job performance and everything to do with his complaints that the tobacco company was spiking its cigarettes with hazardous chemicals and increasing the amount of nicotine in its product to keep customers puffing.

Enraged by his dismissal, a year later Wigand took his story to the top-rated and most respected TV investigative news program in America, *60 Minutes*. He told his story to segment producer Lowell Bergman (Al Pacino), who taped Wigand spilling his guts about the crimes of his former employers. Mike Wallace, the venerable 81-year-old anchor, would be the on-camera "reporter for Wigand's segment."

When CBS learned that Wigand had signed a confidentiality agreement with the tobacco company, network lawyers warned the show's executive producer, Don Hewitt, and Wallace that the segment, if aired, could set them up for a billion-dollar lawsuit from the tobacco giant for tortious interference, i.e., interference with a contract that results in financial loss for the plaintiff. CBS was about to be bought by Westinghouse, and the lawyers feared Westinghouse would back out of the deal if it became liable for damages won by Brown & Williamson. According to the film, money prompted Hewitt and Wallace to accept CBS' decision to kill the story because they owned stock in the company, which would greatly increase in value if the merger with Westinghouse took place.

Mike Wallace was the first and probably the loudest to complain about the film. He was incensed by inaccuracies about his participation in the controversy. An early draft of the script he read showed him making sure there would be a Jacuzzi in his Beirut hotel suite during a trip to Lebanon to interview a leader of the Muslim extremist group Hezbollah. (The scene was pure invention and never made it into the final cut.)

But Wallace was most enraged by the film's portrayal of him as a craven, crass journalist who caved in to CBS' demand to drop Wigand's segment. Al Pacino hero-ically shows his character, Lowell Bergman, single-handedly standing up to the CBS brass in his fight to air Wigand's explosive accusations. (Bergman was a paid consult-ant to the film, and it's his take on the story that ended up on the screen.)

In a series of interviews he gave denouncing *The Insider*, Wallace claimed he had backed Bergman from the start and opposed CBS' legal staff, describing him-self and Bergman as "two peas in a pod, shoulder to shoulder throughout the en-tire exercise." In a letter to director Michael Mann, Wallace lamented his por-trayal as a "soulless and cowardly laggard who lost his moral compass until Lowell set me back on the straight path . . . What's a nice way of saying it? [Bergman] pissed all over us."

The film does excoriate Wallace, who is also depicted as prissy, self-righteous, and barely involved with the reporting of the stories he anchors. In the climactic con-frontation between Bergman, who presses to air the segment, and CBS' chief attor-ney, the film's Wallace caves in, saying, "I'm with Don [Hewitt] on this." Hewitt, who also stood to earn a stock windfall from the CBS-Westinghouse merger, is portrayed as even more obsequious to the network than Wallace. An eyewitness at the meet-ing, Robert Kindler, the CBS attorney in charge of the merger with Westinghouse, said about the network's decision to kill Wigand's interview, "I was there and it was never discussed. It was never an issue." A CBS insider added that Don Hewitt had no power to save the segment, even if he had wanted to.

Director Mann and Marie Brenner, who wrote the *Vanity Fair* piece on Wigand that inspired the film, referred to several interviews Wallace gave to the *New York Times* and other publications in which Wallace defended CBS' decision to kill the segment, although the film does show Wallace eventually siding with Bergman and pushing to air Wigand's interview, but only after the *Wall Street Journal* published an embarrassing account of CBS' cowardly capitulation to Big Tobacco.

The *Wall Street Journal*, however, was also unhappy with *The Insider*. In the film, Bergman, who is the real hero of the piece, is shown leaking internal CBS documents to the *Journal*, which then ran its story. The paper insisted Bergman made no contribution to its piece.

The former Mrs. Jeffrey Wigand, Lucretia Nimrocks, was so enraged with her depiction in the film, she sued the filmmakers. *The Insider* shows her leaving her husband because of pressure the tobacco company brings to bear on her family, including canceling their health insurance, which they desperately needed for their asthmatic daughter's enormous medical bills. (There's a particularly creepy scene in the film in which the then CEO of Brown & Williamson, the late Thomas Sandefur, summons Wigand to his office and threatens to cancel his insurance if he talks to the press. The scene was a total fabrication and Wigand never met the CEO.) The former Mrs. Wigand said the breakup of their relationship had nothing to do with her husband's problems with his former employer, Brown & Williamson. Two pivotal scenes in the movie that drive Mrs. Wigand over the edge never happened, she claimed. After the tobacco company becomes aware of Wigand's dealings with CBS, he finds a bullet in his mailbox. Also, a threatening email pops up on his home computer with the message, "WE WILL KILL YOU." The former Mrs. Wigand said there was no email terrorism and, based on her conversations with FBI agents who investigated the threats, she believes her ex-husband planted the bullet in the mailbox himself!

Even Jeffrey Wigand, the alleged hero of the controversy if not the film, complained that *The Insider* made him look spineless and consumed with self-doubt. Wigand also objected to Bergman's heroic treatment in the film. "The movie gives Mr. Bergman a lot of credit for a lot of things he did not do," Wigand said.

The public had the final say on *The Insider*, and it responded by staying away from the complex character-driven legal thriller. Despite the critical kudos and the Oscar nod, *The Insider* was a major box-office disappointment.

The only person who seemed happy with the final product and its accuracy—other than the director and Bergman—was the journalist whose magazine piece served as the source. *Vanity Fair's* Marie Brenner said, "I have been very impressed with how hard they have tried to be so accurate. It's a movie. It's not a documentary . . . It's emotionally accurate." Bergman added, "It's emotionally and philosophically accurate."

Michael Mann, who created the TV series *Miami Vice* and added that show's eerie atmospherics to the look of *The Insider*, which seems to have been shot in various shades of blue, insisted that the big picture was faithful to events even if little pieces of it were not. "There's very little in this film that's not substantiated," Mann said. "In the realm of drama, you change everything. You change everything to have it mean exactly the same thing it meant before. You do all the typical things. You collapse time, you combine characters." Bergman conceded his depiction in the film was actually a composite of several journalists who broke the Wigand story.

Mann defended his handling of the facts by alluding to another film that got the big picture (Watergate) right while altering details and even fabricating dialogue to make the big picture even bigger dramatically. "Nobody ever said in *All the President's Men*, 'Follow the money,'" Mann noted. "The only guy who said that was Bill Goldman, the screenwriter."

Erin Brockovich (2000)

Directed by Steven Soderbergh
Written by Susannah Grant

CAST

Julia Roberts (Erin Brockovich)
Albert Finney (Ed Masry)
Aaron Eckhart (George)
Marg Helgenberger (Donna Jensen)
Peter Coyote (Kurt Potter)
Scotty Leavenworth (Matthew Brockovich)
Gemmenne De la Pena (Katie Brockovich)

In *Erin Brockovich*, Julia Roberts is the eponymous heroine, a lowly file clerk at a minor suburban law firm who discovers that the residents of Hinckley, a small rural California town, are being poisoned by the corporate monolith Pacific Gas & Electric, which has leaked the deadly toxin chromium 6 into the town's drinking water. Brockovich gets her boss, the ailing, about to retire attorney Ed Masry (Albert Finney) to sue PG&E, and together they win hundreds of millions of dollars for cancer-stricken citizens of Hinckley. Everyone goes home happy (including the moviegoers who ponied up a total of $200 million to see the film) except the evil corporate polluter, PG&E, which is being sued by residents of other towns with claims similar to Hinckley's. Guess who are leading that fight? Our heroine, who earned $2 million as her take of the award, and her boss, who has decided to postpone retirement.

Not so fast, say some of the Hinckley townsfolk. To avoid an even costlier trial, PG&E agreed to settle the case for $333 million in 1996. Masry and his associates, who took the case on a contingency basis and had out of pocket expenses of $12 million that nearly bankrupted them during the suit, got the standard 40 percent of the $333 million award. That meant the lawyers got $133 million, and the plaintiffs $196 million or $300,000 each.

Some cancer victims in Hinckley got much less and were outraged by Hollywood's treatment of the lawyers as heroic do-gooders. "I didn't want to see the movie, but I did. Give me a break! What shit! They depicted the lawyers as concerned about the residents," said an angry Hinckley resident, Diane Zuniga. Her mother only got $40,000, while her father, brother, and sister received no money, despite the health problems they continue to suffer after drinking chromium 6-laced water, which leached into the soil from PG&E's gas transmission plant. "Does Erin really care? I don't know. I just know I want enough money to get this crap out of my body," Zuniga said.

Four hundred of Hinckley's 1,000 residents received nothing from the settlement. One of them, Susan Cordova, believes chromium contamination led to her hysterectomy, but Masry's associates turned down her request for representation twice, telling her she should be "ashamed" because her illness wasn't life-threatening. (The lawyers refute Cordova's allegation.) Thelma Hunter, who suffers kidney cancer and a shoulder eaten away by the carcinogen, and Tom Owens, who has numerous lesions, both got turned down by Brockovich and Masry. Lynn Morris, another stricken resident, said, "Most of us got screwed."

When *Time* magazine told the real Erin Brockovich of these complaints, she said, "What goofballs. It disappoints me."

The details of the settlement were confidential, and many of the plaintiffs felt the amounts had been arbitrarily doled out. "Masry and Brockovich got greedy," said Ron Gonzales, who developed skin cancer and received double his original award of $100,000 after he complained to Masry. Gonzales' sister, who has cancer of the intestines, got $2 million, the same amount Brockovich received. "They could have settled for less and given the money to the people that deserve it. Masry is portraying himself as such a big hero. He and Erin are claiming to be saviors, but Erin got more [*sic*] than my sister did. And my sister's sick," Gonzales said.

Masry, a 67-year-old curmudgeon, dismissed the allegations and scolded the investigative reporter who brought them up. "Why are you being stupid? It was a complicated $333 million settlement. Are you an idiot?"

One hundred ailing children benefited from the settlement, but they got less than is customary. California law allows lawyers to take only 25 percent of awards made to minors, but the judges in the private arbitration gave Masry and his colleagues one-third. The film doesn't mention that some of the judges received an all-expense-paid luxury cruise of the Mediterranean, paid for by Masry's colleagues in the case. Also unmentioned is the fact that in addition to their $133 million cut, the plaintiffs' attorneys took $10 million off the top for "expenses," even though their 40 percent share of contingency cases is supposed to include expenses.

Some plaintiffs were also miffed that they were turned into composite characters in the film, their suffering in effect condensed for easy consumption along with the popcorn. *Erin Brockovich*'s executive producer, Carla Shamberg, pled dramatic necessity. "You're allowed in movieland to fictionalize, but the essence of the story is true. Unless we buy the rights to everyone's story, we have to fictionalize and condense."

Adding insult to injury, director Steven Soderbergh snubbed Hinckley by filming in nearby Boron, California.

The real villain of the piece, PG&E, was left to argue a lame defense in the court of public opinion, having lost in arbitration. "The movie is an entertainment vehicle, certainly not a documentary," a spokesman for the company said.

Attorney Michael Dolan couldn't agree more with PG&E's description of *Erin Brockovich*, even though he is suing the corporation on behalf of Hinckley residents who got shut out of the $300-million-plus payday. "I read the script, and the only true part was Erin Brockovich's name," Dolan said.

The public hasn't heard the last of the title's heroine. Hollywood loves sequels to blockbusters, and the story's epilogue seems tailor made for Roman numeral follow-ups. *Erin Brockovich II* might focus on the tireless Masry's new lawsuit against PG&E. The plaintiffs this time will be the citizens of Topock and Kettleman City, both in California, where two PG&E plants are accused of also leaking chromium.

As for the real Erin Brockovich, despite her $2 million share of the settlement, she's still at Masry's law firm, although the divorced and remarried mother of three with little formal education, who started work there as a file clerk, has a new title, director of research.

AntiTrust
(2001)

Directed by Peter Howitt
Written by Howard Franklin

CAST

Ryan Phillippe (Milo Hoffman)
Rachael Leigh Cook (Lisa Calighan)
Claire Forlani (Alice Poulson/Rebecca Paul)
Tim Robbins (Gary Winston)
Douglas McFerran (Bob Shrot)
Richard Roundtree (Lyle Barton)
Tygh Runyan (Larry Banks)
Yee Jee Tso (Teddy Chin)

AntiTrust takes the geeky preoccupation and belief that computer source code should be free of intellectual property restraints—"all human knowledge should be free," the film's hero, a computer programmer and inventor, shouts—and turns this unlikely subject for drama into a high tech James Bond-type caper complete with a Bond-like villain who has a gadget-filled headquarters and wants to take over the world.

But the bespectacled, sweater-fancying villain Gary Winston (Tim Robbins), the billionaire head of a software behemoth in the Pacific Northwest with a mammoth futuristic house and problems with the Justice Department over antitrust violations, bears an even greater resemblance to Bill Gates than Goldfinger or Dr. No.

Instead of Microsoft, the film's omnivorous corporation is called NURV (Never Underestimate Radical Vision) and instead of Redmond, Washington, its campus-like headquarters are located in Portland, Oregon. And unlike Bill Gates, Gary Winston eliminates inconvenient rivals by having them beaten to death with a baseball bat. Oh, and Winston wants to link and thus control every electronic device in the world with a satellite delivery system called Synapse.

Before Winston and Synapse can take over the world, however, there's this annoying problem with the satellite system. It takes too long to download data. (For a futuristic movie, director Peter Howitt and screenwriter Howard Franklin don't seem to have heard of DSL.)

Recent Stanford grad Milo Hoffman (Ryan Phillippe) is a garage tinkerer trying to attract venture capital to launch his invention, which coincidentally will solve mad Winston's download speed problem. Like many programmers, the idealistic Hoffman believes source code could, and should, be free to all with no copyright protection for software, which makes you wonder how he plans to attract capital or make any money off his own software invention.

But Hoffman is seduced into joining Winston at NURV in a Faustian pact in which Hoffman sells his soul (and his invention) to the Mephistophelean Winston in return for a well-paying job at NURV and a really cool silver Mercedes SUV.

While Tim Robbins is more handsome than Bill Gates even when he's forced to sport Gates' unflattering helmet-like hairdo with bangs and Mr. Rogers' taste in cardigans, some critics felt that Winston and his villainy bore some resemblance to Gates' M.O. by noting that a federal judge trying one of the antitrust suits against Microsoft referred to Gates as "Napoleonic," an apt description of the fictional Winston as well.

Although *AntiTrust* is clearly poking gentle fun at the whole Bill Gates-as-mega-lomaniac phenomenon, MGM, the studio that made the film, insisted on a standard denial that "any resemblance between the film's characters and real people is entirely unintentional and accidental, etc. . . ." Perhaps to avoid a libel suit from Gates, since after all his *Doppelgänger* in the film is called a "fascist monopolist" by an idealistic student, MGM went beyond the standard denial when the studio's spokeswoman, Amanda Lundberg, put out a risible refutation that said, "It's a fictional thriller, and it's not based on anybody real, any company, any events, any people that are real." And *JFK* isn't about the president of the United States.

Some analogies between the film's universe and the real-life Gatesian empire of dot.com bounty were rendered inaccurate by the brief march of time. *AntiTrust* was filmed while dot.com fever still raged, but was released in early 2001 after the dot.com bubble had burst, making many of the lines unintentionally ironic. As in the case where a Justice Department investigator (Richard Roundtree) offers Phillippe's Hoffman $42,000 and a Buick to spy on his boss, Winston. Before the dot-com bust, it seems like a paltry offer compared to Hoffman's Mercedes and stock options in NURV, but after the bust it sounds like a good deal. Other dated incidents in *AntiTrust* include Hoffman's geeky partner getting excited about attracting "eight fifty" in venture capital, which led one viewer at a press preview to quip, "Yeah, eight dollars and fifty cents," referring to the flight of capital away from Silicon Valley start-ups. And when a security guard in the film complains about "stock option billion-aires," he's referring to an extinct species of millionaire secretaries and janitors who owned a piece of now worthless dot.com pies.

Instead of being a futuristic satire of Internet-driven technology and greed, economic reality and history make *AntiTrust*, per the *New York Times'* A. O. Scott, "the first late-90s-nostalgia picture." A prime time series on Fox about the good old days of paper millionaires seems inevitable with a time slot immediately following *That '70s Show*.

BIBLIOGRAPHY

Behr, Edward. *The Last Emperor.* New York: Bantam Books, 1987.

Bernstein, Carl and Bob Woodward. *All the President's Men.* New York: Simon and Schuster, 1999.

Bial, Raymond. *The Sioux.* New York: Benchmark Books, 1999.

Birley, Anthony Richard. *Marcus Aurelius, A Biography.* New Haven, Conn.: Yale University Press, 1987.

Boyd-Smith, Peter. *Titanic: From Rare Historical Reports.* Southampton, England: Steamship, 1994.

Cameron, Kenneth M. *America on Film: Hollywood and American History.* New York: Continuum, 1997.

Carnes, Mark C. (editor). *Past Imperfect: History According to the Movies.* New York: Henry Holt and Company, 1995.

Chada, Yogesh. *Gandhi: A Life.* New York: John Wiley & Sons, 1999.

Collis, John Stewart. *Christopher Columbus.* New York: Stein and Day, 1977.

Conlon, Gerry. *Proved Innocent.* New York: Plume, 1993.

Crawford, Christina. *Mommie Dearest.* Moscow, Id.: Seven Springs Press, 1997.

Diamond, Arthur. *Charlie Chaplin.* San Diego, Ca.: Lucent Books, 1995.

Dutton, Richard. *William Shakespeare: A Literary Life.* New York: St. Martin's Press, 1989.

D'Este, Carlo. *Patton: A Genius for War.* New York: HarperCollins, 1995.

Ferro, Marc. *Nicholas II: The Last of the Tsars.* New York: Oxford University Press, 1993.

Fraser, George MacDonald. *The Hollywood History of the World.* London: Michael Joseph Ltd., 1988.

Gordon, Mary. *Joan of Arc.* New York: Viking, 2000.

Green, Robert. *King George III.* New York: F. Watts, 1997.

Grindon, Leger. *Shadows on the Past: Studies in the Historical Fiction Film.* Philadelphia: Temple University Press, 1994.

Harr, Jonathan. *A Civil Action.* New York: Random House, 1995.

Heimel, Paul. *Eliot Ness: The Real Story.* Nashville, Tenn.: Cumberland House, 2000.

Homberger, Eric. *John Reed.* New York: Manchester University Press, 1990.

Hopkins, Lisa. *Queen Elizabeth and Her Court.* New York: St. Martin's Press, 1990.

Iris, Bary and Eileen Bower. *D. W. Griffith, American Film Master.* New York: Garland, 1985.

Kirsch, Jonathan. *Moses: A Life.* New York: Ballantine Books, 1998.

Lynn, Kenneth Schuyler. *Charlie Chaplin and His Times.* New York: Simon and Schuster, 1997.

Mackay, James A. *Michael Collins: A Life.* Edinburgh, Scotland: Mainstream, 1996.

Mackay, James A. *William Wallace: Brave Heart.* Edinburgh, Scotland: Mainstream, 1996.

Marius, Richard. *Thomas More: A Biography.* New York: Vintage Books, 1985.

Massie, Robert K. *Nicholas and Alexandra.* New York: Ballantine, 2000.

Massie, Robert K. *The Romanovs: The Final Chapter.* New York: Random House, 1995.

Meyers, Jeffrey (editor). *T. E. Lawrence: Soldier, Writer, Legend.* Basingstone, Hampshire: Macmillan, 1989.

Moldea, Dan. *The Hoffa Wars: Teamsters, Rebels, Politicians, and the Mob.* New York: Paddington Press, 1978.

Nasaw, David. *The Chief: The Life of William Randolph Hearst.* New York, Houghton Mifflin, 2000.

Neale, John E. *Queen Elizabeth I.* Chicago: Academy Chicago Publishers, 1992.

Norton, David. *A History of the Bible as Literature.* New York: Cambridge University Press, 1993.

Perry, John. *Sgt. York: His, Life, Legend & Legacy: The Remarkable Untold Story of Sergeant Alvin. C. York.* Nashville, Tenn.: Broadman & Holman, 1997.

Pesci, David. *Amistad.* New York: Marlowe & Co., 1997.

Pious, Richard M. *Richard Nixon: A Political Life.* Englewood Cliffs, N.J.: Julian Messner, 1991.

Porter, Joseph A. (editor). *Critical Essays on Shakespeare's Romeo and Juliet.* New York: G. K. Hall, 1997.

Roquemore, Joseph. *History Goes to the Movies: A Viewer's Guide to the Best (and Some of the Worst) Historical Films Ever Made.* New York: Doubleday, 1999.

Scarisbrick, Jack J. *Henry VIII*. New Haven, Conn.: Yale University Press, 1997.

Sulayman, Musa. *T. E. Lawrence: An Arab View*. London, Oxford University Press, 1966.

Thomas, Bob. *Joan Crawford, a Biography*. New York: Simon and Schuster, 1978.

Toplin, Robert Brent. *History by Hollywood: The Use and Abuse of the American Past*. Urbana, Ill.: Illini Books, 1996.

Trotsky, Leon. *The Russian Revolution: The Overthrow of Tzarism and the Triumph of the Soviets*. Garden City, New York: Doubleday Anchor Books, 1959.

Wilson, Wendy S., and Gerald H. Herman. *American History on the Screen*. Portland, Maine: J. Weston Walch, 1994.

INDEX

ABOUT THE AUTHOR

Nationally known author and syndicated columnist **FRANK SANELLO** has written fifteen critically acclaimed books on history and film, including *Steven Spielberg: The Man, the Movies, the Mythology; The Opium Wars: The Addiction of One Empire and the Corruption of Another;* and *The Knights Templar: God's Warriors, The Devil's Banker* (also published by Taylor Trade Publishing).

Sanello is currently writing *Faith and Finance in the Renaissance: The Rise and Ruin of the Fugger Empire*, a centuries-spanning epic about the influential family of bankers who were the German equivalent of their contemporaries, the Medici.

A journalist for the past twenty-five years, Sanello has written articles for *The Washington Post, The Los Angeles Times, The Chicago Tribune, The Boston Globe, The New York Times*, and *People, Redbook, Cosmopolitan*, and *Penthouse* magazines.

Sanello was formerly the film critic for the *Los Angeles Daily News* and a business reporter for United Press International.

The author graduated cum laude from the University of Chicago and earned a master's degree from the University of California Los Angeles film school. He also holds a purple belt in Tae Kwon Do and has volunteered as a martial arts instructor at AIDS Project Los Angeles.

Sanello lives in Los Angeles with his four cats: Catullus, Cesare, Thisbe, and Pellegrino. The author can be contacted at fsanello@aol.com.